FIFTY YEARS IN CEYLON

FIFTY YEARS IN CEYLON

AN AUTOBIOGRAPHY

THOMAS SKINNER

EDITED BY HIS DAUGHTER
ANNIE SKINNER

GYAN

Published by

GYAN

Gyan Publishing House
5, Ansari Road
Daryaganj, New Delhi-110002
Phone: 011-47034999, 9811692060
E-mail: books@gyanbooks.com

Distribution Network
gyanbooks.com
India, USA, Canada, UK, Australia, France

ISBN : 978-81-212-3379-8 (PB)
First Published, London, 1891

2nd Impression 2020

Printed at: Gyan Press, Delhi.

Fifty Years in Ceylon
Author: Thomas Skinner

FIFTY YEARS IN CEYLON

AN AUTOBIOGRAPHY.

BY THE LATE

MAJOR THOMAS SKINNER, C.M.G.,

COMMISSIONER OF PUBLIC WORKS, CEYLON.

EDITED BY HIS DAUGHTER,

ANNIE SKINNER.

WITH A PREFACE

BY SIR MONIER MONIER-WILLIAMS, K.C.I.E.

LONDON: W. H. ALLEN & CO., LIMITED

AND AT CALCUTTA.

1891.

LONDON:
PRINTED BY W. H. ALLEN AND CO., LIM., 13 WATERLOO PLACE.
PALL MALL. S.W.

PREFACE.

The following autobiography tells its own tale. In my opinion it may be left to rest on its own merits, and needs no introduction to help it to attract readers and admirers. Major Skinner, the writer of it, draws his own portrait vigorously and unostentatiously. The living individual, exhaling British pluck and energy from every pore, seems to stand out before us in sharply defined outline—a typical example of self-help and self-reliance to be noted and observed of all men at a time when the force of our national individuality seems likely to undergo a process of dilution, if it be not already too often "watered down" by the growing desire for combined and corporate action in every sphere of life.

Why then, it may be asked, do you run the risk of spoiling this self-drawn picture by any adventitious or superadded touches? My reply is that the Editor of this autobiography sent it to me just before its publication, with a request that I would write a short preface. I acceded to the request not because the work stands in any need of my imprimatur, but because —as a relative of the family, and as one who has studied the languages, literature, and condition of our Eastern Empire for half a century—I feel it a duty to put on record my appreciation of the value of Major Skinner's services, and of the part he has taken in the task of convincing semi-civilised populations of the advantage of our rule as an instrument of progress and enlightenment.

When I was travelling in the Island of Ceylon in 1877—shortly before Major Skinner's death, and ten years after his retirement—I found the reputation of its great engineer and road-maker still fragrant there. Sir William Gregory was at that time Governor, and through his courteous aid I enjoyed special facilities in gaining a knowledge of the island and in personal association with its inhabitants. I learned that Major Skinner was a man whose memory the Government still delighted to honour, and in travelling from place to place I met many eminent natives who delighted to speak of him as one of their greatest benefactors, and as an officer of unusual administrative ability, indomitable energy, and unblemished integrity of character.

One of these eminent natives was Mr. Alwis, with whom I had more than one conversation. This gentleman was himself, I believe, an able member of the Legislative Government at the time of my visit, though he has since died. The address signed by him and by 1,595 Singhalese chiefs and others, at the termination of Major Skinner's career, is well worthy of attention, and may be taken as a key to the great engineer's popularity and the high reputation which he achieved.

I see that it is printed in small type at pp. 276–278, and in directing attention to this document I here give prominence to two sentences extracted from it:—

> We cannot forget that when you began public life in this Colony, nearly half a century ago, the interior of the country was almost inaccessible, and that roads and other means of communication were then almost unknown. The Colony now possesses a network of roads [nearly 3,000 miles of made roads in an area of 25,000 miles*], such as few colonies can boast of, and this state of things is in no small degree attributable to your indefatigable zeal and energy.

I may here state that Sir Hercules Robinson, who was Governor of Ceylon about twenty-five years ago,

* See p. 265.

has recently written to Major Skinner's daughter as follows :—

44, Ennismore Gardens, S.W.,
27th September, 1890.

DEAR MISS SKINNER,

I am afraid that after a quarter of a century's work in other lands my recollection of Ceylon details is now so faint, that I cannot furnish you with the "particulars" as to your father's life and official work there which you desire.

You must remember that your father's work dated from Sir Edward Barnes's time, in or about 1827, and lasted till 1867, when he retired—a period of nearly forty years—and that it was only during the last two years of his official life that I had the pleasure of being associated with him. All I can now state is, in general terms, that when I assumed the Government of Ceylon, in 1865, I was fortunate in finding your father at the head of the Public Works Department, and that he continued in that capacity till 1867, when he retired. During that period I received from him the most loyal co-operation and efficient aid in carrying out the vigorous public works policy which the circumstances of the country called for, and its financial position rendered feasible.

New roads, bridges, railways and irrigation works were accordingly taken in hand, and energetically pressed forward. I was thus brought into constant intercourse with your father, and formed a high opinion of his ability, industry, sound judgment, and untiring devotion to duty. I saw also enough of the result of the various works which he had carried out before my time, to realise the benefits which his life-long services had conferred on the Colony. We took many a long journey of inspection together, and riding side by side he used to give me the benefit of his intimate acquaintance with the resources and requirements of the country, as well as with the characteristics of its inhabitants. I consider that any success which attended my administration was due in a large measure to the information and sound advice which he thus imparted to me in the early days of my rule.

I wish I could have supplied you with more particulars of your father's official services, but the recollection of these details have waxed dim, whilst I retain only a very grateful and vivid general remembrance of his usefulness and his worth.

Believe me,
Yours sincerely,
(Signed) HERCULES ROBINSON.

Colonel Osbaldeston Mitford, who was under Major Skinner for a time, writes :—

What I admired in Major Skinner was that he was self-made. He went to Ceylon at a very early age to join the Rifle Regiment, and succeeded by his own merit—by perseverance and strict attention to the several duties he undertook—in raising himself till he became Surveyor-General and Commissioner of Public Works. In private he was a delightful companion, and an accomplished gentleman.

Mr. E. L. Mitford, who was for many years in the Ceylon Civil Service, also writes :—

Officially and personally I knew Major Skinner well. He was the pioneer and most efficient cause of the prosperity of one of our most flourishing colonies. When his work began there were but two bad roads in the island, and, when he retired, the island was a network of roads and bridges intersecting every province, all surveyed and made by his industry and perseverance, often under great difficulties.

Perhaps the best tribute which I have myself to offer to his memory is the assertion of my belief that, were he alive, he would deprecate my eulogising him in this

Preface. The performance of his duty was his daily meat and drink. He did it zealously, earnestly, effectively, because it was his duty, and because he took a pride in doing it thoroughly. He desired no other reward than the "witness in himself," and it seems an impertinence on my part to add any words of my own to those of men better qualified than myself to speak of his life-long devotion to the welfare of perhaps the most beautiful—if not the most important—of our Colonial possessions.

All who know Ceylon well in the present day, agree in describing its condition as eminently prosperous and satisfactory. It has now, I believe, more than 180 miles of railway opened and in good working order, and its whole moral and material well-being is rapidly developing. It would be difficult, therefore, for any one to speak in exaggerated terms of the debt of obligation which the island owes to the man who is acknowledged by all to have been the first opener of its means of communication, and the earnest promoter of numerous important works, such as the improvement of irrigation and inland navigation, the encouragement of native talent, and the progress of education.

MONIER MONIER-WILLIAMS.

Enfield House, Ventnor.
October 15th, 1890.

CONTENTS.

FIFTY YEARS IN CEYLON.

CHAPTER I.

BEFORE entering upon the details of my own life, it may be interesting to some of my readers to know a few incidents of historical interest connected with my family in remote times. Those who have the curiosity to hear who my ancestors were, and what they did, will find a short account of them in the Appendix, Note 1.

I was born at St. John's, Newfoundland, on the 22nd May 1804, when my father—an officer in the Royal Artillery—was quartered at that station. I lost my mother in infancy, and was taken charge of, from the age of between two and three, by my maternal grandmother.

About the year 1811, my father was ordered home, and obtained a passage by H.M.S. *Pomone*. How well I remember my excitement whenever the ship "beat to quarters," which occurred always if a strange sail hove in sight, until particulars of her nationality and intentions were ascertained. I invariably rushed to the first lieutenant, Furneux, for a supply of ammunition for my pop-gun, on which I firmly believed the success of any engagement we might enter upon as much depended as on the broadsides of the ship. Five-and-forty years afterwards I met my old friend, Admiral Furneux, at Plymouth, when we had a hearty laugh over my juvenile zeal for the defence of H.M.S. *Pomone*. This voyage excited in me a strong and enduring passion for the Navy, which I have retained to this day, having ever been impressed with the conviction that I should have made a better sailor than a soldier. During the voyage, we had to take on board a strong detachment of French military prisoners of war, to be conveyed to Lisbon. My recollections of that port, and of the Tagus, are perfectly vivid, and have been confirmed as accurate, by persons who have recently visited that place. Indeed, my memory of localities has always been very strong, so much so that, on my return to St. John's, in 1823, I landed and walked through the town—which I left when I was seven years old—to my father's quarters at Fort Townsend.

On his arrival in England, my father found he had to embark for Ceylon. My sister and I were placed at schools at and near Shaftesbury, in Dorsetshire. I was sent to a most kind, worthy old gentleman, the Reverend John Christie. I had no friends or relations in England willing to be troubled with so unprofitable a charge as I should have been during the holidays; so that for six years I remained a permanent boarder at Mr. Christie's, and became so great a favourite with the whole establishment, including my indulgent master and his good lady, that I did just as I liked; and consequently learnt little beyond the most rudimentary branches of knowledge. Hence, when in 1818 I was removed from school, to be sent out, as intended, to join the Navy on the East India Station, I was as ignorant as a boy of my age could well be. On my arrival in Ceylon, my father was so disappointed at my deficiencies that he resolved to send me back to school by the first vessel that presented itself. But communication between Ceylon and England was at that time of rare occurrence.

My father was stationed at Trincomalee, the head-quarters of the Naval Commander-in-Chief, Sir Richard King, whose flag-ship, H.M.S. *Minden*, I had fondly hoped to join. A fine fleet was at anchor in the harbour, of which there was a splendid view from the Flag-staff Hill, where I went daily to feast my longing eyes on the ships, one of which I still hoped to be permitted to join. However, my father was relentless, and back to England and school seemed to be my doom.

I was one evening taken by my family to a ball given by the Commandant of the garrison, Sir Maurice O'Connell, commanding the 73rd Regiment. This indulgence did not seem to promise much pleasure to me, for I was naturally a very bashful boy, and this weakness was a good deal intensified by the knowledge of my extreme deficiencies; however, I had to go, and soon found myself in an unenviable position, for, being a candidate for the honour of wearing the crown and anchor, I was too dignified to associate with any children there may have been of the party, and too young and uncouth a cub to be noticed by anyone else. Mooning about, and wishing myself anywhere but where I was, I was accosted by Sir Francis—then Captain Collier, commanding H.M.S. *Liverpool*—thus: "Who are you, youngster?" In reply, I told him my name, and gave him my parentage. "What are they going to do with you?" "I have been sent out, sir, under an impression that I was to be allowed to join H.M.S. *Minden*; but, on my arrival, my father found me so badly educated, that he is going to send me back to England to school." He walked about with me during the remainder of the evening, with the kindness and consideration of a sailor. I little dreamt of the importance that evening's conversation with Sir Francis Collier was to prove to my future destiny. I went home with my parents, tired and sleepy, and thought little more about the matter.

The next day Sir Richard King and Sir Francis Collier called at my father's quarters, paid him a long visit, and were very energetic in their conversation. My father had always been on the most intimate and familiar terms with the naval officers stationed at Trincomalee. I afterwards learnt that the purport of their conversation, which I had heard at a distance, was their urging my father to apply to the Governor for a commission in the Army for me, as being far better than joining the Navy, and hanging on for years before I could hope for, or expect to obtain, a lieutenancy. The promotion in that service was then so slow that a cousin of mine, Charles Bentham, was then only a mate on board the *Liverpool* after fifteen years' service. The old objection was raised, that my father would not submit to have his family disgraced by putting any member of it into the public service until his education was properly completed; and he maintained his position obstinately, flattering himself that he had beaten off the attack; but on leaving, Sir Richard King said, "We will return and spend the evening with you," to which a ready assent was given.

When they returned in the evening, the Admiral, I was told, intimated to my father that they did not intend leaving the house until their request had been acceded to. I was informed that the besieged held out till about 4 o'clock A.M., when Sir Richard King promised my father that he would not only supplement his application to the Governor with a letter from himself, but that he would send Captain Collier to Colombo with the *Liverpool* to present the papers and to plead himself for his young *protégé*.

A vacancy had just occurred in the Ceylon Regiment when the *Liverpool* reached Colombo, and my father received by the earliest post the *Gazette* with my appointment. Governors of colonies had then the privilege of filling up death vacancies, subject to the approval and confirmation of the Commander-in-Chief at the Horse Guards.

I was ordered to proceed at once to head-quarters at Colombo, and, being a second lieutenant, had to take command of detachments of the 73rd, 83rd, and Ceylon Rifles to march from Trincomalee across the island, through Kandy to Colombo. I had neither time nor opportunity to procure any uniform; so being very small for my age—which was between 14 and 15—I had to start in my school-boy jacket on my first military duty.

The rebellion of 1818 had so recently been suppressed that the country through which our route lay was still unsettled, but we met with no adventure. Arriving at Kandy, I reported myself and the detachments to the commandant, who was not a little amused at so juvenile an authority. I pleaded hard for exemption from attendance at a general parade of troops the following morning; but he would not give me leave, so I had to submit to be the amusement of the whole garrison, when marching from the right, at the head of my detachment, along the whole line to gain my position on its left. I must have looked very absurd by the side of a grenadier ensign of the 83rd Regiment, my stature reaching not far above his elbow. However, I managed to get through this my first ordeal, and next day we proceeded on our march towards Colombo.

The country was truly beautiful, and I was not too young to appreciate it. The second day's march was down the old Ballany Pass, over which, four years before, my father had brought up his battery of heavy guns, one of them a 42-pounder, for the taking of Kandy. It was a marvel to me how he could have accomplished it; I subsequently learnt that he had parbuckled the guns up from tree to tree. I can scarcely imagine anything better calculated to expunge from a son's vocabulary the word "impossible" than this feat: the mountain path was so narrow, broken, steep, and rocky, that it was quite impassable for any horse and rider. My father was an officer full of resources and expedients, and it would have been a strange country through which he would fail to take a battery. I remember once seeing in the Quartermaster-General's office a report of his march from Colombo to the Pearl Fishery, at Aripo, with his battery. He had to cross a famous swamp called "Blue boots," so called because any man fording it sank half-way up his thighs in blue clay. My father reported that it proved an impediment which caused him a little delay, but with fascines, and by breaking up his provision casks and lashing portions of the staves on to the tires of the wheels of his gun-carriages, he passed the obstruction without the necessity of deviating from his route.

In due course of time I arrived at Colombo, and presented myself to my astonished commanding officer, who could scarcely believe his senses, when I informed him that I had marched the detachment from Trincomalee to Colombo. I obtained a few days leave to get my uniform, a no small difficulty in those days; and, having succeeded, I was taken to the fort to be presented to the Governor, Sir Robert Brownrigg, who was most considerate and kind to me. He said:

"If you are not sixteen yet, you will be some day soon, if you live long enough."

From His Excellency I proceeded to report myself to the Commandant of Colombo, Colonel ——, commanding the —— Regiment, who, on seeing my extreme youth, said to me:

"Young gentleman, you are beginning the service at a very early age; it reminds me that this day, forty years ago, my son, now Colonel of —— Regiment, was born on a barrack cot, when I was a sergeant. We have both got on pretty well, you see, and I hope you may do so, too." He added, "Tom —— (a well known major in his regiment) was my first batman, and I have never had my boots so well cleaned since."

The fact was that his regiment, much to its credit, had more officers in it who had been raised from the ranks than any other I have ever come across. They were not a little proud of this, and often talked of it. I can remember seven or eight of them at this distance of time.

Having now equipped myself, as well as circumstances would admit of, I was put to my drill. The adjutant of the regiment was one of the strictest disciplinarians I have ever met with; and under him I was not likely to be dismissed while I had anything to learn. He worked me too hard for my age. I was out at daylight, for three hours before breakfast; at midday, for two hours in barracks: and again in the evening for an hour and a half.

We were commanded at that time by a German officer, a nephew of Colonel Munster; he possessed a good deal of interest, but was an arbitrary and most cruel man. He tried and flogged men for every offence; at the constant punishment parades—sometimes two or three a week—it was a common occurrence to see men faint and drop in the ranks.

My Colonel, who was also on Sir Robert Brownrigg's General Staff, when he presented me to His Excellency, was desired to take me with him to King's House whenever he went there to dinner; consequently, in about a week I received notice from Colonel —— that I was to dine with the Governor that evening, and was duly called for at the proper hour. My sword, an ordinary regulation one, was a serious inconvenience, being out of all proportion, in point of size and weight, to its wearer. I had had a heavy day's drill and felt knocked up. Lady Brownrigg had most kindly reserved a seat for me next to her at dinner; but, directly it was over, my head drooped, and I fell asleep at the table! When the ladies retired, she most kindly took me to her room, disencumbered me of my military paraphernalia, and laid me on her bed, where I slept until my commanding officer was ready to take me home again. This is a sad story to the prejudice of my fitness for the service, but an instance of the motherly kindheartedness of Lady

Brownrigg which I can never forget. I never went to sleep again at the Governor's table, although frequently invited to it!

My drill went on vigorously, and the interest I took in it extracted a compliment from my adjutant, which, he told me, he had never paid any young officer before. He said:

"If you were in the ranks, I might make a lance-corporal of you!"

But my zeal cost me dear; I contracted the disease of the country (dysentery), which caused me to be continually on the sick list. The day I was pronounced convalescent, I was put in orders for regimental or garrison duty to bring up the arrears I had missed when non-effective—a barbarous practice, which I have never known carried out in any other regiment. The consequence was, that over-work and exposure, with my immature strength, too surely sent me back to the doctor's charge after I had enjoyed my freedom for a week; each relapse took me longer to recover from, until at length the illness became chronic. In this condition my regiment was ordered to march to Kandy, and not a cooly, for the transport of baggage, could be obtained for any consideration. In this dilemma, the day before my division was to march, I bethought me of what appeared to me and others a happy idea, which was to invest in a donkey accustomed to carry packs; he might at least, I thought, carry my bedding and a change of clothes. Accordingly my servant went to the bazaar and purchased what appeared to be a promising animal. I was so determined to be in good time for our start in the morning that I had my beast of burden tied up to a verandah post, and, at a very early hour, rose, had my baggage packed in approved form, and sent my servant with it to the barracks, with orders to load the ass before the "assembly" sounded at 3 A.M. His part of the play the man performed extremely well, but unfortunately I had not given sufficient thought as to whether the animal had been properly trained to martial music. No sooner had the bugles sounded the first bars of the "assembly," than off galloped my Bucephalus, dragging my servant with him, and carrying all the necessaries I possessed into an abyss of darkness, never stopping until he had reached the home—three miles off—from which I had torn him the day before. My brother officers who had so admired the sagacious forethought of my arrangement, joined heartily in the laugh at its summary failure, as the donkey scampered over the parade-ground to his own euphonious music—leaving me the unenviable discomfort of sleeping on a bare rest-house table, without a change of clothes for several days and nights. This did not improve the malady from which I was suffering, and, by the time we marched into Kandy, I was completely laid up. The weather had been very wet and unfavourable; of roads there were *none*, and the mountain paths were execrable. It is a marvel to me that I survived the effect of that march, considering the condition of health I was in at the time.

I remained in Kandy for some weeks, when, to get

rid of the scandal of so young an officer, I was sent with a small detachment to Maturatta, an out-station on the Hills under Newera Ellia, to be under the command of an experienced officer of the 73rd Regiment, Lieutenant George Dawson. The quiet and climate of this mountain station were most favourable for my studies. I never forgot the disadvantage under which I was placed by the over-indulgence of my kind, affectionate old schoolmaster, and availed myself of every opportunity I could to improve myself. I was fortunate in being with a kind, fatherly old officer, who, by dint of constant doses of port wine and laudanum, eventually cured me of my illness, of which I have never since had the slightest return. He told me before he administered the first dose, that it might kill me, but that he thought it worth the trial. Directly I got well, and gained a little strength, an ambition seized me to render myself as self-sustained and independent as my men were. The first step in this direction appeared to be to learn to march without shoes. I commenced my training by walking out every morning barefooted to my bath, a short distance off. I had to walk over a portion of the fort covered with sharp quartz gravel, which touched up my sensitive feet considerably; however, I persevered until I made a march of sixty miles over some of the highest, most rugged, rocky mountains in the island, perfectly bare-footed; and such was my appreciation of the comfort of the absence of boot or shoe, that I never would have put on another could I have followed my own inclinations;

and yet, some twenty or twenty-five years later, the authorities had the folly to dress our native troops in ammunition boots. The habits and equipment of the European soldier were introduced one after another till, as I predicted, they utterly destroyed the finest native regiment that any country ever possessed. Instead of limiting as much as possible their artificial wants, and keeping them self-sustained and ready for the field at any moment they have burdened the Malay with all the equipment and barrack furniture of an European soldier, contrary to his tastes, and have made him nearly as costly an appendage.*

I had been some time at Maturatta when my commandant obtained leave of absence for two or three months, and left me in command of the post. A brother officer of his—Lieutenant Blennerhasset—who had been staying with us, accompanied him the morning he started. They left very early, before daylight. About a quarter of an hour after they had gone I heard two shots fired, so I jumped up and prepared to follow my friends, expecting to see them return; but finding they did not, as daylight broke, I went up the road they had taken, to see the cause of the shots. The senior sergeant, who had received instructions from my old mentor to see that I got into no mischief, followed me. The reason of the fracas was soon apparent. A huge elephant had taken up his billet on the road, as his foot-marks plainly showed;

---

* The Ceylon Rifles were disbanded in 1874.

and a broken lantern, a plate of sandwiches, and a broken bottle were the evidences of my friends' flight. I had never seen even a tame elephant at this time, and became so excited at the idea of encountering a wild one that I proposed we should follow him, for the pleasure of only seeing him; but my friend Sergeant Alliff took advantage of my ignorance, and persuaded me that the two shots fired at the elephant would not have checked his flight, and that he must then be miles distant from us. "But," said he, "we will get some plantain trees cut, and place them here; he will be sure to return, and we shall find him at this spot in the morning."

He could scarcely have suggested a greater improbability; but I knew nothing of the habits of elephants, and was obliged to submit, taking care, however, to have a tempting repast prepared for my expected guest should he return. This done, my sergeant seemed quite contented, feeling he had saved me from all present danger, and being persuaded in his own mind that we should see no more of the elephant. I, on the other hand, having every confidence in his assurance, passed a long day of expectation, looking up from the fort every half-hour to the green hill where the adventure of the morning had occurred, to see if the animal had returned.

I went to bed, but had little sleep, the half-hours between the sentries' call of "All 's well" seemed to be immeasurably long. Directly daylight broke I hurried on my clothes and went out to reconnoitre; it was some time before objects were sufficiently clear to enable me to distinguish between an elephant and the rocks, with which the surface of the hill was studded. In a few minutes, however, my doubts and anxieties were satisfied. I could see a huge mass moving along, its size being much exaggerated by the indistinctness of the grey morning light. I rushed to the guard-house, which was pretty near my quarters, seized a cut-down flint and steel musket from the arm-rack, took ten rounds of ammunition out of the sentry's pouch, and off I started to bag my first elephant—my inexperience and ignorance of the danger giving me perfect confidence.

I had no sooner left the guard-room than the alarm was passed speedily to my sergeant, who I soon saw in the distance with a file of men at the double. I was at first a little piqued at his officiousness in supposing I was not a match for my prey without their assistance. I checkmated them to a certain extent by sending two of the men to make a flank movement on the enemy, while the sergeant and I approached him in front. As I advanced nearer, and the light dawned brighter, the proportions of this monster of the jungle appeared to me very appalling. He was a splendid tusker. I thought little of that, supposing that all elephants were thus supplied with ivory, whereas not above one in 300 are so armed. I crept up to a level with the ground on which he was, before I made a direct movement towards him; but he soon discovered me, and gallantly accepting the challenge, rushed headlong at us. The sergeant being better aware of the danger of such a contest than I was, suggested that I should with all speed climb upon a rock close by. The fury with which the beast was rushing at us allowed little time for any evolutions, however simple; but, assisted by the sergeant, I was on the top in a moment, about two feet above the elephant's head, just as he was making for the sergeant. I had only time to cock "Brown Bess," and putting the muzzle on the crown of the monster's head, fired into it. He rolled over with a tremendous crash, to my no small satisfaction. It was not until I saw the huge mass of animal life prostrate and extinct by a momentary act of mine, that I could realise the great danger I had so recklessly run for my faithful sergeant and myself. To kill a huge tusker with an old cut-down flint musket at the first shot I would, at any period of my life, have considered rather a feat; but that the first elephant I had seen, or come in contact with, should fall to a boy of fifteen—for I was not sixteen at the time—was an event. I would have given anything to have remained to gloat over my prey, but at once felt that it would have been unsoldier-like and undignified to appear at all elated at the exploit, specially as the two men the sergeant brought from the Fort, *for my protection*, had joined us from their flank movement: so I coolly directed that the head should be cut off, brought down to the Fort and buried, to enable me to get the tusks out—they were a splendid pair—and I then walked back to my quarters, pretending to be as indifferent as if I had bagged hundreds of elephants before.

The incident created great excitement in the cantonment, all the men off duty rushed up to see the animal their *tuan kilchel*—little gentleman or officer—had shot. I saw the head and tusks brought to the fort by about fifty men, and observed where they intended to bury them, but still considered it would lower me in the opinion of my men if I exhibited the smallest interest in the subject; so I had to bear as best I could the feigned stoicism I thought it right to assume in reference to this strange monster. I waited patiently in my quarters until I thought the whole of the men had returned to the fort for their breakfast, when I stole out quietly and unobserved to gaze in private at my trophy.

On approaching the headless mass I was suddenly arrested by the most unearthly sounds, which appeared to proceed from it. What could it be? Tigers could scarcely have been so prompt in their attendance on the carcase, and that in broad daylight, on the side of an open hill, and yet the noise sounded very like their deep growl. I approached most cautiously. The noise increased as I got nearer; my courage was waning, when it occurred to me that I might ascend the same rock from which I had shot the animal, and reconnoitre my position. I crept up to it by a circuitous approach. Imagine my surprise when, on looking down, I found a large hatchway opened in the side of the carcase, and a couple of Caffres, or African soldiers, in the stomach, most industriously employed. Finding I had no danger to encounter, I descended to the scene of action, and was astonished at the noise their voices made within the body of the animal. When I asked them what they were doing, they told me they were taking out the heart, liver, and lights, which they described as great delicacies in their own country, where they were always used for food. The more I saw of this extraordinarily huge animal, the more astonished I was that he should so easily have fallen to my one haphazard ball, and I began to think I had done rather a good morning's work.

It was not a feat of which to write exultingly to one's father, but several months afterwards he heard of it, and asked me to give him the tusks as a trophy of my first success in elephant-shooting, but I had unfortunately given them to my commandant. They were a very fine pair, and he did not feel inclined to give them up to my father in exchange for another pair, so I never saw them again.

In the years 1819 and 1820, the awful scourge of small-pox for the first time made its appearance in the interior of Ceylon, and was very fatal. Vaccination, or innoculation had not previously been introduced, and the disease spread with fearful rapidity. Directly persons were attacked they were banished from their houses. Sometimes a temporary shed was built for them, in which they were placed, with a little cooked food, to take their chance of recovery. Many poor creatures thus deserted were attacked and torn to pieces by wild animals before life was extinct. Some of them, on being turned out of their homes, tried to crawl up to the fort, in the hope of being buried when they died.

I sent out a fatigue party daily to bring these poor creatures in, and collected as many as twenty-six, most of them in a shocking condition, some temporarily blind, and nearly all in a confluent stage of the disease. I do not remember how I was guided in my treatment of the patients; but I set apart for their accommodation a large spare barrack-room, took the door and window shutters off their hinges to secure perfect ventilation, and spread the floor with clean river sand, on which I placed mats and cloths. I gave to each patient as he was brought in a dose of aperient medicine, such as the post was provided with, and then fed them on congee, or rice water, at first very thin, sweetened with a little coarse palm sugar of the country, increasing the consistency of this rice-water daily as the men improved. I am thankful to be able to state that God blessed my efforts, and supplied my lack of skill, for every individual recovered, though most of them were awfully marked.

None of my troops, fortunately, caught the disease, or I might have got into trouble, having no medical aid within reach. My poor senior sergeant had two remarkably fine boys—twins; they both caught the small-pox together: one of them died, and I had the survivor brought to my quarters. He was placed on a couch by my bedside, but when I awoke in the night I found the poor child was dead. He had passed away quite quietly, without even disturbing me. I was surprised, in the morning, to find how calmly his parents received the sad news of his death; being Mohammedans they were Fatalists, and had made up their minds that the death of one of the twins was a certain indication that they would lose the other. The children were both buried in the same coffin.

I very much admired my men for their extreme independence of all external aid. They were a wonderfully handy set of fellows, and could do anything, from the building of a barrack to the re-tanning of a lady's footstool. They were excellent gardeners, built their own lines, and our mess-house in Kandy, and, as I have before stated, were the beau ideal of Native light troops. Their wives partook of the same hardy nature. A detachment of the regiment was marching from Fort MacDonald, in Ouvah, over the Dodauatta-capella—the Orange Branch Pass—to Kandy, through Maturatta, then the most formidable series of mountain passes in the country—and there were some stiff ones. On the sergeant commanding the detachment reporting its arrival, he stated that he had left a file of his men behind on the road, three miles off, to attend a woman who had been confined on the march, but that they would arrive presently. I ordered a dhooly (a kind of stretcher) to be sent up the hill to bring the mother and infant in, and directed that her husband should have leave to remain with them, instead of marching with his detachment the following day. The next morning, when I got up, I sent my servant to inquire for the woman and her child, and, if it would be acceptable, to give her some warm tea. When he returned, to my surprise, he told me the woman had marched on with the detachment at 4 o'clock that morning, over certainly the worst road I ever saw in my life. I afterwards learned that mother and child reached head-quarters safely.

During the absence, on leave, of my chief, the rains set in very heavily and continuously, and the swollen rivers so intercepted our communications with Kandy that commissariat supplies, which ought to have reached us in three days, were six weeks *en route*, and our stores of grain were nearly exhausted. I at first placed the garrison on half, and latterly on one-third rations, and at last was reduced to the necessity of levying contributions on the villages within our impassable rivers. These villages were not numerous, for in tropical rains little rivulets, which can be jumped across in dry weather, become impassable mountain torrents, and considerably circumscribed our traversable area.

I put off my foraging as long as I could, but after weeks of continuous downpour there seemed no chance of a break in the weather, and, as I feared to entrust the duty to a non-commissioned officer's command, I took charge of the party myself. The idea of protecting oneself against either the weather or the leeches was clearly useless, so I accoutred myself as like my men as I could, the hardened condition of the soles of my feet being much in my favour, for I had to wade through muddy paddy-fields, occasionally far above my knees, in which it would have been quite impossible to have worn either shoes or boots, so I discarded them altogether, cut off the legs of my trousers as short as possible, and resigned myself to the leeches, which in that district, and in such weather, required a more expressive term than "legion" to describe their numbers.

From village to village I proceeded; the first I reached, I drew up my men, called for the elders, and explained to them the difficulty of my position, in consequence of the non-arrival of my convoy of provisions. I had heard of it several weeks ago, and believed it to have been for the last week or so on the left bank of the Bilhooloya, only two or three miles distant, but this was so furious a torrent that it would not be fordable for a week after the rains had ceased. I asked the elders to decide how much grain they could spare me without inconvenience to themselves, and induced them to send an emissary on to the next village to inform the authorities there of my intended visit, and the object of it; I measured out and gave a receipt for the grain I took, and despatched it to the post. At every village I was received courteously, and provided with what I needed.

My legs, throughout the day, presented the most extraordinary appearance—they were literally black with leeches suspended from them; I never attempted to pull them off, as so doing causes the bites to fester, whereas, if allowed to satisfy themselves, the leeches will drop off, and if a little sweet oil is applied after washing, the wounds will heal up without irritation.

I had to repeat this expedition before relief came to us, by the arrival of supplies from Kandy. N.B.—In a country destitute of bridges or roads, see that your stores are replenished before the advent of the rainy season!

My commandant returned to his post at the expiration of an extension of his leave. I reported my doings from the morning he left me until his return, and I had the satisfaction of receiving his full approval. I had now quite recovered my health, and gained much strength from my tour of duty at Maturatta. I had occupied my leisure in striving to improve myself, and was not altogether dissatisfied with the result. Through the kindness of the commanding officer of my regiment, I had been allowed to remain for several months at Maturatta, entirely for my own benefit, for my services were by no means required there.

I was next ordered to Kornegalle, the capital of the Seven Korles, where there was a larger force than at Maturatta. The garrison was under the command of Major Martin, of the 45th Regiment, and consisted of a small detachment of Artillery, two flank companies of the 45th, and a company of the Ceylon Rifle Regiment, of which I was ordered to take command; we had a staff officer and a deputy commissary general.

Amongst the officers of the 45th was an extremely nice fellow of the name of Montgomery, an ensign of about three years' standing, a good deal my senior in age. He was a keen, active sportsman, and we went out elephant-shooting nearly every day. We used to breakfast early and start off to the jungle, on the chance of finding the track of an elephant, which we generally did, and often that of a herd, which we followed up till we overtook them. Sometimes we were led on imperceptibly until, late in the evening, we found ourselves many miles away from the post. The country was well marked by high rocky features, so that as long as it was daylight there was little fear of our losing ourselves; but unfortunately we were often in large deep jungles, far away from home, after dark, when it was quite impossible to return without a guide; many a time we did not get back to our quarters till a very late hour.

The shooting in Ceylon, in those days, was certainly first-rate. Elephants simply swarmed, pea-fowl and jungle-fowl were most abundant, specially in the Seven Korles; snipe, widgeon, and wild duck also in great variety, with curlew and golden plover, were almost everywhere to be found.

My friend Montgomery and I became desperate sportsmen; we were pretty well our own masters, with nothing to prevent our indulging our love of sport to the utmost. It was not much wonder that we were both soon laid up with severe attacks of jungle fever, to which my poor young friend at last succumbed. He died in Kandy, where in the churchyard there is a tomb, erected to his memory by his parents.

I got over my attack, but it was a marvel that I did. One morning my doctor bled me till there was scarcely a drop of blood left in my body; he then gave me forty grains of calomel, and in the evening—as the fever was still raging—he ordered me to be taken out to the yard of my quarters, laid on a bare ratan couch, and buckets of cold water thrown over me, for about twenty minutes! I was then put back to bed, and fortunately fell asleep for several hours. I was awakened by the melancholy call of an owl, named by the natives the "Devil Bird," because its presence is considered a certain precursor of death. It perched itself on the ridge-pole of my cottage, about twelve feet above my head. Our quarters were in the small houses, occupied by members of the Royal Family, in Malabar Street. The descendants of the Dutch are quite as superstitious as the natives, and as the cry of the Devil Bird was heard by them as distinctly as by me, they considered my immediate death as certain. After the severe treatment I had received, the adjutant did not expect me to survive the night, and when he came to see me in the morning was not a little surprised to hear that I had slept for several hours, and was still alive. After some weeks on the sick list, I was able to return to my post at Kornegalle. The death of my friend, and my own narrow escape from the same fate, rather cooled the ardour of my zeal as a sportsman, but had not extinguished it.

CHAPTER II.

A FEW months after my return to Kornegalle two friends—Captain Lloyd, of the 73rd, and Captain Crofton, of my own regiment—came to stay with me. During their visit, I received a letter from an officer of the Quartermaster-General's Department, stating that His Excellency Sir Edward Barnes, the Governor, desired to know if I wished for an appointment on the roads; for that if I did I was to proceed to Ambampettia—when relieved—and open that portion of the great military road which lies between that pass and Warrocopoly, a distance of about eleven miles. This offer surprised me, for I knew that it required no small amount of interest to obtain such appointments, and that, as a rule, the most efficient officers only were selected to fill them.

I showed the letter to my friends, expecting them to congratulate me on my good fortune, but found, instead, that I had to contend with their most determined opposition to my accepting the appointment offered; and I could not help regretting their presence at such a critical time. They used every possible argument against my entering upon any work which involved so much exposure, and so many temptations to intemperance and vice, as were known to characterise the habits of the men employed in road-making, and who were stationed in the neighbourhood of the district which had been assigned to me. The whole day they continued trying to persuade me to refuse. I could not help feeling grateful for the interest these kind old officers took in me; nevertheless, I felt determined not to reject an offer which, I rightly thought, might affect my whole future career. All their warnings and advice were met, on my part, with an assurance that I was quite strong enough to resist the evil examples by which, they affirmed, I should be surrounded. Towards the close of the day—when I had to post my reply—my friends, finding they could make no impression upon me, sought to make a compromise, and asked me if I would submit to "toss up," as to whether I should accept or refuse the appointment. I assented, tossed, and won, and the event influenced my whole future life. I scarcely ever performed regimental duty after this; but I hope I shall be able to show that I have not been a drone in the hive.

My letter, accepting the appointment, was written and posted; the next day I prepared my baggage for a move, in readiness to start as soon as the officer should arrive who was to relieve me; this he did in a day or two, and I handed over my company to him, and started for Ambampettia.

Here I was met by an officer of the Quartermaster-General's Department, who explained to me that I was to descend that pass at a "gradient of one in twenty," and gave me general instructions as to the direction which the road was to take through the Ballapany Valley to Warrocopoly. He was in a great hurry, and took little heed of my perplexity as to the mystery of "one in twenty," if, indeed, he was at all aware of it, when he left me.

I commenced my reconnaissance of the hill, down which I was expected to trace and make this military road. The men I had to work with were totally unskilled labourers, who had never seen a yard of made road in the country—for the best of reasons, that such a thing did not exist. I struck into the jungle from the narrow mountain path by which I had ascended it, but my progress was soon checked by enormous boulders and perpendicular precipices; it was an impossibility to advance fifty yards on a gradual descent, owing to what seemed to me these awful impediments. I began to think I had shown more temerity than judgment in undertaking so responsible a work, of which I was so profoundly ignorant; however, I had accepted it, and it must be done.

Two hundred of the Kandian villagers were ordered to join me in a few days, directly their tools arrived. In the meantime, the first thing which seemed expedient for me to do was to unravel the meaning of "one in twenty." A sharper fellow would, doubtless, have caught it much sooner than I did; or if I had had the candour to acknowledge my ignorance to the officer who came to set me to work, a word of explanation from him would have spared me many hours puzzling over the difficulty. However, the satisfaction of working out a problem of this kind is often turned to good account in the end; it gives a youngster so much confidence and self-reliance on future occasions.

A supply of tools arrived, and also my 200 Kandian villagers, and a more helpless set of mortals than they were at first, cannot be conceived. I had to commence my road-making, but I will not attempt to describe the waste of labour of those first few days, caused by my ignorance of the subject. However, I possessed untiring zeal and an earnest desire to do my best in the service on which I was employed, and I soon acquired, as it were by instinct, various methods for my work.

My Kandians, who had been in open rebellion against the Government only two years previously, were amenable; and I got on well with the headmen. It was up-hill work certainly, for they were relieved from their compulsory service every fortnight, and their successors had to be taught the work over again; but I shortly established a fair character for justice amongst them. A neighbouring officer had managed to get into trouble for coercing his men; but at the inquiry which was held, they said they did not mind "being beaten" by the "little gentleman"—meaning myself—as he never ordered their punishment without their deserving it, but they would not stand unjust punishment from other officers.

Our reports were made weekly to Sir Edward Barnes

and to the Deputy Quartermaster-General. The former, whenever he had an opportunity, would correct our orthography and send back our reports for revision, to remind us of the interest he took in our doings, and this produced the good he intended it should, by keeping us all "up to our work." Sometimes there would be an encouraging remark made with his broad pencil, such as, "This lad with his Kandians is doing well." I also received a letter from an officer of the Quartermaster-General's Department, informing me that His Excellency had observed, and wished me to be told, that with my raw untaught Kandians I was accomplishing a larger quantity of work than an equal number of skilled labourers of a division of Pioneers. This encouragement was far more effective than any amount of fault-finding.

I was much tormented by the wild elephants, which seemed to take a special pleasure in making nocturnal raids on my newly-formed embankments. I had been working near my bungalow, and on a beautiful moonlight night sat up for some time guarding a new piece of road with which I was well satisfied. Later, I went to bed, giving strict orders to my servants to call me immediately if they heard any alarm of elephants, loaded my gun, and placed a supply of ammunition in readiness. I had not lain down more than ten minutes when a servant rushed to my room in great excitement, crying out that a herd of fine elephants was on the road quite close to the bungalow, and that if I got up quickly I might get a shot at them from my door. I jumped out of bed, seized my gun, and was out. The elephants had moved a little, and the night was so clear and bright I thought it worth while to follow and obtain a better aim at them. I dropped one, but the fellow rose again, so disabled that I was led on, little by little, in my state of *déshabille*, till my poor feet—which had grown tender during my civilized life—were so cut that I had to hobble back to my wigwam and attend to them. My night-shirt gave ample evidence of the activity of the leeches, for the Ballapany paddy-fields were fine preserves for them, and at night they simply swarmed. This little incident is scarcely worth recording, but, as years go by, it strikes me now that I should hardly care for a repetition of it.

For some time my employment was at a sufficient distance from other parties working nearer Colombo to render it unnecessary for me to associate much with the officers in charge; but, as I progressed, I was necessarily brought nearer to them—indeed, we were travelling towards each other. It was not until we met that I could fully realise the force and kindness of my friends, Lloyd and Crofton, in striving to guard me against the influences and example of my brother road-makers. Their dissipation was beyond conception. Fortunately it was an impossibility for me to indulge in wine, beer, or spirits—the smell alone of any of them acting upon me as an emetic. Seeing this, there was nothing for it but to let me alone at their dinner-parties; and it was fortunate sometimes that there was one of the party sober enough to take care of the rest.

One night I was engaged seeing my companions stowed away on beds and couches, when I went to poor C.'s room and found him in a heavy sleep. Imagine my horror on perceiving, by the head of the bed on which he had thrown himself, a barrel nearly full of gunpowder for blasting purposes (which he kept there for security!), uncovered, with a bottle containing a lighted candle stuck into it. I could not remove this source of danger to all our lives without a shudder at the risk we had run. In the morning I pointed out the insanity of the proceeding, and declared I would not eat or sleep in the house until the powder was moved to a place of less danger. This they agreed to do.

On another occasion we were dining with H. of the 16th Regiment; he was a literary man, and at one time studied for priest's orders, being a Roman Catholic. His bungalow, which, like all the rest, was constructed of temporary materials, was well furnished, and he had a valuable little library in it. Late in the evening an alarm was given that the house was on fire; we had little time to consider, for in a few minutes the whole was in flames. I do not think that any efforts of ours could have arrested the fire, or that we could have saved much of his property; but, to one who was free from the influence of wine, it was painful to witness the callousness with which the party obeyed the directions of their host in removing the table, chairs, glasses, and a further supply of wine into the road, where they seated themselves and watched the roof of the bungalow fall in with an expiring blaze. The destruction of the whole was accomplished in a short time, and the party proceeded to that part of the building which had been used as a store-room, and therefrom grubbed out some potatoes, which had been roasted by the fire, on which they supped, the whole affair being looked upon as a good joke. Shelter for the night was, of course, gone, and half the party proceeded to officers' bungalows down the road, the other half going in the opposite direction. Such were the scenes and such the reckless style of life prevailing among the first of Ceylon's road-makers, and it would be useless to detail further particulars. They were, however, a fine, devoted set of fellows; their General for whom they worked being their idol, and no pressure was needed to make them do their best. Long before the scene of the work of a division, consisting of about two hundred men, was approached, they could be heard singing, and occasionally became so excited that they seemed more like madmen than reasonable beings.

Sir Edward Barnes often came to inspect the work and to encourage his men. He kept the best table I have ever seen, and always insisted on living better when travelling than when at home in Colombo; in either case, he invariably dined off an entire service of plate. We were always his guests on these occasions, and naturally looked forward to the luxury of a good dinner served in a first-rate manner. I remember on one of these visits there was some urgent necessity for his return to Colombo at once, thereby occasioning considerable disappointment amongst his officers, one of whom gave vent to his feelings that evening at dinner in not very parliamentary language :

"It is too bad of the fellow treating us like this, when we are working for him like mad all day, and getting drunk for him every night of our lives ; we had a right to a feed, instead of his skulking back to Colombo."

His loss of popularity, however, was but of short duration, for it became known along the line of road that he had had a disagreement with the then Chief Justice, Sir Harding Giffard, who, it was reported, was to leave Colombo for Kandy by the new road in a day or two. Without knowing any of the details of their difference of opinion, it was pretty certain what our judgment would be if this dignitary of the law were tried by us, sapient dispensers of justice. A drum-head court-martial was held and a judge advocate appointed, who elaborated a charge against the absent Sir Harding, and sentence was duly passed on His Honour. The road was not completed throughout, and we could easily pass along the unopened breaks without the assistance of the nearest working party. Dreadful plans were proposed and prepared to avenge our General on the Chief Justice, who was to travel in a palanquin, and would most surely have found himself dropped through sundry trap-bridges, laid especially for him, if he had not, luckily for himself, and still more fortunately for the road-makers, changed his mind, and put off his journey. Had he not done so, I fear a few of us would have lost our commissions, for so many were engaged in this illegal proceeding against the head of the law that the plot must have been discovered. We were not, however, to be wholly defeated. Three or four pioneer officers *in cog.* rode to Colombo by daylight one morning, and had the honour of meeting Sir Harding Giffard in his early ride; they carried out their intention of tilting at the Chief Judge, and returned without being found out, fancying they had avenged the cause of Sir Edward Barnes.

There was nothing chivalrous in this act, nor can it be quoted as creditable to the parties engaged in it. I only mention it as a proof of our devotion to our chief. We would have done anything for him. He must have known, as all soldiers should know, the power *true* popularity gives them over their subordinates. In any country or department, progress and improvements will advance, just in proportion to the zeal and energy of the presiding chief. Without his intelligence and activity, Sir Edward Barnes would have found it no easy task to have produced the results which were the fruit of the love and devotion of his officers and men.

I had now been several months "on the roads"; I had opened eleven miles of the main road to Kandy; had exposed myself during the time as much as the men who worked under me, for I was out with them all day, and I felt all the better for it. It enforced regular habits and early hours, and, what I knew to be of great importance to me, I had *not* been able to get over my aversion to stimulants, the taste of which made me absolutely ill.

I was now ordered to move to Allow, on the left bank of the Maha Oya, where a large force was being concentrated under Colonel Brown, R.E. There were stationed at Allow a physician to the forces, Doctor Dwyer, and six or seven subalterns, some commanding divisions of Pioneers, others superintending working parties of Kandians. We had not been there more than two weeks when jungle fever broke out amongst us, and three or four subalterns were removed to Colombo. Then Colonel Brown was attacked and hurried off. Doctor Dwyer followed him, and I found myself alone at the station. The Pioneer Hospitals were crowded; the men along the whole line of road from Veangodde—twenty-five miles from Colombo—were similarly affected, and all the officers had been sent away. I felt very important, being the only effective European officer left. This fact proved t headvantage of my enforced sobriety and temperance.

In the course of my perambulations, I went one day to Warrocopoly, where I heard that Sergeant Hopper of the 16th Regiment was, with his wife and family, laid up with fever. We had by this time heard from Colombo of the deaths of two or three of the poor fellows whom we had sent down from Allow. I found poor Hopper—a huge grenadier sergeant—in a raging fever; his wife and children very little better. I gravely expressed my opinion that he ought to lose a little blood; but the question was, who was to be the phlebotomist?

I had a lancet in my pocket, and offered to do my best for him. He approved, so I prepared for my new duty, and, when all was ready, I made sundry probes at his arm, but found it so immensely fat, I was obliged with my pen-knife to cut a long gash over the vein to enable my lancet to reach it. This done, it bled freely. I then bandaged it up, gave him a dose of aperient medicine, prescribed for his wife and children, and subsequently had the satisfaction of hearing that they had all weathered the storm.

While stationed at Allow, an incident occurred which is illustrative of the life of danger which our reckless fellow-workers ran. C. of the 16th Regiment rode over from Warrocopoly one evening to dine with us, and late in the evening ordered his horse, to return home. We all tried to dissuade him from doing so ; but it was the habit for everyone to return to their respective bungalows, if possible, after dinner, so as to be ready to muster their men and set them to work at day-break. C. thought he was quite equal to the ride, but exposure to the air must have had a bad effect upon him, for he had not ridden a mile before he fell off his horse. At about 4 o'clock A.M., his old Welsh servant, finding he had not returned, started off in search of him, and found him sound asleep on the road, surrounded by a herd of elephants, his horse standing by his side and the bridle-rein in his hand. The elephant and the horse have a great aversion to each other, to which fact in this case our friend owed his safety. Old Thomas managed to get his master home, and in a short time he was sent to Colombo with fever.

He recovered from that attack, but not long afterwards died from a relapse.

I continued for some time the sole representative of authority at Allow, and thought I was proof against the malaria which had proved so fatal to all the other Europeans; but one morning at breakfast I was seized in my turn, my head nearly dropped on to my plate, and I became very ill. In a day or two I was taken away to Colombo. At Mahara, about eight miles from that place, I met O'B. of the 83rd Regiment, who, full of sympathy, tried to save me the trouble of travelling further. He urged me to take up my quarters with him, pointing out with Irish hospitality the uselessness of my going into Colombo, and telling me sad tales from Allow, how one had died that morning, another was buried yesterday, and a third, as I knew, had been carried off a week before. I did not, however, concur in his reasoning, and thought I might as well take advantage of any chance of recovery there might be for me, so with his good wishes I started for my destination in my dhooly (a kind of palanquin, carried on the shoulders of eight men).

I was kindly received at Colombo by a brother subaltern, and was subject for many weeks to the cow-doctoring of the period. Finally, anticipating no benefit from this treatment, a medical board pronounced it necessary that I should be sent home immediately. A ship—the *Globe*—was then preparing to sail for England. I was put on board her, with but a very small amount of vitality, judging from my want of strength. There was no vacant cabin in the ship so I was accommodated, as far as the Cape, on a kind of bunker in a passage just large enough to hold my bed.

As we sailed into southern latitudes, and a cooler climate, my fever and ague—which had for several weeks visited me with precise punctuality at a given hour every alternate day—forgot to return. I soon became able to take nourishment, and improved rapidly.

Our ship was the slowest tub, I should think, that ever made so long a voyage. We were passed at sea by everything that came up with us. A sail in sight astern in the morning, spoke us in two or three hours, and was out of sight ahead in as many more. Our ship was, however, admirably navigated. On landing at the Cape I was hospitably treated by some old Ceylon civil servants, who were residing there on leave. We were nearly wrecked on leaving the Cape, and "rolled down" to St. Helena.

There I had a disagreeable affair to settle with a major of Artillery, who had formerly been in the Irish Brigade, and was nearly old enough to be my grandfather. He had quarrelled with me at the Cape because I declined to give him the cabin which had been assigned to me by the captain of the ship, it having been vacated by an officer and his family who landed at Cape Town. I should not have hesitated to oblige Major B by letting him have this superior cabin had he asked me for it civilly, but I could only refuse his dictatorial demand for it, as he used inexcusably gross language to me, for which he would make no apology. We arranged therefore to meet in a duel the moment the ship anchored. We had but one second between us, who was to make all preparations, and secure the services of the first boat that came alongside, in which we succeeded in getting off to the shore before we were observed by anyone on board ship.

We had little knowledge of the topography of James Town, and it was amusing to see our second with his carpet-bag of pistols leading the way to find a spot sufficiently private for our purpose, and it was some time before he was satisfied with his selection. Eventually the pistols were loaded, the ground measured, and a fool placed at each extremity of twelve paces. I felt very much ashamed of myself, but the fault was not mine. I had been insulted by a man who should have known better, and who could have well afforded to apologise for his loss of temper and discretion. The usages of the Service at that time would not tolerate that any member of it should tamely submit to an insult without demanding "satisfaction" from the aggressor; hence I was permitted this very equivocal privilege of being placed in a position in which I might have taken the life of the father of a family whose children were older than myself, or my own life might have been forfeited.

Our pistols were handed to us and the signal to fire given. I remember aiming low, so that if I hit my antagonist it should not, if I could help it, be mortally.

Our second then declared that all had been done that was necessary for the honour of both parties, and that we must forthwith retire from the ground. This judgment was delivered with the most farcical official solemnity; then Major B. walked up to me, begged me to do him the favour to accept his hand, and expressed the regret and condemnation of his hasty conduct, which would, if admitted before, have saved us this absurd exhibition. He was good enough to tell me that I had acted quite correctly in the matter. This was consolatory, coming, as it did, from "a fire-eater" of the old Irish Brigade. We returned to the ship as friends, and received the congratulations of our fellow passengers and shipmates on our safe return; for directly we were missed on board and seen pulling to the shore, our object was easily conjectured.

All such folly has been swept away by the besom of reform. I wish I could think it had left no dregs behind. Duelling was doubtless a barbarous custom; but, after all, the sacrifices of life which it exacted were but very few. During my forty-nine years' experience in the colony of Ceylon, where there were at times as many as five or six regiments stationed, I can only remember one fatal result. The change in the tone of language and conduct of gentlemen towards each other has been very marked and certainly not improved by the abolition of the old code of honour. Formerly an abrupt and discourteous contradiction could not be given without subjecting the perpetrator to a demand for explanation, or, possibly, for "satisfaction"; and certainly no man dared to talk of women in the way I have heard adopted of late years, or to behave towards them as they do in the present day. I cannot think that this relaxing of the accountability of men for their words and acts has been attended with beneficial effects on society at large, and on military society in particular.

It is surely unsatisfactory to military instinct that, if one man insults another, he should prefer a complaint against him to his commanding officer, or if guilty of an indecorum towards a woman, that redress must be sought in a court of law. I could never be accused of being bloodthirsty or in any degree a fire-eater; but I cannot, on the coolest and most mature consideration, help regretting the changes I have witnessed since duelling has been abolished without creating any courts of honour to supply its place. I am of opinion that in every regiment there should be such a court, consisting of a field officer, a captain, and a subaltern, who should be elected for one, two, or three years by ballot from amongst their brother officers. All cases which could not be otherwise amicably settled, should be brought before them, and their opinion should carry great weight with any authority before whom the affair might be brought. Any man whose conduct was severely censured by this court should be removed from the Service as a dangerous member of it.

After leaving St. Helena we saw no land until, as predicted by the captain, we first sighted the Eddystone light at 9.45 P.M. We were landed at the London docks, having stuck to the ship to the last; for I always felt an instinctive dread of town with excessively small means. I was too unwell, on leaving Ceylon, to have any thought of finances, and my brother officers saw too plainly the necessity which existed for my immediate removal from Colombo, to have thought of the expediency of keeping me until I had the certainty of means to live in London. However, I found myself in lodgings in an offshoot from the Strand. I forget how I got there, but rather think I was taken by Major B., who was never tired of trying to do me any service in his power, or speaking of me to my friends in the highest terms.

I was now placed in an awkward predicament. I had no plain clothes, nor anything beyond what was sent with me when so suddenly put on board at Colombo. I knew no London tailor, and, if I had, my very small stock of ready money would have gone but a short way towards equipping me. I had, at that time, a horror of debt, which would have induced me to prefer living for months in the seclusion of my lodgings to ordering anything for which I had not the means of paying.

Northumberland Court was not a lively place of residence, and after two or three days' contemplation of its limited area, I thought I would venture out of my shell, although I had nothing but my rifle jacket and forage cap to appear in. I had not then learnt how great a sin it was considered for a soldier to appear in uniform when off duty!

I walked down the Strand, and round by the Horse

Guards, without observing that I was attracting the observation of all passers-by, and returned to my lodgings without adventure. Next day I repeated my little enterprise, when, to my surprise and no small satisfaction, I was accosted by a brother officer, the captain of my company, who was at home on leave. He had, it appeared, met me twice the previous day and took me for a young German! He would not hear of my hesitating to order plain clothes until I had the means of paying for them, but walked me off at once to Buckmaster, who received orders to equip me with all possible despatch; and I was confined to my lodgings until I could appear in the streets as other people did. The second morning after this I turned out in an approved suit of "mufty," and walked down to my liberator's lodgings to show myself.

It was a great disappointment on landing, instead of finding my father at Woolwich, to learn that he had been ordered with his battery to Newfoundland again. I had no one in London whom I knew, and felt very cramped with the small remains of the limited sum I had brought with me from Ceylon.

It was true that my passage-money, £49, was due; and, expecting I should be able to draw it, I went to the Colonial Office, where I was to receive it, but was quietly put off for a fortnight, to admit of some official regulations from the Treasury being complied with. This delay was subsequently prolonged another ten days; and even while exercising the greatest possible economy I was reduced to my last few shillings.

Hearing that Sir Edward Barnes was in London, I called on him in Dover Street, and, as I was taking my leave of him, he said :

" How are you off for money, youngster ? "

I replied :

"Very well, sir, and I expect to get my passage-money from the Colonial Office in a few days."

He told me to wait for a few minutes, went up-stairs and brought me down an order on the Board of Green Cloth for £25, which he put into my hand, and told me to pay him when I returned to Ceylon. This generous thoughtfulness quite set me up in the world. I drew the money, and at once settled with Buckmaster for my clothes. It proved a most opportune relief, for, as it turned out, several weeks elapsed before I was allowed to touch my passage-money, which I had called for so often that the Under-Secretary of State, to whom my applications were made, knew my step so well that, with his back towards me, he would address me without looking round.

At length, however, these difficulties were overcome, and I received my due ; but unfortunately, on that occasion, a relative accompanied me to the Colonial Office, and saw me draw my money. He tried very hard to "borrow" a portion of it, but I had the courage to refuse him, and said that the first thing to be done with it was to pay what I owed. To his amazement, I ran off so fast that he could not keep pace with me, and I did not feel myself safe until I gained admission at 7 Dover Street. Sir Edward Barnes fortunately was at home. I was out of breath when I thanked him for his timely aid, and told him I had drawn my money only a few minutes ago. He wanted me to keep the £25 until I could repay him with greater convenience in Ceylon; but I persisted in his allowing me gratefully to repay him then when I could do so, and abruptly left his presence before I had well recovered from the effect of my run up to his lodgings. I always had reason to believe him a noble fellow, but this little incident impressed it more deeply upon me than before. I cannot tell what would have befallen me but for his kindness. When I reached the street again I felt myself to be a free agent, as free as the cool air which refreshed my heated face. This debt had been a cause of great uneasiness to me. I had never owed so much before, and had been longing, day by day, for the means of repaying it. Having escaped the importunities of my needy relative, I had the inestimable comfort of knowing that I owed no man a shilling. Oh, that poor men could know the glorious independence of that feeling! How ill would they be able to bear the wretched slavery of pecuniary indebtedness to anyone.

I now began to be comparatively familiar with London, but had no pleasure in it. I viewed it as a place filled with temptation of every sort, which must be avoided by anyone who hoped to remain master of himself.

The extent of my means was 5s. 3d. a day, an ensign's pay, and to live within this was a problem I had determined to solve, and very tight work it proved; though quite possible to a man who could satisfy the cravings of hunger with simple but wholesome food, flavoured with the sauce of love of independence.

I had never been to a theatre, and determined to avoid them altogether until I could better afford to pay for so expensive an amusement.

I spent my mornings in trying to improve myself—the afternoons in exercise; but I was not long allowed to lead this secluded life, for a number of friends from Ceylon were in town, and they soon found me out. Their society rendered my life more agreeable, but not the less difficult; sociability and strict economy not being very consistent. However, I discovered I had some relatives in England, and received kind invitations from several of them. General Bentham, of the Artillery, living at Canterbury, who had married my mother's sister, asked me to stay with them, and I found there a very happy home. He had four sons—George, a post-captain in the Navy; William, a major of the Artillery; John, a captain in the 52nd Regiment; and Charles, a lieutenant in the Navy. He also had two daughters, Fanny and Maria; the latter was a great beauty, and married the Rev. — Gipps, afterwards one of the Canons of Carlisle. I visited Canterbury not long ago, and went to see the old house and the Dane John; they are close to each other. The door of the former was open, and so little changed that I could have fancied I had but just left it. The Dane John was precisely the same as I had known it fifty years previously; even the trees seemed to be of the same size and unchanged; but what had that time done for man? General Bentham and my aunt had, of course, passed away, but so had also every one of their children; the youngest, Mrs. Gipps, having died very suddenly a short time previously. Mrs. Bentham lived to attain a very old age—upwards of a hundred years. When more than ninety she used to introduce her eldest son, Admiral George Bentham, as her elder brother, which, in truth, he looked more like, and she would laughingly say, "If I admitted he was my son, people would think I was becoming an old woman!"

After remaining for more than six weeks at Canterbury I paid a long visit to my old schoolmaster, the Reverend John Christie, at Belmont, near Shaftesbury, where all the old servants were still to the fore, though some of them were married. My host scarcely knew how to show me enough kindness. He had given up his school; but I could hardly believe my senses at the enormous reduction in the size of everything I had so recently left behind me. The house, grounds, rooms, and play-ground were dwindled down, by my experience of the world, to a tithe of my boyish estimate of their dimensions. I was still but a boy according to the present acceptation of the term; but the three-and-a-half years since my departure from Shaftesbury had given me a large amount of experience of the world. In the retrospect, the time seemed scarcely a span's breadth, though so full of incidents; yet where I had been accustomed to be treated as a child, I was now received everywhere as a travelled man. There were not, in 1822, many lads of eighteen to be found in Dorsetshire who had been to India and bagged their half-a-dozen elephants.

CHAPTER III.

In the spring of 1822, I embarked, at Bristol, on board the schooner *La Hogue*, for St. John's, Newfoundland. I paid £10 for my passage, it having been arranged with the captain that, for that sum, I was to expect nothing more than ordinary ship's fare, such as he had himself. We progressed fairly till we reached mid-Atlantic, where we encountered a succession of tremendous gales; however, I amused myself by learning to work the ship's reckonings and observations. For many days we could do nothing but "lie to" under bare poles, unable to light a fire or cook anything; our bulwarks were carried away, and our long boat was washed from her position on the deck, up between the rigging and the fore-mast, under our futtock shrouds, and I became at last very tired of this state of inactivity. One day we found ourselves sailing through a shoal of whales; some were playing together, others floating on the surface of the ocean, sound asleep. We passed quite close to one of the latter, which appeared to be much longer than our vessel. We saw numbers of huge icebergs as we approached the banks of Newfoundland; but I may here observe that, long before we reached that place, our splendid system of reckoning had placed us some degrees up in the woods, though mine had not reached so far inland as that of the master of the schooner. I cannot tell where he received his nautical training, for, one day, in confidence, he informed me that a few years previously he had been a shoemaker in Newfoundland.

The fog was so dense that we literally could not see from one end of our vessel to the other. We could carry but little sail, and had to keep the danger bell going continually to prevent, if possible, our being run into; though the bell could have availed us very little, had we been in the track of any other vessel.

At length we reached St. John's harbour, just before it was blocked up with icebergs in the narrows; had we not managed to get in at that nick of time, we should have been long kept out, the entrance was so choked with ice. Attempts were made to break up these masses, which prevented communication with the harbour, but without any result. It is a fact not generally known, that heavy ordnance has little or no effect upon an iceberg. My father, commanding the artillery at St. John's, totally failed, with 42-pounders, to make any impression on them, although the distance was very short; the round shot fell dead from them into the water, as if the ice had been a huge mass of india-rubber. My late neighbour, General Thorndike, R.A., then a subaltern in my father's battery, reminded me of this incident shortly before his death.

I landed with a perfect recollection of the locality which I had left as a child, and walked up to Fort Townsend, where I had the happiness of taking my family by surprise, for ours was the first vessel of the season which had arrived, and during their long winter they had heard no news from England.

Directly the men-of-war could get out of harbour, the whole fleet was sent away in search of disabled vessels, which were overdue; the state of the weather had been such that all the early spring vessels were more or less damaged. The *La Hogue* was, I believe, the only one that reached port without assistance.

I seemed to know as much about St. John's as if I had only left it the year before. My first impulse was to go out fishing, though it was still cold—so cold, that I could not prevail on anyone else to accompany me; but I had inherited my father's love of the rod, and took instinctively to the sport. Early in the season the fish are so ravenous that it required very little dexterity to fill one's kreel with fine trout.

Whether it was the fact that Newfoundland was my native climate, or that I had not yet thrown off the caloric imbibed in Ceylon, I know not; but certainly I was able to endure a very low temperature, with perfect impunity, and to this day I enjoy cold weather, while suffering great inconvenience from the heat of summer. During the greater part of my life, however, I have borne a fierce tropical heat, and have constantly been exposed to the direct rays of the sun, in a cloudless sky, for six months of many years, while employed in my reconnaissance of the mountain zone of Ceylon, and in the construction of the map of that island, often not sheltering under a roof from daylight until dark.

As the summer advanced, fishing in Newfoundland became no easy matter, for the mosquitoes on the lakes and rivers were so great a nuisance. As I could not willingly relinquish the sport, I was obliged to adopt some antidote to these abominable pests; they were far more venomous than the mosquitoes of India, for they of the West speedily bunged up one's eyes, if they had the chance. So the next time I went out with my rod I took with me a mixture of hog's lard and Stockholm tar, wherewith to lubricate my face, neck, and hands. Two artillery gunners who went with me declined to submit to this disagreeable ordeal, though I cautioned them as to the consequences of their unprotected condition. I had not been fishing long when I saw my men getting very fidgetty, owing to their soldierlike objection to disfigurement from my horrid mixture. A little later their faces were frightful objects, being so swollen that they could scarcely see; and there was nothing for it but to lead them to a fisherman's hut not very far off. They learned afterwards to respect my kalydor.

One of the battalions of the 60th Rifles was stationed at St. John's during my visit there. I knew most of the officers well, especially the Honourable George Harvey, a son of the Earl of Bristol. With him and some others I went outside the harbour one day for sea-fishing. Our bait was simply a bit of red or white rag tied on to our hooks. With this we hauled in cod as fast as we could lower our lines, until our hands were quite raw with pulling in the fish. We were obliged, in the end, to throw a quantity overboard, in order to lighten our boat, and so take her back in safety. This was not true sport, and I never indulged in it again.

On one occasion a party started to visit a very large iceberg, which was grounded in deep water outside the harbour. I did not accompany them, preferring my rod-fishing; but on my way to the river I had to pass near the coast to the northward of the harbour, when I heard an appalling noise, like a prolonged and very heavy clap of thunder, but there was no appearance in the sky to justify such atmospheric disturbance. When I returned home in the evening, I found the sound had proceeded from the breaking up of the iceberg into two pieces, just as the boats containing the party were approaching it. Fortunately, they were some distance off, and only felt the shock slightly, for had they been nearer their boats would probably have been swamped. The noise was described as having been tremendous.

It was in Newfoundland that I received from my relative, then Colonel Lewis, of the Royal Engineers, my first lesson in surveying, in which he said I showed great aptitude. I little expected at that time that I should subsequently be employed in the triangulation, survey, and sketching of the island of Ceylon.

I remained with my father and family at St. John's until the end of the summer. Two men-of-war, H.M. ships *Sir Francis Drake* and *Egeria*, were under orders to sail for England. My brother John joined the latter as a midshipman, and I was to sail in the former.

The day of our departure at last arrived, and I took a sorrowful leave of home, feeling pretty certain I should not again see some of the dear ones I was leaving, even should I return from Ceylon myself. I never again met either my father or step-mother, my beloved sister, or my brothers.

The voyage to England in a large ship, like the *Sir Francis Drake*, was most agreeable compared with my outward trip; its size, the companionship of the officers, and also that of some of my own relations, made it especially pleasant.

On my return to England, I visited my step-mother's sisters, Mrs. Moore and Lady Wood, the latter at Isleworth, near London, where they were near neighbours of Sir Benjamin Hobhouse. We were a merry party of young people. I remember one day we were all weighed, and, to everybody's astonishment I was the lightest of them all, being only 7st. 7lbs.

In the winter of 1823 I was preparing for my return to Ceylon, when I received a subpœna to remain in England as witness in a distressing trial with which I had no personal concern, but I managed to get off.

In January 1824 Colonel Muller was appointed to the command of my regiment, and before his appointment he did me the honour of calling on me. He was a German officer, a nephew of Count Munster, and had been Equerry to the Duke of Kent, in which capacity he went over to Germany to marry by proxy, and bring to England the bride of His Royal Highness, and the future mother of our beloved Queen.

Colonel Muller was very kind to me. He had the private *entrée* at Kensington Palace, the residence of the Duchess of Kent, and one day wrote to the equerry in attendance to say he would be at the palace the following morning, Sunday, to breakfast, and that he would take me with him. We were unfortunately late in arriving, the Duchess and young princess having retired to prepare for church.

Shortly after this he asked me to accompany him to Paris, with Mrs. Muller, and he also took with him another young subaltern of the regiment, who was at home on leave. This proved a most amusing trip, and I wish I could recount some of the incidents that occurred, but I fear my memory now is too little to be depended upon. We crossed the Channel to Calais in one of the early steamers, and arrived there at low tide. Directly the steamer was made fast, the people on shore very politely lowered ladders for us to ascend by. I was the first passenger to land, and on reaching the quay was stopped by a set of fellows who crossed their hands, and held them thus, to prevent, I suppose, my landing until I had paid for the use of the ladder. I did not possess a very exalted impression of Frenchmen, and with the greatest effrontery closed my fists and hit out right and left, with all my small might. In amazement at my impudence, I conclude, they fell back and made way for me.

We had to undergo a minute inspection of our baggage at the Custom House, every article being examined. Here I found ample justification for the opinion I had formed of French manliness, for there were two horrible men in uniform, with enormous cocked hats, put on "athwart ships," and profuse beards and moustaches, hugging and kissing each other in the Custom House. It was the first occasion in my life on which I had witnessed such a spectacle, and it was no longer a wonder to me that I should have been permitted so easily to clear a way for myself through a crowd of such so-called men!

We next proceeded to the Diligence Office to secure our four seats for Paris; all the others had been taken, and our party just filled the extraordinary vehicle. On approaching Abbeville in the morning we were surprised at the crowded state of the road for many miles outside the place. Numbers of women were riding, and, in many cases, two on one horse. When we drove into the town, we found a guillotine erected in the *Place*, where there was to be an execution that morning. The crowd around the scaffold at nine o'clock was so dense, that by eleven o'clock, when the execution was to take place, and at which time the travellers on the road would have arrived, the scene must have been that of a closely wedged mass of human curiosity.

This journey called forth no ordinary degree of patience. The snow was deep upon the ground, and the smallest ascent was pronounced by the postillion to be "une grande montagne," and was an excuse for the slowest pace at which his horses could crawl. However, in course of time, we reached the French capital, and at first took up our quarters at Meurice's Hotel in the Rue de Rivoli.

My colonel's wife was an exceedingly tall woman, with very light hair, and would have been conspicuous anywhere. Her dress was out of fashion in England, but in Paris, even to our indulgent eyes, we knew that she was an object of universal observation, especially as there were very few English women there at the time. She was, however, quite unconscious of the sensation she was creating, and adhered to her antiquated bonnet and dress. Before a week had passed she was caricatured—no, faithfully represented—in every print-shop in Paris. Both she and her husband must have seen these full-length portraits, but they never noticed them, and she had the pluck to brave them all, for she continued to wear her English costume the whole time we remained abroad.

We enjoyed our visit to Paris, and benefited much by the experience we gained there, coming back to England in time to make our preparations for our return to Ceylon. We embarked on board H.M.S. *Princess Charlotte* on the same day, the 10th April, and from the same place, Gravesend, that I did on the first occasion of my going to Ceylon. We took out the head-quarter division of the 97th Regiment, under the command of Colonel Christopher Hamilton, and had besides a large and very agreeable party on board. I have a list of the names, and will insert it, though very few, I fear, are now alive :—

Sir John Sinclair, Bart., Madras Artillery.
Lady Sinclair.
Sir Robert Comyn, Chief Justice, Madras.
Colonel and Mrs. Muller, Ceylon Rifles.
Colonel and Mrs. Hamilton.
Major and Mrs. Haddock (the former was afterwards killed by an elephant in Ceylon).
Captain Darrah.
Lieutenant O'Neil.
,, Macintosh.
Ensign Chesney.
,, Stannus.
,, Handcock.
Assistant-Surgeon Austin.
Mr. Abbott, Madras.
Mr. Bathie, Madras.
Lieut. and Mrs. Armstrong, 45th Regiment.
,, and Mrs. Sidley, 45th Regiment.
,, and Mrs. Metge, 45th Regiment.
Ensign Lascelles, 45th Regiment.
Doctor Stewart, M.D., Bengal.
Mr. J. Stewart, Bengal.
Mr. Gibbings and Mr. Walker, Cadets, Madras.

Mr. Brownlow, Cadet, Bengal.

Mr. Burridge and Mr. Snoak, Madras.

Mr. Turton, and myself.

I had a splendid cabin, with a large port where I could have three chess-tables. We were a large party of chess-players. Colonel Hamilton was the best; next to him were Sir Robert Comyn and Mr. Abbott. We formed ourselves into a club, and met twice a week in my cabin. It was great presumption in me to join it, for I was by far the most indifferent player of the party, and at first had to endure many defeats from them all; but after a few weeks' practice I was sometimes successful, and then the game began to engross my thoughts to such a degree that I constantly dreamt of chess, and played whole games in my sleep. So wonderful is the power of the brain, when undisturbed by other things and intently absorbed with one subject, that, when suffering from fever, I have passed most painful nights in working out logarithms, keeping every figure of a whole theorem in my mind; but this left me in a fearful state of debility when I awoke.

Our chess club became a matter of interest on board, and was fully discussed every day of our meeting, when we went up on deck before dinner. Before I left the ship I had the satisfaction of beating Colonel Hamilton in nine games out of a rubber of eleven, and thereby became the champion of the club. This honour I had made up my mind if possible to attain; and on the mornings of our club meetings in my cabin I never left it till the day's work was over. I had a roll and a cup of tea brought to me for my breakfast, and by thus isolating myself kept my mind entirely free from other subjects.

In going through the Bay of Biscay, a little girl was born on board our ship. Her father was in the 97th Regiment, and, when she was christened, bestowed on her a number of names, which I hope she bore well through life—"Christopher Hamilton Charlotte Biden Biscay," the first two in honour of her colonel, the third the name of our ship, the fourth after our worthy captain, and the fifth from the locality in which she made her advent into this world.

The 97th Regiment had only recently been raised. They were a fine set of young fellows, the average age of the men being only nineteen. They retained their health in Colombo better than some of the other regiments, though they were subjected to very unfavourable treatment. As I was Staff Officer of the Garrison for a few years after the arrival of this regiment, I was tolerably competent to judge. My orders were to give the effective strength of the troops three nights in bed each week. With so much garrison duty as there was at Colombo, this was not always an easy matter. In England, I believe, the troops are always supposed to have six nights in bed each week. This can only be because garrisons at home have so few military duties to perform, and a turn of home work may be intended to set a regiment up, and therefore the less night-work they are subjected to the better.

I think that the English theory of the undesirableness of enlisting young recruits is carried to excess. A young thoughtless lad may require more looking after than one of more mature age; but if the system and discipline of a regiment is really good, and officers and non-commissioned officers take an interest in their men, I should prefer a recruit of eighteen or nineteen to one of five-and-twenty years old. He would require a year or two of feeding and training, but he is more likely to turn out a satisfactory soldier than a man who has passed several years in another occupation.

There is also a quantity of twaddle talked, in reference to the unhealthiness of tropical climates. I am myself an instance of a boy, not fifteen years of age, put into the Service; and I was always far too restless a spirit to save myself in any way. From the age of sixteen, when I was first employed away from my regiment, scarcely any labourer could have worked much harder, or have gone through greater exposure, than I was subject to during my forty-nine years' service in Ceylon. I shall soon be seventy-three years old, and have paid more than double the amount, £3,000, for which I insured my life twenty-six years ago.

In support of this opinion, I will mention my father-in-law's regiment, the 18th Royal Irish, which was stationed at Trincomalee when the order was received for active service in China. When I went to the former place to take leave of Colonel Burrell, there were no men in hospital; and, when they embarked for China, every man marched on board the ship with his arms and knapsack on. How seldom is this the case with regiments serving in England or elsewhere!

My father, when quartered for four years at Trincomalee, with a strong detachment of artillery, kept two very good boats, both schooner-rigged, in which he often went out sailing or fishing. They were manned by his own men, and, during the S.W. monsoon, were anchored near the Sally port, in Back Bay, close to their barracks. These boats were the pride and amusement of the battery. In consequence of the men having plenty of work to occupy their time, they scarcely knew what it was to be ill, and did not lose one of their number during their tour of duty there.

It would be difficult to describe the regret with which everyone on board the *Princess Charlotte* contemplated the approaching termination of our happy voyage, and our separation from Captain Biden, one of the best and most kind-hearted sailors that ever trod a quarter-deck.

The captains of the old East India Company's ships were a very superior class of men, well educated and accomplished, of whom Christopher Biden was an unusually fine specimen. He was for many years afterwards master attendant of Madras, and came once to Ceylon to pay me a visit.

I have already stated the extraordinary coincidence of my having embarked for Ceylon on two occasions from the same place on the same day; still more remarkable is the fact that on the same day of the month we dropped anchor on the same spot in Back Bay, Trincomalee.

15th April 1818, embarked off the "Falcon Hotel," at Gravesend.

10th August 1818, anchored in Back Bay, Trincomalee.

15th April 1825, embarked off the "Falcon Hotel," at Gravesend.

10th August, anchored on same spot in Back Bay, Trincomalee.

The distance run in 1825 was 13,581 miles.

On our arrival at Trincomalee, we were met by Major Anderson, of the Ceylon Rifles, Staff Officer of the Garrison, who assisted us in our preparations for the journey to Colombo, round by Jaffna, the extreme north of the island. We proceeded as far as Jaffna by water, but from thence we had to travel by land, and a very tedious affair it was.

When we reached Colombo, one of the first pieces of intelligence I heard was, that on Captain Mainwaring's promotion, the adjutancy of the regiment had been kept open for me. It was in vain that I protested I did not want it, as I heard that a most efficient officer, Lieutenant T. W. Rogers, had applied for it and was most anxious to obtain it. At length, after several days' negotiations, I agreed that Mr. Rogers should be brought to head-quarters, that we should both work together for three months, and, at the termination of that time, the more competent of the two should be appointed.

The morning after this arrangement had been made, Colonel Churchill, Sir Edward Barnes's Military Secretary, called on me, by order of the General, and said the latter officer advised me on no account to accept the adjutancy, but desired to know whether I should prefer to be one of Sir Edward Barnes's A.D.C.s, or to be made Staff Officer of Colombo? My reply was thoughtlessly given, expressing my feelings on the subject: I said I never wished to be an A.D.C. to any man in time of peace, but that if His Excellency would make me Staff Officer of Colombo, which involved constant active military duty, I should be very proud of the appointment. The garrison then consisted of—

A Troop of Dragoons.
A Detachment of Royal Artillery.
A Detachment of Royal Engineers.
A Company of the Royal Staff Corps.
16th Regiment. A portion of this regiment detached.
78th Regiment.
83rd Regiment.
97th Regiment.
Ceylon Rifles.
Gun Lascars.
Armed Lascoryns.

Several detachments were drafted from these regiments, but still the garrison was large, and its duties were conducted on the most strict and rigid principles. A field officer and two subalterns were on garrison duty every day; guard-mounting was done with the utmost formality; guards were "trooped" every morning, and not the slightest deviation from established forms was permitted without the field officer of the day being called upon to give his reasons in writing. The commandant was present at guard-mounting about three days in each week. I do not believe that the garrison at Gibraltar could have been under stricter discipline than that of Colombo at this time.

It was not till half-an-hour after I had sent my message to the Governor that I reflected on its impertinent character, and thought I had completely done for myself, and had no chance whatever of getting any appointment. My surprise was the greater, therefore, when, the following morning, I found myself in General Orders as Staff Officer of Colombo. The officer who had previously held the appointment being sent to Point de Galle, where the garrison was smaller and the duties lighter.

When I went to thank His Excellency for my promotion, imagine my surprise at his asking me to take up my quarters at King's House, and to become a member of his family. I began to think I had not done so far wrong in being honest and straightforward in my dealings with men in authority. My error would have been in thinking that I should always meet with so great and noble-hearted a man, and such a true soldier as Sir Edward Barnes, whose equal, for largeness of views, generosity, and nobleness of mind, I have never known in any position of life. He was a commander for whom any soldier would have considered it the highest privilege to have served even unto death. It was impossible to ride in his *cortège* without being inspired with the most devoted enthusiasm. How well any man who ever served under that perfect soldier can realise the description the late Sir Robert Arbuthnot gave of a desperate attack which he once saw Sir Edward make on a French position. The scene of the attack was an orchard, walled all round, to which he took his brigade up in open columns of companies; when at the proper distance he wheeled them into line, and then, having fired his men with his own enthusiasm, he rode his charger at the wall, and, cocked hat in hand, cleared it in the most splendid style. Sir Robert Arbuthnot said it was the finest sight and most effective attack he had ever witnessed. Sir Edward was, at the time, an exceedingly fine, handsome man.

I was now of age, having attained my twenty-first year, and for the next four years I acted as Staff Officer, which comprised every military department. The Staff Officer had charge of all military buildings, quarters and barracks, barrack furniture, and equipment of every description in the district, as well as performing the duties of brigade major of the garrison; he was assistant to the Deputy Adjutant-General, to the Deputy Quarter-master-General, and to the officer commanding the Royal Engineers whenever they required his services.

I was a very active little sprite, and was *never* late for one of those 6 A.M. guard-mounting parades, or for any duty, though I must not say how often, during those four years tenure of office, I did not go to bed till after guard-mounting. One morning Sir Edward Barnes came down to the billiard-room, as he usually did, between 12 and 1 o'clock, where we all congregated after breakfast. Seeing me intent on a game, he said:

"What are you doing here, youngster? I thought you would have been at Negombo by this time."

"What to do there, Sir?" I asked.

"What! Have you not received your orders from the Quartermaster-General?"

"No, Sir; I have not seen him to-day."

"Go to him at once, and be quick in what you have to do."

It was nearly 2 o'clock before the Quartermaster-General could be found. When I caught him he directed me to proceed to Negombo—an old fort twenty-three miles north of Colombo—to make a plan of the barracks there and to prepare an estimate for their repair, so as to fit them for immediate occupation.

This was rather a bore, for I was engaged to a very pleasant dinner party that evening, to which I knew the Governor and Lady Barnes were going. It was 2 o'clock when His Excellency saw me ride out of King's House grounds. I knew I could depend upon my grey arab charger, so the moment I got clear of the fort I started at a moderate hand-gallop, drew bridle for a minute or two at every sixth mile, and found that I reached Negombo within the two hours. There was no time to lose; I hooked my reins to a tree in the barrack square, and took out my field-book and tape; measurements for the plans were soon made, data for estimate all taken within the hour, my horse girthed up, and I in my saddle on my return to Colombo. I allowed my arab to go his own pace, which was always good, and found he had done the twenty-three miles home faster than on going out. I had my bath, dressed, and jumped into the buggy of one of the A.D.C.'s, and arrived at the dinner party very nearly as soon as the Governor and Lady Barnes.

The moment Sir Edward saw me he came up to me; there was no mistaking when he was displeased, though he had never found fault with me before. However, I thought to myself, "I will have a bit of fun; for I see you think I have neglected my orders." I was not left long in doubt on that point, for the following dialogue took place between us:

"Well, youngster; what the —— are you doing here? I thought I told you this morning to go to the Quartermaster-General for orders."

"So I did, Sir."

"And what did he tell you to do?"

"He ordered me to proceed to Negombo, Sir, to take plans of the barracks, to report the number of men they could accommodate, and to submit an estimate for their repairs."

"And what do you mean, Sir, by neglecting those orders; you ought to have gone off instantly. Colonel —— should have given you your orders yesterday evening."

"I have not neglected them, Sir; I have been to Negombo, and your Excellency will have all the information you require laid before you to-morrow morning."

"You have been to Negombo?"

"Yes, Sir."

"And taken plans of the barracks?"

"Yes, Sir."

"And framed an estimate for their repair?"

"Yes, Sir."

"At what time did you leave King's House?"

"Two o'clock, Sir; reached Negombo at nine minutes to four; and left it at a quarter to five."

"And what did you ride?"

"My own charger, Sir."

I saw the satisfaction he felt by his expression; he turned round, and although I pretended not to be looking at him, I saw the glee with which he was repeating my little exploit to our host, the Honourable Mr. Granville, and other members of the party. It was a fair ride and amount of work against time, but much more credit was due to my dear little horse than to myself.

I was only a pound or two over eight stone, and never tired of riding if allowed to go the pace. This little incident pleased my patron immensely; he was a perfect horseman himself, and there was nothing he liked better than to have things done quickly.

Not very long after this, we were sitting over our wine one evening, when one of the aides-de-camp, a brother of Lady Barnes, told us of some feat which a man of his regiment, the 10th Hussars, had performed in England, namely, riding a given distance against time in the dark. I ventured to say it was a good ride, but I thought nothing so very extraordinary, and that the same thing might be done in Ceylon. Little Churchill, the military secretary, took me up at once, and in his most sarcastic manner said :

"Oh, I suppose you imagine you could do it?"

"I do not *imagine* anything about it, I feel sure I could do it if I tried, but would rather not attempt it," I replied.

"Ah! do you think you could ride to Veangodde and back before guard-mounting?"

That took place at 6 A.M., and it was now past 11. Churchill went on bullying me until I could stand it no longer, and at last I asked Sir Edward if he would excuse my leaving the party if I accepted Churchill's bet of £50.

He struck the table with his fist and exclaimed, "Well done, youngster! I thought you could not stand it much longer. Certainly, take his bet and win."

The bet was that I could not ride my charger to Veangodde, which was twenty-five miles distant, and back again to Colombo before guard-mounting at 6 o'clock the following morning. I went down-stairs, threw off my coat, went to the stable, roused and saddled my poor little horse, who had eaten his grass for the night, and was sound asleep when I disturbed him—poor little beast, he had been out with me the whole previous day. I tied a small feed of corn in my handkerchief, round my waist, and vaulted into the saddle without cap or coat. I allowed the horse to go his own pace, drawing bridle at seven and a half miles to put the saddle back and tighten my girths; he then went on briskly till we reached Veangodde, when I looked at my watch and found he had done his twenty-five miles in just two hours and a half.

I knocked up an old bazaar woman who made me a cup of coffee while my horse was eating his feed of grain. I re-saddled and gave my grey the reins, he went off at his usual pace—we were never very slow in our movements—and when I had nearly reached the Bridge of Boats I got a light from a bazaar man to look at my watch, and found we had returned faster than we went out, so I was enabled to go into Colombo and reach the fort at half-past 5 o'clock, where most of the Staff were waiting up to congratulate me on my success. I had my bath and attended guard-mounting parade as fresh as need be.

When I met Churchill he paid me my £50, condemning his folly for having made a bet which I was enabled to win with so little trouble. The fact was my charger could do almost anything but fly; he was one of the most spirited and enduring animals I ever met. On field-days and at reviews we used to be the amusement of many and the dread of a few. The little creature quite enjoyed his work, and entered into it *con amore.* In throwing out points for the formation of a line he would, at full speed, interlace any number of covering sergeants, going alternately to the right of one and to the left of the next; he would go round a flank at a gallop so that I might touch the outer file, or, in taking orders to a commanding officer of a regiment, he would tear furiously up to him, and then stop dead short, so that our stirrup-irons touched, the old gentlemen sitting uneasily in their saddles until the fear of a collision had subsided. It was very wicked of me to startle them like this, but I knew my arab so well that I was perfectly sure there was no danger to be apprehended.

Sir Edward Barnes was himself the best mounted officer I have ever seen, he rode a magnificent bay arab charger with black points, whose coat shone like satin. Lady Barnes presented this Nigitte arab to her husband; he had cost her between £400 and £500, and was thought to be cheap at the price.

For a staff officer to appear on parade badly mounted was considered almost a military offence. One morning after a field-day, Sir Edward called "Mounted officers to the front."

They accordingly trotted round and formed a semicircle before him, when he thus addressed them: "Gentlemen, the next occasion on which I have the honour of meeting you here, I shall expect to see you all properly mounted. Outward face. To your respective corps. Trot; canter; gallop!"

The scene that followed was amusing.

Riding was not considered as essential to an officer in those days, as it is now, and young fellows were not taught before entering the Service. Swimming should, in my opinion, be as necessary an accomplishment in the army and navy as riding or walking. The first drill for a recruit should be his swimming lesson; and as for a sailor, he should be able almost to live in the water. Every child, if I had my will, should be a proficient in that art.

I had not held my appointment very long, before Sir Hudson Lowe arrived as second in command, and after some persuasion assumed the duties of Commandant of Colombo. He had not held any command of the kind for some time. A general impression prevailed that Sir Hudson Lowe was a surly, austere man, but never was a character more maligned; a more kind, I may say tender-hearted man, I never met with. For a military commander it almost amounted to a fault, for it was with extreme difficulty we could get him to notice irregularities, or to punish breaches of discipline. If I had not had the support and co-operation of his A.D.C., Oliver De Lancy, the discipline of the garrison would soon have fallen off under his command.

He was terribly undecided, and I have often wondered how his wavering mind could have carried him so far through the service, or enabled him to perform those delicate duties which were imposed upon him. I retained until very lately a striking proof of this characteristic. He was involved in a correspondence with the Government on an important question connected with the duties of his command. On my waiting on him one morning, he desired me to sit down and write a letter from his dictation. He paced up and down a long room, the whole width of his house, and in three hours finished and corrected his composition. I read it to him, and he desired me to take it home, copy it, and bring it to him for his signature. I obeyed his orders, but was far from obtaining his signature. I had to sit down again "to make a few verbal alterations," and this was repeated until I had seven copies of the letter; the one to which he finally attached his signature proved to be a very slight deviation from the original draft.

I never could understand why none of Sir Hudson Lowe's works were ever published, for he had undoubtedly several on hand, and a very large quantity of MS. ready for the press. Two or three amanuenses were continually engaged by him, and *many* reams of foolscap paper were filled, and so arranged in his private room as to indicate that there were at least three subjects to which his attention at the time was devoted. No circumstances could have been more favourable to quiet reflection than those of his life. He was very hospitable and generous; kept an excellent table, and first-rate cellar.

Sometime about the middle of the year 1826, an incident occurred to me illustrative of the kind-heartedness and generosity of my brother officers. I was at the time, I think, fifth or sixth lieutenant, and there was no one before me for purchase. One evening the members of the staff and of Sir Edward Barnes's family were in the A.D.C.'s room, when Captain Dawson, C.R.E., said it was a scandal I should not have my company for the want of a few hundred pounds, and at once circulated in the room a proposition to make up the required amount. I was not made aware of this proceeding until it was announced to me that the sum was made up and at my command. I was very deeply grateful to my brother officers for their most kind impromptu suggestion, but positively declined their generous offer, for I knew full well that there were those present who could ill afford to contribute.

Later in the year, or more probably it was in the beginning of 1827, I was surprised one morning by Sir Edward Barnes sending me a message that he wanted to see me directly. I began to take a retrospect of my late life, wondering what I could be required for, at that early hour. When I went to his dressing-room, which was immediately over my own bed-room, I at once saw I was about to "catch" it. The difficulty which presented itself to my mind was to determine for which of my many peccadilloes I was to be brought under His Excellency's displeasure, for, I must own that while I was acknowledged to be a good, smart officer, in all matters of duty and punctuality, I was a very wild one. Always consulted, and the first to be referred to, when any piece of mischief was wanted, I had had so many little adventures lately of which I was the originator, that I was fairly puzzled when confronted by the Governor. With his face covered with lather and a razor in his hand, he exclaimed in a very angry tone :

"What have I done, Sir, to deserve this treatment from you?"

I had never seen him look so angry, or heard him speak with such austerity before; and I had some difficulty in restraining my feelings, for I felt extreme sorrow and contrition for having offended the best friend that any youngster ever had. Every naughtiness I had been guilty of seemed instantly to crowd upon my memory, as a personal offence against the kindest and most partial of patrons, and I was overcome.

I fancy I see him now, with his arm up, his razor just as he had taken the first sweep from his chin, as I stammered out:

"I am extremely sorry, Sir, that I have done anything to displease you; will you be so kind as to tell me what it is? Be assured I would not intentionally have incurred your reproof."

"I feel it very much, and thought better things of you——"

I could not help interrupting, and implored of him to tell me in what respect I had been so unfortunate as to displease him.

"I hear, Sir, that you are allowing a man to purchase over you."

I replied: "Yes, Sir; but I have no money, and you know I am too thoughtless and extravagant a fellow to borrow it; I might never be able to repay it."

"Why did you not consult me? You must have known I could have helped you, and might, I should think, have been sure that I have the inclination to do so. I cannot easily forgive you for your want of confidence in me."

He laid down his razor, and, with his face covered with shaving soap, sat down and wrote the address of his banker, desired me to take it instantly to my adjutant, return my name for purchase, and state that he had already ordered the money to be paid on being applied for. He then told me to mount my horse and ride out *at once*, before breakfast, as a ship was about to sail, and I must not lose the opportunity.

I did as he desired me, and a supplementary return of officers for purchase was instantly prepared and submitted, but not in time to catch the ship, whose departure for England was earlier than the Governor supposed.

The consequence of this failure, by an hour or two, in the despatch of the regimental return of my name for purchase, lost me nearly nine years rank as a captain.

My friend Rogers got the step. I never regretted it, or envied him his good fortune. We—*i.e.* his brother officers and friends—were very fond and *justly* proud of him. A nobler fellow, a finer soldier, or a truer friend could hardly be imagined. Sir Robert Wilmot Horton, Sir Edward Barnes's successor in the Government, who had seen as much of life as a very large experience of European society could afford, was one day speculating on what would be the effect of the possibility of beginning life anew, with his matured knowledge of the world, and the privilege of personating any character he had met with in life. He was himself a most able and accomplished man, and it seemed strange that his self-esteem could admit of his preferring any character to his own ; but, to our surprise, he declared that if it were possible to adopt another's identity, that Captain Rogers was the one he would select of all the men he had ever known. This was a grand compliment, and as high a tribute to the merit of my friend as one man could pay another.

This splendid fellow, Rogers, was struck dead by lightning on the Happootella Pass on the 8th June 1845. At the time of his death, he was performing, *most efficiently*, and to the entire satisfaction of the Government and public, the offices of Government Agent of the district of Ouvah, District Judge, Commandant of the District, and was also my assistant in charge of the roads of that province—duties which, after his death, required four men to perform, with far less efficiency, promptitude, and punctuality than when they were administered by him alone.

He was also a keen and successful sportsman, and had bagged more elephants than any man in Ceylon; I cannot state with accuracy the number, but am under the impression it was about fifteen hundred.

The Kandian population of the Ouvah district—all Buddhists—paid the highest compliment in their power to their late energetic chief, by erecting, to his memory, a pretty litttle Christian church in the town of Badoola, the metropolis of the district. It has always appeared to me very beautiful, that their love and regard for Captain Rogers should have been so great as to overcome their religious scruples.

I have already stated that Rogers got his company when my name was too late to be returned for purchase. It was nearly nine years between the dates of our respective promotions, during which time eleven officers were promoted, or placed on full pay, over my head, besides fourteen being senior to Rogers when he got his company, so that it was a curious fact that when he was killed I occupied his position of senior captain of my regiment. It is not often that so many captains are disposed of so quickly.

This loss of time gave my kind patron far more uneasiness than it did me; he appreciated, better than I did then, the great advantage of early promotion.

CHAPTER IV.

In the years 1827–8–9, whenever elephants made their appearance within thirty or forty miles of Colombo, I received notice of their arrival from the headmen, and when I could get leave, exercised my privilege of taking some of my brother officers out shooting. A good many absurd incidents occurred on these occasions, on one of which Captain Forbes, of the 78th Regiment—he has since taken the name of Forbes-Leslie—and myself started after a herd, which was reported to be about forty miles off. We got up to the elephants, killed, as we thought, one of them, and gave chase to the rest. It was awfully hot weather, and the pursuit turned out unfavourably for us, and the elephants beat us; so we returned to our defunct friend, whom we imagined as dead as "Julius Cæsar," he having resigned to us his tail as a proof of death; but he soon began to show signs of animation, which signs were increased by our repeated discharge of balls into his head. To our no small dismay the animal presently discovered a tree, up which a native had climbed for safety, rushed at it with great fury and brought it to the ground; in his fall from the branches the poor fellow's skull was terribly fractured, in fact, completely opened. I did all I could for him with my small amount of medical skill and appliances; I cut off his hair and bandaged up his head with strips of wax cloth, which we used for the protection of our guns. In the course of the morning he seemed to us all to have passed away; we felt glad the poor fellow's sufferings were over. With my official notions I went through the form of recording the circumstances attending the accident. We passed an unanimous opinion that the deceased had met his death accidentally, having been killed by a wild elephant. This nice little bit of formality had not been long completed when my attention was drawn to the fact that, like the elephant who had injured him, the man we had pronounced to have been "accidentally killed," was showing unmistakable evidence of life, and we had to cancel the proceedings of our impromptu coroner's inquest. I am sorry to be obliged to add that the poor man, as well as the elephant, departed this life the following day.

A few years later I was extending my trigonometrical points in this direction, and overheard one of the attendant headmen giving rather an amusing account of this affair, and especially of myself, who had taken a prominent part in it. There was a large concourse of idlers standing round the instrument, and, as I corrected some of the details of the story, the narrator asked me how I could know anything about it, as there were only two gentlemen present, one of whom was very tall and the other extremely small. They were very much amused when I proved to them my identity. I heard from Colonel Forbes-Leslie a few weeks ago, when he reminded me that it was upwards of fifty years since our shooting party just referred to.

On another occasion my old friend, the Hanwell modelair, sent to tell me there was a fine herd of wild elephants near Avisavella, about twenty-eight miles off. Accordingly I, with three other friends, Colonel Lindsay, Captain Forbes, and Lieutenant Holyoake—all belonging to the 78th Regiment—rode out to the Avisavella Rest House, where we dined, and made our preparations for an early start the next morning. We were all up long before daylight, and divided our forces; Colonel Lindsay and Holyoake holding one Pass, while Forbes and I took charge of the other. The herd was a fine large one, and we looked forward to a glorious day's sport. Presently the elephants came on with a splendid charge, when suddenly a man came running to us crying out, "Gentleman plenty sick, Sir!"

Forbes gave the man his brandy flask, and desired him to take it to the "gentleman." We had hardly got rid of this fellow before another came tearing down in a frantic state, saying—

"Gentleman soon will die. Elephant catch him!"

We went at once and found poor Holyoake in a sad plight. He had been charged most viciously, and while making his retreat down hill the elephant caught him, and attempted to "butt" him with his forehead, but in doing so over-reached Holyoake, and thus enabled him to crawl under the body of the elephant and creep out from between his hind legs. No sooner, however, did the enraged animal find he had lost his victim, than he gave chase again, and this time he caught poor Holyoake and took his revenge, breaking his arm and collar bone and smashing in his ribs on one side. In this state we found him, and had some difficulty in taking him back to Colombo. We managed to carry him to a boat, and conveyed him by the Kalanyganga river, getting him back to his quarters at about 2 A.M., when we had to call in the surgeons to patch him up.

As none of us had tasted any food since very early morning we were pretty well tired and done up; so when we had received the report of the medical officers that no danger was to be apprehended, and that in due course of time our friend would be as well as ever, we separated and went off to our respective quarters, anxious to get to bed.

Forbes went with Colonel Lindsay, as his wife was staying with Mrs. Lindsay during his absence. On entering the dining-room his host poured out a glass of what he imagined to be first-rate curaçoa, which Forbes drank off before he discovered that he had taken a large dose of castor oil. His disgust was too great to be restrained until his host had also partaken of it, and he hurriedly exclaimed, "It 's castor oil you have given me!"

Colonel Lindsay was a most absent-minded man, and

was often known to go into a house, or committee-room, holding a dripping wet umbrella over his head until relieved of it by someone.

With reference to elephant-shooting, I have heard men who have never come in contact with these animals assert that in their wild state they are never dangerous; but the two cases I have mentioned, and also those of Major Rogers, who was very badly wounded by one, young Wallet, a very fine young fellow of my department, who was killed close to the place where Holyoake was so mauled, and the death of Major Haddock of the 97th Regiment, are a few evidences of the expediency of being well prepared for mischief.

Elephants are strange animals. I have seen many little traits of which I have never read any account in books on natural history. One thing I noticed, that the larger and more powerful they are when first captured and brought to the stables, the quieter and more docile they appear. The largest captured elephant I have ever seen was one in the possession of Mr. Cripps, the Government Agent of the Seven Korles; he was a full-sized animal, and yet he fed from our hands the evening he was brought in. He was very docile in his training until the day he was first put in harness, when he could not stand the indignity of being expected to draw a waggon. He dropped in the shafts and died—the natives declared of a broken heart. This was by no means a solitary instance of casualties from a like cause. I have had several animals in my own department who have died when first put into harness, and who, apparently, had nothing the matter with them before.

Another peculiarity in the elephant it may not be amiss to mention is that I have often witnessed at kraals* very small elephants used for catching the wild ones; and remember one case in particular at the Three Korles, in which Molligodde, the first adigar†, took a prominent part. He rode a very small animal, so small that his head did not reach the height of several of the elephants about to be captured; but he went into the kraal with the utmost confidence, and was very active during the business. Many large elephants were taken without any of them using the least violence towards the little animal ridden by the adigar. This adigar possessed numbers of large tusked elephants, any one of which, one would have supposed, would have been far more formidable and efficient for the work than the puny animal which he rode. I have never seen the mahout‡ of the small elephants at kraals ill-used or in the smallest danger, however violent the wild ones might be.

A scene I witnessed of a herd of elephants bathing, while I was surveying in the central forest, is described in Sir J. Emerson Tennent's book, *The Wild Elephant*. He writes :—

---

* Kraal, a strong enclosure, in the heart of the forest, formed of trunks of trees, for the capture of wild elephants.

† Adigar, Kandian chief.

‡ Mahout, elephant-driver.

The following narrative of an adventure in the great central forest toward the north of the island, communicated to me by Major Skinner, who was engaged for some time in surveying and opening roads through the thickly-wooded districts there, will serve better than any abstract description to convey an idea of the conduct of a herd on such occasions :—

"The case you refer to struck me as exhibiting something more than ordinary brute instinct, and approached nearer reasoning powers than any other instance I can now remember. I cannot do justice to the scene, although it appeared to me at the time to be so remarkable that it left a deep impression in my mind.

"In the height of the dry season in Neuera-Kalawa, you know, the streams are all dried up, and the tanks nearly so. All animals are then sorely pressed for water, and they congregate in the vicinity of those tanks in which there may remain ever so little of the precious element.

"During one of these seasons I was encamped on the bund or embankment of a very small tank, the water in which was so dried that its surface could not have exceeded an area of 500 square yards. It was the only pond within many miles, and I knew that of necessity a very large herd of elephants, which had been in the neighbourhood all day, must resort to it at night.

"On the lower side of the tank, and in a line with the embankment, was a thick forest, in which the elephants sheltered themselves during the day. On the upper side and all around the tank there was a considerable margin of open ground. It was one of those beautiful bright, clear, moonlight nights, when objects could be seen almost as distinctly as by day, and I determined to avail myself of the opportunity to observe the movements of the herd, which had already manifested some uneasiness at our presence. The locality was very favourable for my purpose, and an enormous tree projecting over the tank afforded me a secure lodgment in its branches. Having ordered the fires of my camp to be extinguished at an early hour, and all my followers to retire to rest, I took up my post of observation on the overhanging bough ; but I had to remain for upwards of two hours before anything was to be seen or heard of the elephants, although I knew they were within 500 yards of me. At length, about the distance of 300 yards from the water, an unusually large elephant issued from the dense cover, and advanced cautiously across the open ground to within 100 yards of the tank, where he stood perfectly motionless. So quiet had the elephants become (although they had been roaring and breaking the jungle throughout the day and evening), that not a movement was now to be heard. The huge vedette remained in his position, still as a rock, for a few minutes, and then made three successive stealthy advances of several yards (halting for some minutes between each, with ears bent forward to catch the slightest sound), and in this way he moved slowly up to the water's edge. Still he did not venture to quench his thirst, for though his fore feet were partially in the tank and his vast body was reflected clearly in the water, he remained for some minutes listening in perfect stillness. Not a motion could be perceived in himself or his shadow. He returned cautiously and slowly to the position he had at first taken up on emerging from the forest. Here in a little while he was joined by five others, with which he again proceeded as cautiously, but less slowly than before, to within a few yards of the tank, and then posted his patrols. He then re-entered the forest and collected around him the whole herd, which must have amounted to between 80 and 100 individuals—led them across the open ground with the most extraordinary composure and quietness, till he joined the advanced guard, when he left them for a moment and repeated his former reconnaissance at the edge of the tank. After which, having apparently satisfied himself that all was safe, he returned and obviously gave the order to advance, for in a moment the whole herd rushed into the water with a degree of unreserved confidence, so opposite to the caution and timidity which had marked their previous movements, that nothing will ever persuade me that there was not rational and preconcerted co-operation throughout the whole party, and a degree of responsible authority exercised by the partriarch leader.

"When the poor animals had gained possession of the tank (the leader being the last to enter), they seemed to abandon themselves to enjoyment without restraint or apprehension of danger. Such a mass of animal life I had never before seen huddled together in so narrow a space. It seemed to me as though they would have nearly drunk the tank dry. I watched them with great interest until they had satisfied themselves as well in bathing as in drinking, when I tried how small a noise would apprise them of the proximity of unwelcome neighbours. I had but to break a little twig, and the solid mass instantly took to flight like a herd of frightened deer, each of the smaller calves being apparently shouldered and carried along between two of the older ones."*

Although on the garrison staff of Colombo, where the duties were carried on with the utmost punctiliousness, I was often employed by Sir Edward Barnes in surveying and tracing new roads; my garrison duties being at these times provided for. In 1828 I traced the Newera Ellia road from Rangbodde to Gampola, having previously laid down a line from Colombo to Chilan and Putlam.

I have seen controversies in newspapers on the subject of the curing of the bites of poisonous snakes, some medical officers stating that it was impossible to do so. My own experience convinces me to the contrary. In tracing the Newera Ellia road above mentioned, near to Poocellawa, we were at work, the clearing party in advance opening the jungle, when a cry was heard that a pioneer had been bitten by a tic-polonga, the most venomous snake known in Ceylon, said to be much more so than the cobra de capello. I was at my instrument in the rear when the man was brought to me. What was I to do with him? In half an hour, at the most, we all supposed he would succumb to the poison; but listlessly to resign ourselves to inaction seemed too hard-hearted. My powder-flask

---

* *The Wild Elephant*, p. 51.

contained the whole extent of my field *materia medica*. How was it be applied? I laid the man down, and with my pen-knife deeply scored the bitten arm. I then emptied a charge of gunpowder over the wound, and applied a match to it. I repeated this several—it may have been five or six—times, and sent the man away to the camp, never expecting to see him alive again. After our day's work was completed I returned to my wigwam, and, on going to look up the invalid, to my surprise and immense delight I found him alive and moving about. In two days more he was as effective as any of my party.

It was curious that the day this man returned to work another fellow was bitten in the foot by a splendid specimen of the same description of snake, which was killed and brought to me with the disabled man. This seemed intended to be a confirmation of the previous experiment, which I followed out exactly, but with considerably greater confidence. Neither of the men suffered pain from the surgical treatment, the parts operated upon having been numbed by the poison of the snakes. In this second case, the man left me for his camp in better spirits than the first-named, and he was at work with the rest of the men the following morning.

I was too much engaged with my work to take much notice of this at the time, but I mentioned it in subsequent discussions on the subject. Sir Robert Wilmot Horton, who was then Governor of Ceylon, thought the information so valuable to the public that he induced me to publish an account of it in a local paper. I have, since my retirement from Ceylon, sent an account of these facts to the London *Times* in reference to a correspondence in its columns on the subject, with the object of refuting the assertion of some Indian medical officers that there was no known cure for the bite of venomous snakes.*

It would, I think, be worth while for some analytical chemist to determine what element of gunpowder could have had the curative effect in the cases of the two pioneers just mentioned, as having been bitten by large full-grown ticpolonga. I am disposed to attribute it to the charcoal, for I sent home, through Sir James Emerson Tennent, specimens of snake-stones with which I had seen cases cured; and the result of Mr. Faraday's analysis of the "Pamboo-Kaloo" was that it appeared to be animal charcoal. If this be the case, surely a specific might be discovered which might diminish the mortality at present attributable to the bites of venomous

---

* Extract from Sir J. Emerson Tennent's book, vol. i., p. 193. "Major Skinner, writing to me, mentions the still more remarkable case of the domestication of the cobra de capello in Ceylon. 'Did you ever hear,' he says, 'of tame cobras being kept and domesticated about a house, going in and out at pleasure, and in common with the rest of the inmates? In one family, near Negombo, cobras are kept as protectors, in the place of dogs, by a wealthy man who has always large sums of money in his house. But this is not a solitary case of the kind. I heard of it only the other day, but from undoubtedly good authority. The snakes glide about the house, a terror to thieves, but never attempting to harm the inmates.'"

snakes. Sir J. Emerson Tennent says, in his book on Ceylon :—

The use of the Pamboo-Kaloo, or snake-stone, as a remedy in cases of wounds by venomous serpents, has probably been communicated to the Singhalese by the itinerant snake-charmers who resort to the island from the coast of Coromandel; and more than one well-authenticated instance of its successful application has been told to me by persons who had been eye-witnesses to what they describe. On one occasion, in March 1854, a friend of mine was riding, with some other civil officers of the Government, along a jungle path in the vicinity of Bintenne, when they saw one of two Tamils, who were approaching them, suddenly dart into the forest and return, holding in both hands a cobra de capello which he had seized by the head and tail. He called to his companion for assistance to place it in their covered basket, but, in doing this, he handled it so inexpertly that it seized him by the finger, and retained its hold for a few seconds, as if unable to retract its fangs. The blood flowed, and intense pain appeared to follow almost immediately; but with all expedition, the friend of the sufferer undid his waistcloth, and took from it two snake-stones, each of the size of a small almond, intensely black and highly polished, though of an extremely light substance. These he applied, one to each wound inflicted by the teeth of the serpent, to which the stones attached themselves closely, the blood that oozed from the bites being rapidly imbibed by the porous texture of the article applied. The stones adhered tenaciously for three or four minutes, the wounded man's companion in the meanwhile rubbing his arm downwards from the shoulder towards the fingers. At length the snake-stones dropped off of their own accord, the suffering appeared to have subsided; he twisted his fingers till the joints cracked, and went on his way without concern. Whilst this had been going on, another Indian of the party who had come up took from his bag a small piece of white wood, which resembled a root, and passed it gently near the head of the cobra, which the latter immediately inclined close to the ground; he then lifted the snake without hesitation, and coiled it into a circle at the bottom of his basket. The root by which he professed to be enabled to perform this operation with safety he called the *Naya-thalee Kalinga* (the root of the snake-plant), protected by which he professed his ability to approach any reptile with impunity."*

* * * * *

On the 28th of March 1829, I lost a very dear friend, and the service a most invaluable officer, in Captain W. Dawson, commanding Royal Engineers. The poor fellow died in my arms. The whole island mourned him. Wherever he was known, he was dearly loved. Sir Edward Barnes had, notwithstanding Dawson's junior rank, selected him for the position of C.R.E., which was a colonel's command, for Sir Edward knew, from his Peninsular experience of him, the great merit Dawson possessed as an officer. A singular coincidence occurred in reference to the monument erected to his memory on the top of the Kaddoganawa Pass, which was one of the triumphs of his skill. The foundation of this column was laid at the same time as that to the memory of His Royal Highness the Duke of York, late Commander-in-Chief, at the entrance of the Park at the end of Waterloo Place. The dimensions of these two memorials are identical, the only difference in them being that Dawson's monument is built of brick, whereas that erected by the nation to the memory of the Commander-in-Chief of the Army, in a conspicuous position in the metropolis, is of granite, surmounted by a statue of His Royal Highness. Dawson's remains were interred in a vault in Saint Peter's Church, Colombo.

* *Ceylon*, by Emerson Tennent, vol. i., p. 197.

On the 25th of November in the same year, we lost another good officer, Lieutenant W. Moore, of the Royal Staff Corps. He was Deputy Assistant Quartermaster-General. Being very ill, a medical board decided that he was immediately to be sent to England. I had therefore embarked him on board a ship which was to sail for England the following day. In the morning the captain wrote to me suggesting the expediency of my landing the poor fellow again, as he had become much worse during the night, and the captain thought he could not long survive. I went off at once and brought him on shore, and was glad I did so, for he died during the night, and was buried the next day.

On the morning of the 27th of November 1829, Colonel Churchill, the military secretary, brought me a message from the Governor to the effect that he intended giving me the appointment now vacant by Moore's death in the Quartermaster-General's Department. I ran off instantly to Sir Edward Barnes, told him what Churchill had just communicated to me, and said:

"You know, Sir, I am quite ignorant of the scientific duties of the department. I literally know nothing of them."

He answered: "Do you think I do not know that as well as you do? Will you promise me that you will do what you can to qualify yourself?"

"Certainly I will, Sir."

"That is quite enough; go about your business." And he turned on his heel and left the room.

This was an awful responsibility I had taken on

myself. I knew my new chief to be one of the most talented officers in the Army, very scientific and extremely exacting, and I felt quite sure that he would never tolerate inefficiency in an assistant. However, the thing was done. I had accepted the appointment, and all my life I had thoroughly believed that any man with ordinary abilities could make himself anything he liked, unless he acknowledged himself infirm of purpose or idiotic. So off I started at once, knowing I had everything to learn.

I had not been in General Orders a couple of days before I was ordered to relieve Lieutenant F—— of the Royal Engineers, who was employed in the construction of a rope suspension bridge over the Ambepoose river, midway between Colombo and Kandy. The Governor was very much interested in this work, on which the communication with Kandy and the Seven Korles route depended. The consequence was he frequently visited it, and was pleased to approve of the mode in which I proceeded. My taste for everything connected with the sea gave me a facility in the management of tackefalls, &c., which had its advantages in helping me with my present work.

Having completed this job, I was placed in charge of the roads of the interior, under the Quartermaster-General, all public works being at that time conducted by the military. This employment gave me plenty of riding, and compelled me to be as nearly "ubiquitous" as possible.

CHAPTER V.

I WAS now to be employed on rather important special service. In August 1830, I received instructions that His Excellency the Governor required me to proceed to the Eastern Archipelago on a special service, for which I was to prepare. The Government barque *Anne* was to be armed, and I was to proceed to Trincomalee to take on board guns, ammunition, and necessaries for the expedition, and thence to embark for Prince of Wales Island, Malacca, Singapore, and Java, to hold a conference with the Governor-General of Netherlands, India, and to regulate my subsequent movements by the result of this conference.

Having received my final instructions, and taken leave of the Governor on Saturday, the 28th of August, at daylight on Sunday I embarked on board the Government barque *Anne*, with the detachments, 1 subaltern, 1 sergeant, and 15 rank and file of the 58th Regiment, to act as marine artillery in charge of the guns and stores, and 61 of all ranks of the Ceylon

Rifles, a staff surgeon, and a good crew. The 58th Regiment were well drilled to artillery practice, and could work a battery of guns most efficiently.

At half-past 7 we got under weigh and sailed, according to orders, in company with the Government barque *Wellington*, which was conveying Sir Hudson Lowe to Batticaloa. With fresh, steady breezes, we reached the latter place at 3 o'clock on the 31st of August, when I bore down to the *Wellington* to ask, by signal, if Sir Hudson Lowe had any orders for me. Not having any, he released me, and authorised my making sail for Trincomalee, where I arrived, and anchored in Back Bay, at 7 o'clock the following morning.

Having mounted an European guard on board, and given the necessary orders regulating their duties while in harbour, I landed, and waited on the commandant, my old friend Colonel Hamilton, of the 97th Regiment. I then lost no time in putting myself in communication with the departments for the purpose of getting on board our guns, ammunition, and small stores. I dined with Colonel Hamilton at the 97th mess, and during the evening a bet was made by the Colonel and Lushington on Major Hall's and my rifle-shooting, which was to be decided the following day, and was settled by my beating Major Hall in the best of seven shots at 100 yards.

Early next morning I inspected the guns, and discovered that the carronade carriages were made so much too large that there was no possibility of working the guns. I was obliged to have them dismounted, and sent the slides and carriages on shore immediately to be altered. This detained us until the 9th of September.

Sir Hudson Lowe arrived in the *Wellington* on the 3rd, and was received with the usual salute and honours. During my detention here, I joined a party, one afternoon, and went an excursion in the inner harbour; we had a delightful sail, and much enjoyed the beauty of the scenery.

I wrote to His Excellency and explained the cause of my delay, naming Thursday, the 9th, as the probable day for sailing. One evening, the non-commissioned officers and soldiers of the 97th Regiment acted *Paul Pry* and the *Liar* wonderfully well. The greater number of the performers were men who had come out with me, in the *Princess Charlotte*, five years previously. I was much gratified to find that many, who came out as raw recruits, had, by their steady, good conduct, been promoted to the rank of sergeants, and had grown fine soldier-like fellows. I never could have imagined it possible that the 97th Regiment, as I knew it three years before, could have so rapidly risen to its present state of appearance and discipline. Corporal punishment, which used to be almost an every-day occurrence, was now seldom known in the regiment.

On the 9th September we took on board our ammunition, and prepared for sea. Just as we were starting, H.M.S. *Crocodile* came in, and "hove to" in Back Bay; she had arrived from New South Wales and Batavia; and finding that the Admiral, Sir Edward

Owen, was in the Straits of Malacca, Captain Montague asked me to be the bearer of despatches to him, for which I waited. My old friends, Wilson, Dan Mackinnon, and Frith, of the 58th Regiment, came on board. At 6 o'clock, having received the despatches from the *Crocodile*, or, rather, seeing her boat putting off with them, we weighed anchor, set sail, and started on our course before the boat was alongside, for we had so many hands on board, we could work the little ship like lightning; she was a beautiful craft, and sailed remarkably well. On leaving, our friends gave us three hearty cheers, which we returned with interest.

From the 10th to the 17th September 1830 we had days of calm and a tremendous swell from the S.E.; a steady breeze then sprang up, but with it dirty weather, and, the wind being aft, we rolled immoderately and shipped a great quantity of water, the pumps going every hour. We were too late in starting from Ceylon, the S.W. monsoon having nearly expended itself.

At daylight on the morning of the 17th the island of Pulo Rondo came in sight about fifteen miles distant, and at 8 o'clock we saw the high land of Acheen Head. The sea here assumed the most curious appearance, occasioned by what Horsburg describes as a "ripple." There was very little wind, and that little variable; to this was opposed a swell, sometimes short and irregular, at others long and continuous, which broke with considerable violence, and in the former instance was not unlike the effect produced on the water by a sudden hurricane.

On Sunday 19th we paraded for divine service, and I officiated in a clerical capacity for the first time.

On Tuesday 21st, we made Penang or Prince of Wales Island, at 2 o'clock, but in consequence of light winds could not get into the harbour, so anchored off the northern point of the island. At daybreak the following morning we got under weigh, although there was wet, dirty weather, with light contrary winds. We passed a Company's brig at anchor, and I afterwards learnt Lord and Lady Dalhousie and their retinue were on board, returning from the Straits to Calcutta, His Excellency having been on a tour of inspection to these settlements.

We anchored about 12 o'clock in the harbour, where we found six ships, eighteen brigs, and a number of Chinese and other small vessels. I went on shore directly to deliver despatches from Sir Edward Barnes to the President, Mr. Ibbetson, who kindly invited me to take up my quarters with him during my stay at Penang, which I agreed to do. From Mr. Ibbetson's I proceeded to the Admiral to report my arrival and to deliver despatches. Sir Edward Owen was most kind, and desired me to call upon him for any assistance he could render me in furtherance of the service on which I was engaged. We all dined with the Admiral, and much enjoyed the society of Lady Owen and her niece, Miss C.

The mess arrangements of the native regiment—the 25th Madras Infantry I think it was—struck me at the time as being peculiar and undesirable. They had no establishment, every officer's servant brought his own table equipment; if it did not arrive in time, the officer had to wait and look on till it came. I do not know, however, that it was not a less objectionable *extreme* to go to than the opposite one of extravagant luxury and display which most of Her Majesty's regiments now indulge, in placing upon their tables more costly plate than they can possibly accommodate. I know a regiment, which has not long returned from foreign service, which has burdened itself with a centre-piece for the table which cost £500, although it was acknowledged before they bought it that they possessed more plate than they could possibly use. Is it any wonder that so many young men are ruined by such encouragement to extravagance? I think as many as five or six officers have had to leave that regiment and sell out. The commanding officer and seniors of regiments should be made a great deal more responsible than they are for the mess expenses of their juniors; but so little are they now responsible that it frequently happens that the colonel and field officers of a regiment spend much less on the mess than many of the subalterns, who are impressed with the idea of the necessity of "keeping up the *credit* of their regiment." This would be much better preserved by a prudent regard to economy than by any amount of reckless entertaining involving, as it so often does, the necessity for their selling out, and becoming heavy burdens to their family and a discredit to the reputation of their regiments. When will the Horse Guards become alive to the expediency of looking into this subject?

But to return from this digression. Much as I had been led to expect from the extremely beautiful approach to this superb little island, I was agreeably surprised in my expectations being more than realised. The first object which strikes the visitor on arriving at Penang is the excellent landing-place or jetty, projecting for a considerable distance into the harbour; it is built of cut granite, having an inclined plane about twelve feet wide in the centre and a flight of steps on either side; it is paved with slabs of granite and covered in with a substantial tiled roof, affording delightful shelter. The jetty is about one hundred feet by forty.

Directly we landed we were assailed by "link boys," who contended for our patronage of their master's vehicles, which are exactly similar to the palanquin carriages used throughout India, drawn by small Sumatra ponies and led by a horse-keeper or "syce." The palanquins are extremely clean and comfortable, and the greatest convenience to strangers; they seemed to be in much requisition, for the natives use them as much as the Europeans. These ponies—there are very few horses in Penang—are small but extremely hardy, equal to heavy weights, and able to go through an incredible amount of work. They are very sure-footed little animals; I scarcely saw one with a broken knee. They are never shod, which confirms the opinion I have always entertained, that half the falls that horses meet with are more often due to bad shoeing than any other cause.

The streets, roads, and dwelling-houses of this island all claim an equal share of admiration; but the little English-looking church, which attracts the attention of the stranger, is truly beautiful; it is surrounded by a number of very fine trees not unlike the cypress. Its appearance is sufficient to inspire one with a feeling of devotion, and enough to make one fancy for the moment that he is at home; the interior is quite in keeping with its exterior, only more beautiful and chaste.

I went for a delightful ride one day with Mr. Ibbetson to the top of Flag-staff Hill, which is 2,500 feet above the sea, and is reached by a bridle-path. On the summit is the Governor's bungalow: the grounds are laid out with great taste, and the scenery from there is truly exquisite; the view comprises nearly the whole island of Penang and a considerable portion of the opposite shore of Quedah, which near the coast is richly cultivated. Our possession there is called Province Wellesley, and is bounded on the north and south by two rivers, which can be seen from Flag-staff Hill, winding from the densely-wooded country of the interior to the sea-shore, the whole scenery being enriched by the numerous small islands with which these seas are studded.

On the 23rd I landed the recruiting parties, and sent them to different parts of the island for a week. During that time a few men offered themselves; but I was under the necessity of rejecting them, as they were very inferior specimens. Penang is, in fact, the worst place for raising recruits. The Malay population is principally composed of men from Quedah, who possess boats or small vessels, and lead a roving, lawless life, and will not for any consideration leave it for husbandry or any other employment. Piracy was considered by the Malays not only legitimate, but an honourable mode of gaining a livelihood; so much so that the younger sons of Rajahs, who could not be independently provided for, almost invariably adopted it as their profession. There have been several cases of piracy in the Straits this year. Men-of-war have been sent in search of the pirates; but as yet with little or no success.

So daring are these fellows that while we were at Penang there was an instance of a fleet of their vessels passing through the harbour in the night and capturing a boat. They murdered the crew with the exception of one man, who escaped badly wounded and brought the intelligence to Penang. Not long since, the wife of a celebrated pirate resided here, and was the agent through whom the prisoners, taken by them, were ransomed.

The size of Penang is twenty miles long, the greatest width is nine miles, and only three miles at the narrowest point. It is for the most part hilly, the only level space being that on which George Town is built, and on the highest point of which—2,500 feet above the level of the sea—the Governor has his bungalow. The whole range of hills is covered with jungle, except where cleared for cultivation.

The climate is extremely healthy and the atmosphere moist, except in February and March, which are the driest and coolest months. The temperature is very regular, its extremes in George Town being 76° and 78°, and at Flag-staff Hill 64° and 76°.

The soil on the low ground is generally of a white sandy description, the hills being composed of a red, soapy clay and cabook, with very little appearance of rock throughout the island.

The only cultivation carried on as yet is that of nutmegs, cloves, pepper, coffee, sugar-cane, paddy, cocoa-nuts, and beetle-nut, for which the soil appears well adapted; of the foregoing, cloves and coffee are found to thrive best on the high ground, the others are confined to the valleys. The proportion which the cultivated bears to the uncultivated land is estimated at about one-tenth. Ground is of little or no value, and is given by Government to all applicants almost unconditionally. The exports are nutmegs, cloves, and pepper; of rice, coffee, and sugar-cane there is not a sufficient quantity grown for the consumption of the island.

The only extensive proprietor is Mr. Brown, the son of the man who first introduced the cultivation of nutmegs. The remainder of the land is subdivided, principally amongst the Chinese, who are the chief cultivators. English implements of husbandry are scarcely known here; the Buffalo plough and mamoty being used as in Ceylon.

The island produces abundance of fine timber for purposes of house-building, also a tree called poon, suitable for mast-poles; but there are no ornamental woods. The roads are numerous and good in the vicinity of the town, and the island is intersected by them in all directions. The population amounts to 35,000, the greater proportion being Chinese. Of the aborigines there are none. When the island was taken possession of in 1786 it was merely a haunt for pirates, who immediately vacated it for Pulo Dinding, a large island to the southward, which is still their favourite place of rendezvous.

Convicts from all the settlements of India are sent to Prince of Wales Island, and a few to Malacca and Singapore. There are at present at Penang 1,200; the best behaved of these, numbering about 500, are hired out as servants, horse-keepers, and grass-cutters, the others being employed on the roads and public works.

The settlement of Province Wellesley extends for thirty miles along the opposite coast, and to the distance of three miles inland. Its population is 25,000, and the chief product is rice, with which Penang is supplied.

On the 1st October I took leave of my hospitable host, Mr. Ibbetson, to whom I am indebted for the greatest kindness and attention. On the following day we sailed for Malacca, and had a most tedious passage of seven days, arriving on Saturday the 9th. In consequence of the caution given me by Sir Edward Owen, I made arrangements for an officer's watch being kept at night, to be taken alternately by Mann, Brook, and myself. We had scarcely been at anchor ten minutes when a fresh gale sprang up from the north-east, and our ship dragged her anchors a considerable distance. This is not unusual at Malacca, the ground being of a soft, muddy description, not adapted for secure anchorage; but, at the same time, ships are seldom damaged, although they are frequently driven on shore.

I landed as soon as possible, and waited on Mr. Fullerton, the Governor, with despatches from Sir Edward Barnes, Sir Edward Owen, and Mr. Ibbetson. Mr. Fullerton, readily granted me permission to raise men, but held out no hopes of my being able to procure any of a desirable description. This opinion was confirmed by other residents at Malacca, so I decided not to land the recruiting party, but gave directions for proceeding to Singapore directly the ship had taken in water.

Malacca, as well as Penang, belonged to the East India Company. The former settlement consisted of an area of about thirty-six square miles, extending to the base of Mount Ophir, the altitude of which is 4,000 feet above the sea. It bears traces of great antiquity as an European settlement. In an old church on the Flagstaff Hill, just over the Stadt House, as Government House is still called, there are some tombstones with Dutch inscriptions bearing dates from 1650 to 1760. The Chinese burial-ground, situated just behind the town, is five miles in circumference, and is very interesting.

The Anglo-Chinese College is also worth visiting.

The number of Chinese boys educated in English at this college is thirty-two. They have a Chinese printing establishment, and also an English Press. About ten miles from Malacca in the south-easterly direction, there are some hot wells, which vary in temperature.

We sailed from Malacca on Monday, 11th October, at 8 P.M., but the winds being light and contrary we were four days working down to Singapore, the usual run occupying from thirty-six to forty-eight hours. The scenery was very beautiful. We were continually sailing between wooded islands and narrow channels, and the number of vessels which met and passed us enlivened the otherwise monotonous voyage. The passage into Singapore, leading through groups of islands, was very fine, the town and harbour opening abruptly immediately on rounding St. John's Island, which forms the western boundary of the harbour.

Perceiving a sloop of war at anchor, we ran in ahead of her; had every brail, down-haul bunting, and leach-line manned and ready, and came to anchor two cables length inside H.M.S. *Zebra*, Captain Pridham. Sails were furled, yards squared by lifts and braces in the shortest space of time, and our little craft sat like a duck upon the water; she was a perfect beauty, the *Zebra* by her side looking like an old hulk.

There were ships of all classes in the harbour: European square-rigged; Chinese junks of enormous size; buggis prows from Celebes, Borneo, and all the islands of the Malayan Archipelago; no less than 349 sail at anchor ; but of all the vessels assembled there, ours was acknowledged the "belle." She created a little jealousy, I fear, on board the man-of-war, our neighbour, for the morning after our arrival a boat came alongside from H.M.S. *Zebra*, with a lieutenant, to ask if we had a Governor on board, for, if we had not, the lieutenant informed me, we were transgressing in flying the "Union Jack" at our main, which, he said, is the flag of an "Admiral of the Fleet."

I had, with great modesty, forborne to fly the pennant, which our vessel carried in her own waters, and had hoisted the "Union Jack," which is always used on forts and military positions when a flag is used at all. I informed the lieutenant that on the coast of Ceylon, where our ship was constantly under the observation of the naval authorities, she invariably wore a pennant and the colours of the Commander-in-chief of the station, but, to avoid any question on the subject, I had hoisted the flag I should use if on shore. I requested, therefore, that before hauling down my flag I might see the regulations which justified this interference. He gave me a seat in his boat, and on reaching the *Zebra* I found Captain Pridham was on shore. The first lieutenant received me very politely, and showed me the regulations on the subject, begging me not to make any change until I had seen his captain ; but the regulations seemed to me perfectly clear, and on returning to my ship I ordered the offending flag to be hauled down.

When Captain Pridham became aware of the fact he

was much annoyed at the officiousness of his first lieutenant, and begged me to re-hoist my flag, or to wear the pennant which our vessel always carried in Ceylon waters. At first I thought it wiser not to run the risk of further question on the matter, but the naval Commander-in-chief, hearing of it, issued a General Order that vessels belonging to colonial governments were to be allowed to fly the blue ensign.

On Sunday morning, the day after our arrival, I received a very kind letter from the Resident, Sir George, then Mr. Bonham, requesting me to become his guest during my stay at Singapore, which invitation I accepted, and delivered to him the despatches from Sir Edward Barnes. He offered me every assistance, and held out hopes of success in procuring men for enlistment.

Singapore is a wonderful instance of the advantage of the unrestricted enterprise of free trade : so late as the year 1822 there was scarcely a native hut, certainly not one European habitation on the island ; in eight years it had not only grown into the most important settlement in the whole of the Malay Archipelago, but was the emporium of more trade than the whole of the other ports put together. The trade is almost exclusively one of barter, the English merchant procuring profitable exports in exchange for English goods. The annual value of importations in 1830 was five millions sterling.

The advantages the native merchants experience in finding free trade established at Singapore has withdrawn the whole commerce from the neighbouring

Dutch ports. On my subsequently going to Batavia I found the harbour there perfectly denuded of native vessels, while at Singapore there were between 300 and 400 at anchor bringing produce from every island in the archipelago.

The society of Singapore was tolerably extensive, and most hospitable, and conviviality and good fellowship reigned pre-eminent. During the fortnight I was there we only dined at home three times, and on each occasion there was a large party. Mr. Bonham was extremely popular. The merchants form a conspicuous portion of the society at Singapore. As at other Settlements, early hours were adopted for dining, which I should have supposed very objectionable for men of business, as no work was ever done after the 3 o'clock dinner. Cigars and an evening drive closed the daylight occupations ; people meeting again in the evening till about 10 o'clock. Ladies were very much in the minority in 1830.

Government House was situated on elevated ground, commanding a fine view of the whole harbour. Captain Pridham and I spent much of our time looking through a very fine telescope, belonging to Mr. Bonham, and in rival criticisms of each other's vessels. I had a very quick eye for anything which was out of place or order, and often worried the naval commander by pointing out a slack rope or a yard that was not quite square. On one occasion he challenged me to go on board and overhaul his ship, to see if I could detect anything wrong in her.

I said: "That is all very fine; of course, you will have her in the order she would be in for an admiral's inspection."

However, I accepted the invitation, and promised to lunch on board "the day after to-morrow."

Accordingly, the captain's boat was sent for me, and on our way to the ship I looked her all over, and, to my delight, observed that by some accident her pennant had not been hoisted to the truck, but was half-way down her top-gallant mast. I was in a great fright lest the midshipman should detect it, so I kept him in constant conversation, never looking again at the *Zebra* until we were alongside of her.

I was received by Captain Pridham and his officers, and directly after was invited to go round, and pull her to pieces. I pretended not to have observed anything; but, on being taken aft to the stern of the vessel, I looked aloft, and coolly suggested to them that unless they were in mourning they had better hoist their pennant to the mast-head, as at present it was only "half-mast"!

If a live shell had fallen on the deck, I do not think it could have caused greater consternation than did this remark. Had it not been for this—to me fortunate—accident, I might, with a microscope, have looked in vain for anything to find fault with, for the *Zebra* was in first-rate order. It was an unfortunate incident for poor Pridham, for he had, laughing at my passionate love for everything connected with the sea, told all his other guests the object of my visit. He never heard the last of it; everybody chaffed him unmercifully, but he was such a good-tempered fellow that he was not put out about it.

During our stay at Singapore Mr. Bonham gave a delightful picnic for us on a beautiful island, called Battoo Battoo Ballia. After a very pleasant lunch, at which enough champagne was consumed to swamp the discretion of some members of the party, my subaltern, poor John Mann, began to boast most absurdly of my rifle-shooting, and suggested that I should have a shot at one of Mr. Bonham's pretty little crystal salt-cellars, if he would allow it, offering him ten Spanish dollars if I missed it.

Under any circumstances, it would have been a most foolish engagement to make, for Mann could gain nothing if by accident I should succeed; but after such a lunch it was simple madness. To add to his folly, he insisted on putting the salt-cellar on the crown of a new black hat for which, the day before, he had paid eight dollars. I tried to back out of the affair, but was allowed no choice; so I loaded my rifle, the mark was put up, and the distance measured. I felt the odds were at least 500 to 1 against my subaltern, and I would have given a good deal to have let him off; but he insisted as obstinately as, in the first place, he had heedlessly made the arrangement. My rifle hung fire, but I kept the salt-cellar covered, and when it did go off, by the most extraordinary accident not a vestige of the salt-cellar was to be found, and Mann's hat had escaped without a ventilator having been made in it.

8

I have always been a fair rifle shot, but by this *complete accident* I acquired such an undeserved reputation, that I determined not to risk it again by any further attempts at practice.

A short time after our arrival I received a curious message from Tankuah Parahsah, son of the Sultan Bermah, and nephew of the Sultans of Singapore and Rhio, to the effect that, if I would remain long enough to allow him to sell off his property, he would enlist with the whole of his followers, and bring with him as many Buggis men as I would take. There were several objections to my accepting his offer. He was himself under age, and not one Buggis man in a hundred would have been of the standard height required by Government, although the build of these men for strength and endurance is more like the little Coorgh soldier of the East India Company's army than any I have met with.

I was, for the reasons assigned, unable to entertain Tankuah's proposals. He and his father sent me some very beautiful and valuable specimens of arms, peculiar to the Malay Archipelago—spears with male rattan shafts, mounted with gold and red horse-hair heads; shafts of worked steel; varieties of Borneo and other swords; a great number of creses, one very handsomely set with brilliants. The former of these I gave to Sir Edward Barnes, the latter had all the brilliants and gold picked out and stolen while I was away from home on a reconnaissance.

Of the natural productions of Singapore little can be

said, it being covered with a mass of jungle from its shore to the very centre of the island. Sufficient timber is grown for building purposes, and enough grass to feed a small number of ponies and cattle. The population is between 18,000 and 19,000. Of roads there are none which deserve the appellation, but a few are in progress in the vicinity of the town.

The Resident's, or Head Commissioner's House and the Jail, are the only public buildings, the ground-floor of the latter being used as Court House, Treasury, and Offices. The private dwellings are numerous and extremely good. The spot on which the town is built appears to have been an immense swamp, but it has the advantage of two rivers about a couple of miles from each other, on the banks of the largest of which are built the principal mercantile houses and godowns. This river is at high tide navigable for a short distance, for small craft, even a vessel of 180 or 200 tons, may be brought a little way up its entrance.

Malacca and Singapore are both under the Governor of Penang.

Having arranged to stay at Singapore till the end of November, by which time I hoped to accomplish the object of my mission, I gave orders for the ship to be in readiness to sail early on the morning of the 1st of December; but, in consequence of the arrival of the Governor, Mr. Fullerton, and Mr. Ibbetson, for whom I had to wait, I could not get on board till later. With a moderate but fair breeze, and a favourable tide, we soon lost sight of Singapore on our passage to Batavia.

We made the mouth of the Strait of Rhio the same evening, and there fell in with a ship, the *Triumph*, bound for Point de Galle. Her captain kindly offered to take letters or anything else for us, so I wrote to Mr. Bonham requesting him to send the despatches I had left with him.

Calms and contrary winds beset us in every direction. The consequence was we did not reach the town of Rhio till the following day, and were obliged to anchor there, the wind being strong and adverse. Rhio is a Dutch settlement on the west of the Island of Bintang, insignificant in appearance and equally so in reality. We found at anchor here a Dutch sloop-of-war, the *Laisle*, just arrived with a commodore to relieve Colonel de Loul, who had for some years administered the Government of the settlement.

We had not been long at anchor when the report boat boarded us, from which we received the first intelligence of the death of King William IV. Immediately I ordered the ensign and pennant to be lowered to half-mast. The breeze freshening, we continued our course. As usual, it played us false, but we were enabled to take advantage of the tide when it turned in our favour. We were carried by adverse winds amongst a group of islands in the straits of Dumpoo, communicating with those of Drion; from thence we coasted along the eastern shore of the beautiful island of Linga, with its two peaks in the centre called the "Ass's Ears." On leaving this, we for some time lost sight of land, Pulotogu, or the Seven Islands, being the only ones we sighted between Linga and Banca.

After a most tedious passage, destitute of any incident of interest, even that of a moderately fair wind, of which we had had but very little experience since our departure from Ceylon, we arrived on the 9th December in the Straits of Banca, off Minto, also a Dutch settlement on the west coast. We here found the English brig *Agnes* bound for England, which left Singapore a week before we did. We all sent letters home by her. Captain Miln dined with us; in the evening we parted company, and before morning we had run her out of sight.

While beating down the straits on the 11th, we fell in with H.N.M.'s schooner the *Windhund*, commanded by Lieutenant Kettervil. She is stationed in these straits as a cruiser, and carries twelve four-pounders, and has a crew of twenty-five Europeans and fifteen Javanese. The second lieutenant Pècké and the assistant surgeon dined with us, and were little disposed at 10.30 to obey their recall to their vessel, which fired a gun for that purpose. The following morning the *Windhund* got under weigh with us, and politely piloted us through the eastern Lucepara, the southern entrance to these straits, which are little known and seldom frequented by vessels. After getting well through them, she "put about" and we parted company.

We had scarcely entered the Java Sea, when, on the 14th, we experienced a heavy gale from the S.W., dead against us. Our ship laboured much, and we had one of our boats carried clean away, with her davits, which were snapped short off.

On Wednesday the 17th December, we sighted two brigs ahead, beating to the southward. When we came up with them, we found one to be the *Agnes,* which we parted from on the 9th. She had taken the western Lucepara channel, which gave her a better position, and enabled her to weather the gale of the 14th better than we had done.

On Friday the 19th, we found in the morning that the current had driven us to near a rock close to the Thousand Islands, from which point to our anchorage our sail was truly beautiful, passing through numerous small islands, and within a "stone's throw" of some of them. Many of these did not exceed a few acres in area, but all were most richly wooded, with here and there a fisherman's hut, under a canopy of luxuriant and variegated foliage, conveying to my mind the most perfect idea of tranquillity, independence, and repose.

The last island we passed before reaching our anchorage was Onrust, where the naval yard is situated, and where the *Ruffle,* a fine Dutch 28-gun frigate was then undergoing repairs.

CHAPTER VI.

On taking up our berth in Batavian waters, I saluted the Fort with thirteen guns, which salute was duly returned. About 5 P.M. two Custom House officers came on board, intending to remain with us while we stayed at Batavia, but, ours being a king's ship, I protested against there being any necessity for their presence, politely showed them to their boat, and heard no more of them. I then went on shore, and had to appear at the Custom House, where I was closely interrogated as to whether my vessel was a king's ship, or belonging to the East India Company's Marine. On assuring them that I had no connection with the latter, but belonged exclusively to His Britannic Majesty, they became more civil.

Our pull to shore was a most tedious one; the water for three quarters of a mile, before we reached the canal—or, as the Dutch call it, the boom—was so shallow that our gig, which was by no means a large one, ploughed up the mud for the whole of that distance. We saw several alligators, with which this shallow water abounds. We now entered the canal, which extends for about a mile, at the head of which is the landing-place, the Custom House, and Master Attendant's office.

This canal is formed partly by excavation inland, but principally by two treble rows of huge piles driven in on either side, strongly braced together, and running a considerable distance out to sea. On each side of the canal, which is not less than 60 feet wide, is a roadway, or towing-path, formed by filling in between the three rows of piles, already described; that part of the canal which has been carried out to sea has been deepened, the excavated soil serving to fill up the sides.

I went to the French hotel, a short distance from Batavia, on the Welterfreden road, considered the best there; the *table d'hôte* is at 4 o'clock, and they seemed startled at my ordering my dinner at 8 P.M. After dinner I adjourned to a large well-lighted billiard-room, with two tables, one of which seemed devoted to English, the other to Dutchmen.

Being anxious to select a desirable companion from my own countrymen, I made the acquaintance of, and played a game of billiards with, a major of the Dutch service, in order to reconnoitre the group. My observations did not leave me favourably impressed with the gentlemanly demeanour of my own people, who were loud and boisterous, and not very particular in their choice of language. I have always had great faith in my use of physiognomy in judging of character, and bringing that to my aid on the present occasion, I selected one whom I thought the most quiet, polished man of the party.

I entered into conversation with him, and asked him to have supper with me. I would have defied anyone to have supposed, from his pronunciation and language, that he was a foreigner; but before we parted company, towards the small hours, he informed me he was not an Englishman.

"If you are not," I said, "you must, at any rate, have been born in England, and brought up there."

He replied: "No, I cannot say that I have never been in England, for I landed in the north of Scotland, and travelled south. I may have been in England for about three weeks, but feel sure that I understood and spoke English as well before I left St. Petersburg as I do now. At the Russian Military Colleges every student is obliged to pass an examination in three European languages, besides his own, before he can leave the college."

After he told me that he was a Russian, I fancied I detected in Mr. Fearon a certain degree of pedantry in his conversation, but his language was always critically correct in its application. He gave me some valuable local information which I much needed.

Having ascertained that Messrs. Miln and Haswell

were the oldest established and most respectable mercantile house in Batavia, I called on them to secure them as my agents, and also to seek their advice, should I require it. I then wrote to the Chief Government Secretary, Mr. Van Schoor, at Bintenzorg, enclosing Sir Edward Barnes's despatches for His Excellency the Governor General, and stating that I would wait on His Excellency on any day he might be pleased to appoint.

I next went to the head of the police, to obtain his authority to land some "time-expired" men, Javanese, whom I had brought down in the ship with me. The permission being granted, I went to the Master Attendant, to request him to send off boats for the men; this he promised to do, and I returned on board to settle with them, and give them their discharges.

Mr. Miln having offered to accompany us to Bintenzorg, kindly asked me to dine and sleep at his house the night before we started. John Mann was anxious to go with me, so on December 20th we dined with Mr. Miln, where we found a party assembled to meet us, chiefly composed of men who had resided many years in the island, and who remembered our army which had held the country from 1811 to 1816. Their inquiries for their old friends and acquaintances were more numerous than we could satisfactorily answer. It was, however, a pleasing proof of the high appreciation in which they were held by all parties, Dutch as well as Javanese; indeed, the sight of our red uniforms created quite a sensation, especially amongst the natives, who had but recently been subdued in a very serious revolt, when the Dutch nearly lost possession of this magnificent island.

The Javanese, who undoubtedly are much impressed with the idea of our prowess in arms, have a saying which they are rather found of using, particularly before our countrymen ; it is to this effect : " When the rain comes, the goats run away ; when the English come, the Dutch run away "—referring to the peculiar and very strong antipathy the goats have to rain, and the efforts these animals always make to get under shelter from it.

For some little time a report had been spread that we were part of an advance guard coming to take over the island again for our sovereign. It should be no matter of surprise that the liberal and enlightened policy of Sir Stamford Raffles's Government should have been preferred to that of the Dutch, or that the natives should have risen in revolt against the latter, whose Government appears to us to be both narrow and most oppressive. They exact from the native population sixty days labour, or 16 per cent. of their entire time, in each year. The whole staple produce of the soil—coffee, sugar, indigo, and rice—is required to be sold to the Government at rates which it fixes, and which, of course, reserves a large margin of profit for itself.

But to resume my story. At daylight on the 20th December a lumbering post-carriage drove up to the door. The four little ponies which were attached to it would scarcely, I thought, have strength to draw the empty carriage, much less when encumbered with the heavy load it was destined to bear. In the first place, there was a very fat Javanese coachman, of at least fifteen or sixteen stone in weight, who, with his inverted wash-hand basin shaped hat, rope reins, and peculiar long Javanese whip, amused us not a little; next on the list, who shared with "Coché" the honour, though unfortunately not the comfort, of his elevated position, came my friend Lieutenant J. B. Mann, a grenadier officer of no mean stature or weight. The driving-box of this vehicle was not constructed for the dimensions of its present occupants.

"Coché," without much courtesy, availing himself of his official supremacy, seated himself with little solicitude for his companion's ease, who, having only just half the space necessary for his accommodation was most inconveniently situated *on* the iron rail which surrounded the box. In this unenviable position we travelled for some twenty or thirty miles, when poor Mann's discomfort was somewhat ameliorated by the demolition of the railing which yielded to his weight. The inside freight was composed of the following:—Messrs. Haswell, Young, and myself, two servants, and also a kind of guard, footman, or groom attached to the coach behind, and the boot full of luggage underneath. Thus we were eight in number, a good load for horses of any size. The little ponies, at the well-known crack of the driver's whip, started off, and in a minute were at full speed; this, I thought, could not possibly last long, but they never slackened their pace till they had accomplished the first stage of six miles, which they did in less than half-an-hour. The whole distance of forty pauls, equal to thirty-six English miles, was accomplished in three hours and a quarter; this included stoppages at every sixth mile. The time occupied in changing horses was so unreasonably long that the pace at which we drove must have been more than twelve miles an hour, which would have done no discredit to any horses in England.

The road to Bintenzorg is extremely good, about thirty feet wide, covered throughout with small, washed, river gravel. The manner in which the roads are kept in repair throughout the island is by dividing it into certain portions, which are given in charge to the several districts; this portion of each district is again subdivided until it eventually becomes allotted to individuals, who are then responsible each for his share being kept in the most perfect state of repair. Buffalo-carts and waggons—the universal mode of transport in Java—are not permitted on the high roads, a space being allotted for them on either side of the road, which, from never having been made, is merely distinguished by the ruts of mud, often up to the axle-trees of the waggons, which mark its track. This system must be very bad for commerce, and quite contrary to that adopted in Ceylon, where the roads are opened to facilitate the trade of the country, quite as much as for any other traffic.

The scenery on the way from Batavia to Bintenzorg is in many places so similar to that of Ceylon, that at times it was difficult to realise that one was not travelling between Colombo and Kandy, though I must admit that the general appearance of the scenery is more open, with undulating pasture lands, and numbers of fine residences situated on the different estates, which give to the country a more civilized and European appearance.

On our arrival at Bintenzorg Mr. Haswell very kindly took us to the house of an acquaintance, M. Diard, a French naturalist in the employment of the Government. He was a favourite pupil of the celebrated Cuvier, and is highly spoken of in *Finlayson's Mission to Siam.* Having taken him by surprise, we found him hard at work with his establishment of silk-worms, in which he is succeeding remarkably well. The whole process, as described by him, appeared extremely simple.

Having sent up to the aide-de-camp in waiting to ascertain at what hour His Excellency could give me an audience, I received in reply a most courteous and polite note from M. Knorle, by desire of the Governor-General, inviting me to take up my quarters at the Palais during my stay in Java, and appointing 12 o'clock as the hour he wished to receive me

Having breakfasted with M. Diard, I repaired to the Palais at the appointed time, and was shown into a very spacious state drawing-room, where Lieutenant-General J. Vanden Bosch soon joined me. He was about fifty-six years of age, of neither a martial nor very dignified appearance; he wore what I afterwards discovered was a household uniform of his own—a lightish green coat without facings, gold embroidery round the collar, cuffs, skirt, and down the front, with a large gilt button, on which was the letter W; two epaulettes with three small plain silver stars forming an equilateral triangle on each strap.

Having previously submitted to him, through the Chief Secretary of the Government, Sir Edward Barnes's despatch, he opened the conversation on the business of my mission by saying that the letter which he had had the honour of receiving from His Excellency Sir Edward Barnes notified to him that I had brought a certain number of old soldiers, "time-expired men," discharged from the British service, to be landed at Batavia, but that he was sorry to inform me this had been prohibited by an Order in Council, passed some time since, forbidding the return to their country of any Javanese or native of any of the Netherlands possessions in India, after having been in the service of another foreign power.

I explained to His Excellency that the men had all received their discharges from me, had been finally settled with, and that I had therefore no more authority over them than I had over soldiers in the Netherlands Army; that I had not ventured to land them without the authority of the Head of the Police and the Chief Magistrate of Batavia, who had kindly ordered boats to be sent off by the Master Attendant, by whom the men were in fact landed.

He exclaimed: "Has Master Venn been so indiscreet as to take this upon himself?"

I expressed my regret and astonishment that, with the existence of such a regulation, the Chief Magistrate and Head of the Police should, immediately on my application, have granted my request. It was clear that I had no power to correct the error that had been committed. After a moment's hesitation, he said that the men should be provided with quarters and taken into the pay of the Government. This was one way of keeping a hold upon them!

His Excellency could not help showing his mortification and displeasure at being thus checkmated, while I could not help congratulating myself that I had so cautiously but successfully got to windward of this narrow-minded policy; had I delayed for a day in getting rid of the men, I should undoubtedly have been involved in a most perplexing difficulty.

I begged the Governor to communicate the Order in Council to which he had referred to Sir Edward Barnes. He explained to me that the reason which had prompted this prohibition arose from the difficulty they had experienced in quelling the insurrectionary war, which had been much prolonged by the knowledge of military tactics which had been acquired by men who had served in our army while we held possession of Java, and who had received their discharge from it on our handing over the island to the Netherlands in 1816.

With regard to Sir Edward Barnes's wish to recruit men in Java, he said, if we were in any military difficulty he would ask the Council of Netherlands India to rescind their resolution and permit the enlistment;

but as the case stood, he much feared the possibility of his being able to carry the Council with him in his desire to meet Sir Edward Barnes's wishes.

In placing me under such restrictions, General Vanden Bosch evidently tried to do so in as conciliatory a manner as possible. Not having the candour to say that it was contrary to their policy to allow their people to serve another Government, he tried to shelter himself under the plea of an Order in Council which, I firmly believe, had never been passed. His Excellency imagined, I suppose, that any tale would be plausible enough to "gull" a youngster in diplomacy, such as he thought me to be; he therefore indulged me with the following speech:

"So much were we impressed with the necessity of making the regulations I have quoted, that during our late troubles, although sorely pressed and in a critical and dangerous position, we could not ask for assistance either from Bengal or Ceylon, knowing that in return we could not assist you with men as you now desire."

General Vanden Bosch little thought I was aware that they had on two occasions made applications for help, which he now tried to make me believe they had not done. They first applied to the Governor-General of India for the aid of troops, which request was declined, and subsequently for permission to recruit in Bengal, which was freely acceded to; but the Government distinctly refused to enter into any responsibility with the men. Permission to recruit they gave willingly; but all engagements must be made between the Government of Netherlands India and the men.

My reasons for doubting the existence of the Order in Council quoted by the Governor-General were these: In the first place, in so rigid a Government as that of the Dutch, it appeared to me to be extremely improbable that one of the first Civil authorities in Batavia should not have been furnished with a copy of the order, and should so unhesitatingly have acted in direct violation of it. This, however, might possibly be attributed to an oversight, had I not subsequently to my interview with His Excellency at Bintenzorg called on a gentleman (Mr. De Puis) who was formerly in our service when Java was in our possession. Until lately he had been the Chief Secretary to the Government at Batavia, but now held another office. Thinking he would have some influence and likewise inclination to be of service, I called on him, and without informing him of the result of my interview with the Governor-General, I asked him if he thought there was any probability of my succeeding in raising a force of Javanese, and whether there was any prohibition to my doing so, or to the Javanese enlisting in our service? He immediately replied:

"There is no regulation against their enlisting; but, of course, the previous permission of the Java Government would be required, and I doubt your being able to obtain that, seeing that so recently in our great emergency the assistance of troops was refused by the Bengal Government."

Having for the time finished our business, General Vanden Bosch entered into private conversation on various subjects. He was much struck with the mourning we wore, especially when he learnt it was a mark of respect shown throughout the army for our late sovereign William IV., of whose death we heard at Rhio. Personally, nothing could exceed the Governor's kindness: he repeated his invitation that I should take up my residence at his palais during my stay in Java; he gave me splendid apartments; provided me with a carriage and four greys, which I was given to understand were for my exclusive use whenever I required them; saddle-horses *ad libitum*; and an A.D.C. was always ready to attend me, a distinction which would certainly not have been extended to an officer of far superior age and rank to mine who should visit any of our colonies.

After leaving the Governor I went to the quarters of Captain Du Bus, one of the A.D.C.s, to join Mann and M. Diard, who accompanied me to the grounds of the palais. It would require an abler pen than mine to do justice to this fairy scene. The palais is a splendid building, and deserves its dignified appellation; it is built in the form of a segment of a circle, two stories high, with an octagonal dome in its centre. It was erected by Marshal Darndelles, but considerably added to by Sir Stamford Raffles, who took the palace of Calcutta as his model, which this one at Bintenzorg much resembles in miniature.

The grounds on which this palais is situated are not

sufficiently extensive, but the beautiful surroundings and extreme taste with which they are laid out go far to compensate for this defect. In front of the palais is a park with some fine timber and crowded with deer, of the same description as those in Ceylon. The other side of the palais faces the S.W., and commands one of the most beautiful scenes that can be imagined; the grounds in this direction extend to the banks of a river, which sweeps round the base of the hill and forms the boundary. This river can be seen for a considerable distance up the valley, and is a most beautiful feature in the foreground of this truly lovely scene. After visiting the baths, grottoes, fountains, and other objects of interest, we were taken by M. Diard to see his valuable collections of Natural History. They are very extensive and beautifully preserved.

I then returned to the palais, while Mann went with M. Diard to his house. At 4 o'clock young Knorle, the A.D.C. in waiting for the day, came to announce dinner and attend me to the drawing-room, notifying that I was to have the honour of taking in Miss Vanden Bosch, and on joining the party assembled in the drawing-room the General introduced me to his wife and daughter. At dinner I found, to my embarrassment, that our conversation must be limited, owing to the fact that neither of us was a good French scholar. My fair friend could not speak English, and I could not converse in Dutch. However, the time passed pleasantly in trying to instruct each other.

After Sir Edward Barnes's magnificent table equipment, that of the Governor of Netherlands India appeared extremely plain. He was, however, very hospitable, and the dinner, which lasted about an hour, was better than the appointments. Afterwards we adjourned with the ladies to the balcony. Cigars, very first-rate ones, were handed to His Excellency, who begged me to join him in smoking. Thinking it best to comply with all the Dutch habits I took one, rather at the expense of my conscience, for it appeared to me sacrilege to the fair sex to smoke before them. However, having accepted His Excellency as my model, I followed his directions implicitly. Smoking in the presence of ladies cannot be considered by the Dutch in any way disrespectful to them, for you *never* see a Dutchman in a carriage with ladies without a cigar or pipe in his mouth, and a coil of "tali appi," or lighted slow match, being carried by a "tiger" behind the carriage.

After an hour's pleasant lounge in the balcony the Governor said, that if it would be agreeable to me, the ladies would like a "promenade in the gardens." Besides a variety of beautiful and curious birds, with which the aviaries were stocked, there was a number of wild beasts. We paid a visit to a fine tiger, which had been caught in the neighbourhood of Bintenzorg, a few days before. It was not quite so large as a royal Bengal tiger, nor did his colours appear so bright; but they told me he was not quite full-grown, which may have accounted for this. He was destined for a fight with a buffalo, a species of encounter they are very fond of in Java. I was invited to witness the fight, but business in Batavia called me away. The result of it was, I learnt, as is generally the case, the defeat and death of the tiger.

During our walk in these beautiful grounds the Governor entered into conversation with me on the subject of my interview with him in the morning. He said he had been considering the point, and the best advice he could give me would be to go to the Island of Bally, from whence he had himself procured some men, whom he considered well adapted for soldiers. If I decided on going there, he offered to give me a letter to their Resident, ordering him to assist me. I asked His Excellency if he thought I should find any difficulty in enlisting men with our system of recruiting, which I explained to him. He replied:

"You will be able to get as many men as you require, but you will be obliged to buy them from the Sultan; each man cost me about £8 sterling."

I informed His Excellency that this would not only be deviating from my instructions, but also endangering my neck, for I feared that such a proceeding would bear no other construction in England than that of trafficking in the slave trade. No sooner had I said it, than I realised what an unfortunate and ill-timed speech it was, for it implied an accusation against His Excellency to that effect. I saw that he evidently considered it such, and hastened to change the conversation. I told him that I hoped, in the event of his not being able to grant me permission to recruit in Batavia, he would not extend the restriction to all Java, but that he would allow me to go to some more remote part of it. His reply was that the rule applied equally to all the Netherland possessions, and that Bally was only an exception from its being independent of their Government.

I then asked whether I might be permitted to land a few of my men daily for recreation and exercise, to which he made no objection.

Madura and Bally, two islands to the eastward of Java, are still Buddhistical in their religion, being two of the very few countries in the East which were never subject to the Mohamedan conquest. His Excellency made me a most tempting offer, which required all my powers of self-denial to resist. He said:

"If you will send your ship round to Sourabaya, the eastern extremity of the island of Java, I will send you in my own carriage with an A.D.C. from here. We have post horses stationed at short stages the whole distance. Up Marshal Darndelles Pass you will be obliged to travel rather slowly, with buffaloes to drag your carriage up; but in all other parts of the line you can travel at the rate of from nine to twelve miles an hour. The road runs from west to east, the entire length of the island."

It would have been a glorious opportunity of seeing the country; but I knew my vessel was needed in Ceylon for the pearl fishery in March, therefore I could not reasonably have wasted my time for my own gratification, and I felt obliged to refuse the offer.

I was surprised to see at what a distance the officers of the Staff were kept by the Governor and his family. The General's little son took a violent fancy to my red uniform and appointments, and afforded some amusement to the party by the extravagance of his admiration.

The Dutch Staff are very peculiar in their adaptation of native habits and costume. The whole of the A.D.C.s, some three or four, always in the mornings, went about their rooms in sarongs and shirts—the sarong being a Malay cloth, wound round the waist and reaching nearly to the ankles.

On retiring from the drawing-room I adjourned with M. Monton, Du Bus, and Knorle, to M. Diard's rooms, where we should have spent a very pleasant evening but for that uncivilized practice of employing dancing-girls. The Javanese music is soft and plaintive, much more so than any other Oriental music I had heard. The dancing-girls I thought very inferior in grace and appearance to those I had seen in Ceylon, and I soon tired of their performance. Their voices were, however, soft and melodious, and some of the airs were extremely pleasing.

Amongst a number of agreeable persons whom I met that evening was a Major Mourelle, who had long served under Napoleon in Italy and Spain; but, unfortunately for his own interests, had adhered a little too long to Napoleon's cause. It was Major Mourelle who took Sir

Edward Paget prisoner at Henbra, near Ciudad Rodrigo, on the 17th November 1812. He wore a seal which was given to him by Sir Edward Paget, and was a fine soldier-like fellow. After the peace of 1815, he was reduced to the rank of captain. When I met him he was in command of the troops at Bintenzorg.

The drives in the neighbourhood were truly beautiful, but impossible for me to describe. I went about in great style in my carriage and four; but I fear I did not appreciate as I ought to have done the constant attendance of my A.D.C., whose presence I would sometimes have willingly dispensed with. The fact is that at the age of twenty-six it is not so pleasant to be continually on your dignity, but Dutchmen are much too matter-of-fact ever to relax when they consider themselves on duty.

I had now to return to Batavia to visit my ship and make arrangements for sailing, for I found I could make "no way" with His Excellency. He would talk to me on the subject of my mission to any amount, but never gave me the smallest satisfaction on any point. I asked his permission to allow me to present my officers to him on the first occasion of his being in Batavia, and he appointed a day. He also was kind enough to order that I should inspect his troops at Welterfreden, and arranged with Colonel Krieger, the second in command, Colonel Reas being on duty at Bintenzorg, to receive me at the barracks at an early hour on Tuesday, 23rd December. I was, of course, punctual to my time, and was received with all state by the whole of the officers in full dress. But I fear their uniforms were totally eclipsed by ours, which at that period were very handsome. The uniform of the 58th Regiment was particularly so; and a finer specimen of a British grenadier in his "bear-skin" could scarcely be found than my friend John Mann.

The troops were paraded in "fatigue" dress in their barracks. The proportion of officers to men appeared larger than in our service, and they were much older men in their respective ranks.

The principal barracks at Welterfreden are five in number, of two storeys each, forming a square of about 150 yards, used for drilling. The buildings are of masonry, extremely commodious and well ventilated, capable of containing 200 men each, and were in excellent order. They were furnished with a most admirable description of cott or stretcher; it is made of canvas, having only a bar of wood on each side. The head of the cott fixes into a strong batten in the wall, the foot resting on a form sufficiently long for the breadth of two cotts. During the day, when the cotts are not required, they are unshipped, rolled up and placed against the wall; the forms then become available for other purposes, and, the barrack being cleared, is used for parades in wet weather, drills in the heat of the day, or for recreation.

But this arrangement did away altogether with the home-like appearance of our barracks, and deprived the men of the possibility of lying down to rest in the heat of the day, when tired with the early drills. For four years I had the charge of the barracks in Colombo, and knew tolerably well the habits of our soldiers; and I certainly would not, for the comfortless order of the Welterfreden barracks, have deprived our men of the use of their standing cotts.

The European troops stationed there were almost entirely French or Belgians. There were some very fine young men among them, though they were not well "set up" as soldiers. Their appearance led one to think they had a more intimate acquaintance with the plough than the drill-corporal. Two or three companies of the native troops were attached to each battalion of Europeans. All the native troops I saw were Buggis men from the island of Celebes. They are undoubtedly the finest of all the Malay tribes, and it is said of them that the word of a Buggis man is more to be depended on than the oath of any other man. They are a short, thick-set race, of immense muscular build. It would be unfair to judge of them, as they appear in the Dutch service, where soldierly bearing and smartness find little favour.

The arms then in possession of the Dutch troops were all French, long, bright rifle-barrels, secured to the stock by clumsy iron hoops encircling both. Colonel Krieger, however, informed us that they were about to issue new rifles and pistols. The former had bronze barrels, and were detonators, the nipple, instead of being placed at the side of the barrel, was in the centre of the breech, the hammer striking it horizontally, so that although not a breech-loader, the Dutch had used the "central fire" for upwards of forty years.

After the usual schiedam and bitters and cigars had been handed round, we took our leave of Colonel Krieger and drove to Colonel de Sterlers. He had been for four years the Dutch Resident or Ambassador in Japan. The Dutch were at that time the only European nation admitted to that country. Colonel de Sterlers had, therefore, advantages which rarely, if ever, come within the reach of an European for collecting curiosities, and of which he appears fully to have availed himself. He had kindly promised to show them to me, and had them all laid out and arranged ready for me to see. His collections were so extensive, and of such infinite variety, it would be useless for me to attempt to describe them, but the articles which most attracted my attention were the wonderful varieties of every costume of the country, many of which had belonged to, and were presented to him by, the Royal Family of Japan; a most curious and ingenious clock, quite unique in design, a number of weapons, drawings, and embroidery. The sword-blades appeared remarkably good, and the engraving on steel was exquisite. The china, cotton, and silk fabrics were rich and costly, as were also a great variety of metallic wares, telescopes, japanned and lacquered goods in endless variety. In fact, Colonel de Sterlers's house was no contemptible museum of the productions of Japan. Sir Edward Barnes had commissioned me to purchase for him any valuable curiosity I might have the opportunity of buying, but, fortunately, I did not purchase any, for, had I done so, they would have been within eight-and-forty hours at the bottom of the Java Sea. I suspect it was the magnitude of the investment which prevented my accomplishing it.

Under a sense of great obligation to Colonel de Sterlers, we took our leave of him, for he had gone through a very laborious day's work on our behalf and had afforded us great gratification.

We next visited the Harmonic, or Assembly Rooms, a fine building which joins that of the Society of Arts and Sciences, the whole presenting an imposing pile. The Assembly Rooms are very spacious, consisting of a vestibule, on either side of which are two long rooms, one a ball room, the other with card tables in it. Besides these, there are fine billiard rooms, and an extensive apartment for suppers.

Then we proceeded to the theatre. Its exterior was not pretentious, but its interior was neat and commodious, capable of accommodating 500 people. We had subsequently an opportunity of witnessing some very good amateur theatricals. The Governor who was present, had invited me to bring my officers to his box, which is well situated in front of the stage. All his family and staff were with him. To our surprise, we found that the ladies alone occupied the dress circles and boxes; the gentlemen being in the stalls and pit. We could only account for this curious arrangement by the unattractiveness of the former. I never before had seen such a gathering of plain women. The stage dresses and acting were good, but in the after piece the wit and allusions were so broad and low, I could not understand the Governor being able to tolerate it.

I had a long conversation with His Excellency that evening, but with the same result as regarded any portion of my official mission. His kindness to me was extreme. He said that though we might not meet again in the East he trusted at no very distant date that he might have the pleasure of meeting me in Europe, and that if ever I were near him I should not forget to make myself known; adding that he hoped my stay in Java had been made as agreeable as it could be, notwithstanding the disappointment which he so much regretted I had been subject to.

Amongst other topics His Excellency touched upon that of the French Revolution, news of which had just been received. "Should the Republic be permanently established," he said, "there are few of the Continental Powers that will not be influenced by its effects. For Holland it is the worst possible news."

He went on to remark that their Brabant States had long been ripe for a revolt, and were only waiting for the opportunity or example to act. Prussia was, in his opinion, in even a still more critical position, and, unless Frederick granted a freer Constitution to his people, he would, in all probability, share the fate of

Charles X. In fact, he gave a most gloomy view of the whole politics of Continental Europe. England, he thought, was internally safe, but would have to take up a powerful position, and act a very decided part, if she wished to stay the democratic tendencies of the day. I told him I was too little of a politician to venture to form an opinion on such general questions, but thanked him for the expression of his views, which I told him I should remember with much interest as the consequences of the recent news were developed.

One morning we rose early, and, accompanied by our kind friend, Mr. Lowdon, who had been of great assistance to us on many occasions, we went to see—I must say without much ceremony—the person and residence of a Mr. Mackiel, said to be one of the "lions," if not *par excellence the* lion of Java. He enjoyed the largest income in Java, upwards of 400,000 rupees, equal to about £40,000 sterling a year. He had inherited his vast wealth from his father. His town house, which we visited that morning before breakfast, is a fine specimen, we were told, of the best description of the old Dutch houses, of which it now stands the solitary representative. The apartments are *very* spacious, paved with marble, and otherwise as magnificent as the most liberal display of gilding and costly furniture could make of them. One of the old man's hobbies was collecting musical clocks and watches, in the purchase of which he indulged in the most fabulous extravagance, and had certainly succeeded in accumulating some exquisite specimens of workmanship. The variety was endless; each room, the vestibules, halls, passages, and every spot where a clock could be placed was furnished with one.

I was more anxious to see his stud than anything else, but he was indifferent about showing it, saying that just now it was so small it was hardly worth looking at, as he had only about fifty horses in his stables. There were amongst them some beautifully-matched teams of fours from the Island of Timour, celebrated for its breed of horses; in fact, he had some from all the surrounding islands. I asked the price of four well-matched dark cream-coloured horses, which I thought of purchasing for Sir Edward Barnes, and found I could get them for 1,000 Rs., or £100, and four well-matched jet-black beauties for £80. I would have bought both teams, but had no accommodation on board for horses, and there was no opportunity of sending them likely to offer. He next took us to see his carriages, of which he had nineteen of different descriptions; and then showed us his enormous establishment of slave-girls, some of whom were the best specimens of the Malay genus we had seen.

Having received a hint that we were to be profuse in our expressions of admiration of all we saw, we were lavish in our praise, and never forgot to give him his full rank of "colonel." Before leaving, he invited us to his country residence at Tjietrap, about twelve miles on the Batavia side of Bintenzorg. A day was fixed, and his invitation was accepted; and we took our leave of Colonel Mackiel, returning to breakfast with Mr. Hawell.

At 6 o'clock on Saturday morning we started for Tjietrap, in two carriages, and, being less heavily laden than those we before used, the four post-ponies seemed to fly with us. The stages were so short, six pauls apart, that we seemed to be for ever changing horses. At the twenty-seventh paul-stone from Batavia, from which the road to Tjietrap branches off to the left, we found four of Colonel Mackiel's horses waiting to take us to his hospitable mansion, about three miles off. At a sudden turn in the road the tri-coloured flag was to be seen waving in the breeze over the house, this being the usual practice for Dutch gentlemen at their country seats to show they are at home.

Our approach was announced by an excellent band of Javanese music, placed in a raised stand over an arch, through which we passed. Shortly after we drove under another triumphal arch, and near it, in a lodge evidently erected for the purpose, another band greeted us, playing European music. This arch was at the entrance of the quadrangle, around which were the different buildings of this curious residence, the centre being laid out with fountains, in which were the choicest fish, selected as much for their beauty as for their delicacy at table.

Much as we had heard of this extraordinary place, it far surpassed anything the imagination could conceive. In the centre of this open area—quadrangle is far too limited a term for it—were these fountains and reservoirs containing rare and beautiful flowers, as well as the fish above mentioned. There was nothing very striking in the architecture of the place, which was built with more regard to oriental comfort and luxury than for effect.

On our alighting from the carriages we were shown into the principal building, in the wide verandah of which breakfast was prepared for us. Our host had driven over to the Palais of Bintenzorg to invite some members of the staff to meet us, and had not returned; we were requested to sit down without him. This we were not sorry to do, as it afforded us a better opportunity for enjoying the novelty of the scene. Our repast was substantial and good, every luxury which the country could produce was on the table; but the height of a Dutchman's ambition is the display of his servants, who generally are slaves. The attendants on our small party of three were no fewer than a dozen male and half that number of young female slaves, who are always distinguished from other servants by their white dresses, which is the badge of domestic slavery. The making and handing of tea, coffee, milk, sweetmeats, pickles, sauces, and the changing of plates was exclusively the duty of the latter.

Our meal was rather a protracted affair, but at length it came to an end. We lighted some very choice cigars and went for a stroll. A number of boys are always in attendance with lighted *tali api*, or slow match, in case the cigar goes out! We wandered through various buildings, which consisted principally of sleeping apartments for the many visitors who sometimes congregate here, as many as fifty and sixty at a time; amongst the number was Governor-General Van Bus, whose presence was so highly appreciated by our host that he built and furnished, in the most regal style, a house for his exclusive use.

The baths, billiard rooms, stables, and everything were on a scale commensurate with the rest of the establishment. We were all tolerably tired with the heat and exertions of the morning, so availed ourselves of the habits of the country and took a siesta.

At half-past four the bands at the lodges announced the arrival of our host and his friends from the Palais of Bintenzorg; at 5 o'clock dinner was served; we were most graciously received by Colonel Mackiel with every demonstration of kindness. There was nothing strikingly peculiar in the dinner, beyond its extreme luxury and the fact that a plate of cold rice was placed by the side of each person. Our sable host shovelled it into his mouth with all the primitive simplicity of his ancestors prior to the invention of spoons and forks. The table was surrounded by three circles of servants of both sexes, one-tenth of whom had nothing more to do for us than make a most minute scrutiny of everything we did. The music was softened by judicious distance, and was very pleasing. Some of the Javanese airs are plaintive and pretty.

After dinner Colonel Mackiel attended to one of his most important daily occupations, that of feeding his fish, with which the reservoirs literally swarmed. This

10 *

he did with the red Hybiscus or shoo-flower, basketsful of which were brought to him. No sooner were the flowers thrown into the water than hundreds of fish immediately rose, and in two minutes the flowers were devoured. There was one reservoir with peculiarly large and brilliant gold-fish, of not less than a pound and a half in weight. These fish were fed with oil-cake, suspended through the centre by a piece of bamboo, half immersed in the water, which spun round as the fish nibbled at it. These reservoirs were ornamented with handsome marble statues and vases.

The evening was pleasantly spent with several of the Governor's staff in playing billiards and cards, and in other amusements. The Javanese band was replaced by an European one, which played with great taste and execution. Nor were they strangers to "God save the King" and "Rule Britannia," which they played in our honour. The "Colonel's" band in town consists of fifty-six men.

Having made arrangements to wait upon the Governor-General the following day, I started, after breakfast, with Mann for Bintenzorg; but as we did not reach the Palais till 1 o'clock, His Excellency was having his mid-day nap and could not see me, but had given instructions that I should be invited to dine with him, and in the evening he would discuss business matters with me.

Accordingly, after dinner the Governor informed me that he had submitted to his Council, the day before, the object of my mission, and he was sorry to say with the result he had anticipated. It was therefore out of his power to grant my request to raise men in any part of Java, or at any settlement in possession of their Government; at the same time repeating his advice to me to proceed to Bally, where, His Excellency assured me, I should find no difficulty in procuring as many men as I could require, promising to send me a letter for the Resident at that place, to whom he would give directions to afford me every assistance in his power.

I informed His Excellency that, having received his final answer, and consequently having nothing now to detain me, I should, if he would oblige me with his despatches for Sir Edward Barnes, sail on Tuesday morning. These he promised to let me have that evening. I told him I hoped he had mentioned to Sir Edward the restrictions he had been obliged to place me under, in regard to the service on which I had been sent, and further, that he would fully enter into the subject of any regulations of Government that might exist, prohibiting the return to their country of such Javanese soldiers who had enlisted in our army during our occupation of Java, and who were desirous of returning.

As I had promised to go back to Tjietrap the same evening to admit of my reaching Batavia early on the following morning, I was unable to accept the Governor's pressing invitation to make a longer stay with him previous to my departure from the island.

On Monday the 29th December, finding I had no alternative but to proceed to Bally, I came to the determination that I would request two or three of the oldest and most respected merchants, who had been there, to meet me for the purpose of giving me their opinions on several subjects, which I considered essential, previous to my start. On my way to town, however, I met Mr. Brook, who put in my hand a letter, in which he represented the impracticability of this voyage at the present season of the year.

Having ascertained that the two persons from whom I could procure the best information on the subject were Mr. Milne and Mr. Davidson, two of the first merchants in the place, I wrote to them enclosing Mr. Brook's letter. In consequence of their official reply I was compelled to relinquish all idea of proceeding eastward, and decided to return to Singapore and the Straits of Malacca. I therefore became doubly anxious to get away, every day being of the utmost consequence in "saving a passage" at this season of the year, for after the N.E. monsoon breaks the voyage to Singapore becomes extremely difficult and tedious, sometimes taking as long as two months.

I had given orders that the ship was to be ready to sail on the 30th December, as I expected to receive the Governor's despatches on the 29th; but finding they did not arrive, I sent an express to Mr. Vanschoor, at Bintenzorg, representing my anxiety to sail, and informing him I only waited for despatches and a reply to a letter I had written to him on the subject of a prisoner, which I begged might be forwarded to me as soon as possible. The Governor's despatches arrived at Batavia during the night, and were instantly sent on board to me, but still no communication from Mr. Vanschoor. Consequently, I had to land again the next morning, and eventually found him at the Governor's Palais. Apparently he had no idea of answering my letter, so if I had waited for his reply, I might have been detained many days! As it was, we were delayed until the 3rd January.

I may here give an account of the Skutiri, or kind of militia, or which our late host was a colonel. The Dutch had lately received a severe lesson in attempting to extend their influence in Celebes, which not only humbled their pride, but was nearly proving fatal to their existence in the East. It originated in the folly of the then Governor-General, Baron Vander Capellen, the predecessor of the late Commissioner-General Van Bus. The Baron, in making a tour of the various settlements, visited Celebes, where he required the whole of the chiefs to wait upon him to pay him homage as the representative of majesty. They all complied, with the exception of an old woman, the Queen of Born, who objected. On her reasons being demanded, she asked Baron Vander Capellen how he could be so inconsistent as to call her "Her Majesty the Queen," and at the same time require her to pay homage to him as Governor.

The Governor-General sent Her Majesty word that, if she did not comply, her message would be considered a declaration of war: this, unfortunately for the Baron, was just what the Queen was only too ready to avail herself of.

To reduce this old lady to reason, 3,000 European troops were withdrawn from the Eastern districts of Java; but even with their assistance the result proved a complete defeat to the Dutch; they were obliged to withdraw to their garrison at Macassar without even the shadow of a treaty.

Withdrawing the troops from the districts of Sourabaya, Samarang, and Solo, gave a favourable opportunity for a revolt, which it cost the Dutch five years to suppress; nor did they then accomplish it without the aid of treachery—unheard of in an enlightened, civilized enemy. Their loss during the war is estimated at upwards of 40,000 European troops, and it is said to have involved them in pecuniary difficulties, from which it took them many years to extricate themselves.

The loss of troops for such warfare, where most of them must have fallen victims to the climate, appears incredibly great; but it will not seem out of proportion if compared with the mortality of one regiment, the finest employed in Java. It was termed the Corps of Expeditionaires, and was raised expressly for this service, being engaged only for the limited period of three years, and under the agreement of the Government to send them home again at the expiration of that time. They landed at Batavia 3,500 strong, and are said to have been the finest body of men ever seen in that service, principally composed of French and Belgians. At the expiration of their period of service the remnant of the corps was embarked and only amounted to forty men (!) who had survived the three years. None of the regiment had been previously sent home or drafted into other corps.

During this protracted insurrectionary war the Dutch were so critically situated that they were obliged eventually to withdraw nearly the whole of their troops from Batavia, for the defence of which place they raised a militia, or what they term Skutiri, both horse and foot soldiers, in which were enrolled the whole of the inhabitants of the city, jumbling together Dutch, English, other Europeans and natives, without the slightest discrimination as to class, character, respectability, or the reverse.

When there had existed an absolute necessity for such a measure, no objections were made to it—in fact, the contrary feeling was so strong that the English merchants, of whom there were a great many, having perceived the probability of such an emergency, were the first to volunter their services for the protection of the city. Instead of appreciating this act, or the feelings which suggested it, the Governor-General scarcely acknowledged it; but told the deputation who waited on him that he had already contemplated the necessity for raising such a body of men, and that arrangements had been made for carrying it into effect.

They were all immediately enrolled, dressed in some uniform, and forthwith placed on duty on the Governor's guard and on various other posts in the town; the whole were subject to martial law, by which the most influential individuals, who ranked as privates, were constantly tried for imaginary offences. An acquaintance of mine—one of the most respected men in Batavia—was once taken from his bed, where he was lying very ill, to appear before a court-martial for being absent from parade. Although he produced the medical certificate showing his inability to attend, he was fined, and subsequently pensioned on account of his age and incapacity. He considered himself fortunate in being treated with such lenity (!), though the "pension" was certainly rather a novel one, for he had to purchase his exemption.

Another man was fined and imprisoned for attending the funeral of his friend instead of a parade. This system was carried to so obnoxious an excess that a wealthy merchant was not infrequently placed on guard, with a set of natives who might the following day be employed as his coolies. At last a deputation on the part of the English waited on Baron Vander Capellen to remonstrate against their being compelled to perform the duties and submit to the indignities to which they were subject, now that there were ample troops in Batavia for all the duties that could be required, and the latter had absolutely nothing to do, while gentlemen were called upon to do their work. The Baron at first was obdurate and would listen to no argument, until a member of the deputation told him that whatever the consequences might be, he would no longer submit to the degradation; that he spoke not only for himself but for many of his friends as well, and that they had all made up their minds that they would leave the Colony at once, however great the sacrifice might be. This show of determination had an immediate effect, the deputation were invited to dinner that day and several of the English merchants were exempted.

Mr. Milne, the gentleman with whom I stayed while I was in Batavia, was one of this deputation, and on going to dine with the Governor that day the two sentries he passed at the Governor's door were the *Chief Judge of the Island* and a friend of his own. This almost surpassed my powers of belief until I was assured that the Chief Justice was even still in the ranks of the Skutiri, the drills of which he is obliged to attend as regularly as his shoemaker or his tailor, probably standing next in the ranks to one or the other. So much for the independence of a Dutch Judge!

In making a retrospect of my visit to Java, I think it was one of the most agreeable incidents which has occurred to me for years; the novelty and interest of the visit were not a little enhanced by the great kindness and attention which I universally received not only from my own countryman, but from all the official authorities. From the Governor-General downwards, everyone with whom I came in contact treated me with a kindness and consideration far beyond what I could have expected.

I cannot help regretting that my limited stay, and the various duties which required my attention, prevented my seeing as much of this beautiful island as I might otherwise have done. Java is perhaps one of the most interesting countries to which a traveller can direct his attention; it is considered not only one of the most beautiful, but also the richest island, for its size, in the world.

CHAPTER VII.

On the 3rd January we embarked. Our medical officer, Surgeon Kennis, had occupied himself, while we were rattling about the country, in making a natural history collection, to which object he was devoted. He had asked for, and I had granted him, permission to take his collection to the vessel ; but until I went on board and found his cages piled half-way up the main mast, I had no conception of the extent of his zeal in his favourite hobby : every bird, animal, and insect he could obtain in Java was represented in duplicate. How long they were to live, or how to be cared for on the voyage, were problems to which he had seemingly given little heed, but which were to be summarily settled before the evening closed in.

Directly we embarked we got under weigh, made all sail, and left the harbour in good style. We threaded through, and ran close to numerous beautiful islands, until we got well out to sea, when we had fair weather, and made a rapid run, as we thought mid-way between some islands, of which I now forget the names, and a reef of covered rocks called the "Brewers."

We had just finished our dinner when the look-out from the fore-yard sung out "Breakers close ahead"; the helm was instantly put down, but, having at the time all sail set, and a leading breeze, before the vessel could answer her helm we were hard and fast upon the "Brewers." On sounding we found we had only two fathoms of water under our bows, but a considerable depth under our stern. The ship bumped heavily, her masts each time bending like a whip over her bows; we instantly furled sails, and lowered our boats; placed a couple of anchors astern, and got a good purchase on them to prevent her driving farther on to the reef. We then lightened the ship as quickly as possible, by throwing guns and everything that could be spared overboard, and so disappeared poor Kennis's valuable collection of tigers, apes, monkeys, and birds of all kinds and colours. He only saved one or two orang-outangs, most extraordinary burlesques on human nature; which he subsequently taught to sit at table, to eat with a knife and fork, to help themselves, to take wine with him, in fact, to behave far better than many human beings sometimes do.

We hauled up our stern anchors without starting the vessel, and repeated this operation three times, when about 1 o'clock A.M. Mr. Brook, our navigating master, made a confidential communication to me, that if I wished to save the lives of those on board, it would be necessary without any loss of time to prepare several rafts, for the vessel was lightened as much as she could be; she would not move with any power we had on board, and she could not hold together another hour. Besides this, we knew our complement of boats could not hold one third of the people we had on board. I ordered him not to repeat his apprehensions to anyone else, and warned the captain to the same effect. I then directed that every anchor in the ship should be taken out astern by the captain, who was to have them all carefully dropped one over the other. This took some time to accomplish, but eventually we got our boats back to the ship, when we applied capstan windlass, and every tackle fall to be found in the vessel, every ounce of strength, and every particle of mechanical power was brought to bear upon the cables. Every soul on board plied with all his strength, but for an hour without the slightest effect, when, just as the sun showed a bit of his "limb" on the eastern horizon, we felt the ship move, gave three cheers, and, with a long pull and a strong pull, and a pull all together, we had the satisfaction of feeling her gradually grating off the reef; but the anxious moment was when she floated into deep water. The pumps were worked to ascertain whether or not we could keep her afloat, to run her back to Java, or whether we could prosecute our voyage to Singapore.

The divers we sent down to examine the ship's bottom, reported that the greater part of her fore-foot and false keel were gone, and two large holes rubbed away in her bottom beneath the fore-chains; but still, as she did not make more water than we could keep under with our ordinary ship's pumps, I resolved, if we had saved enough water and provisions to carry us, with extreme economy, to Singapore, to sail instantly for that place, knowing that the expense of repairs and outfit in a foreign dockyard would be very heavy.

Our inspection of provisions and water proved sufficiently encouraging to justify the experiment; and, therefore, without waiting to recover our guns, we made sail to the northward and reached Singapore without further serious adventures, and immediately applied to Captain Montague, of H.M.S. *Crocodile*, for officers to inspect our vessel, and for any advice and assistance that they could give us. For the official inspection we had her beached at spring tide, and found the report of the divers was quite correct. There were two large holes six feet by three and a half, rubbed right through her copper and planking; but the vessel having been built in one of our Admiralty dockyards, her timbers were all close and well caulked between, so that, though she had lost much of her outer planking and copper during the twelve hours she was bumping on the "Brewers" reef, she still continued to float in safety; had she been differently constructed she must have gone to pieces.

The report of the committee appointed by Captain Montague, of H.M.S. *Crocodile*, placed me in a new difficulty. It was to the effect that the vessel was unfit to cross the Bay of Bengal without an amount of repairs, which would have detained us at Singapore for an indefinite time. I therefore issued a notice to all on board, with a copy of the report, stating that I did not require anyone to go back to Ceylon in her, who thought the risk too great; that I would provide all such persons with a passage in another ship, but stated that I intended to return to Ceylon in the vessel, and called for the names of any who were willing to share the voyage with me. Every man on board volunteered to go, and I am thankful to say we all arrived safely at Colombo without any further misadventure, about the end of March 1831.

I reported the result of my mission to Sir Edward Barnes, submitted my accounts, which were duly passed in audit, and resumed my duties in the Quartermaster-General's Department, by taking charge of the public works—the roads and bridges, in the interior of the island.

This year, 1831, His Excellency Sir Edward Barnes was appointed Commander-in-Chief in India, and left Colombo for Calcutta on the 13th of October. He was kind enough to tell me that he would have taken me with him, but that he conceived I should, both to the colony and to myself, be much more beneficially employed in Ceylon than I could be in India.

"That may be, Sir," I replied, "but I hope, if ever I hear of your being on active service in the field, you will allow me to join you on leave."

Sir Edward Barnes was succeeded by Sir Robert Wilmot Horton, Bart., who became a very great friend of mine.

In 1832 I was ordered to open a road from Aripo, on the western coast, where the pearl fisheries were situated, to Anarajapora, the capital of the district of Nuwarakalawa, about which less appeared to be known than about the most recently discovered lake in Central Africa. In the latest maps of the island then published, this district was described as a mountainous unknown country, so that to ascertain its position I had to survey into it in the first place. This was a very slow operation, for this part of the country was so flat I could not triangulate it; moreover, it seemed to be the policy of the Kandians in those days to keep this sacred retreat as inaccessible as possible to Europeans; the low overgrown jungle paths, which alone led to it, were so extremely tortuous, that it was difficult at times to pass along them.

My astonishment, therefore, was the greater, when I reached the place, to find *extensive* ruins, large dagobas, magnificent tanks of colossal dimensions, and instead of the "mountainous country" represented in the, so-called, maps, I found a thickly-populated district, with evidence of its having been, at some remote date, the granary of the country. This all the more surprised me, for, when I received my orders to execute this work, I naturally tried to obtain some information regarding the country, but could gain none; no one that I could hear of had ever travelled through it, not even a Government Agent; and from the fact of its being so completely a *terra incognita*, I took an unusual interest in exploring it.

In addition to my military duties, the Governor conferred upon me the civil appointment of Government Agent, with revenue and judicial powers, but without civil pay or remuneration.

Taking my field books and data to Aripo, I commenced my operations from the "Doric," a fine building, so called from its style of architecture. It was erected by Lord Guildford as a temporary residence for the Governor when he visited the pearl fisheries. I laid down the forty-seven miles of jungle path on paper. Of all the innumerable bearings and short distances, in most cases of a few yards only, there was probably not one really accurate; but so completely had these inaccuracies counterbalanced and neutralised each other, that in protracting the new line of road, which frequently crossed the tortuous old native jungle paths, I was surprised to find how correct the work was in the end. The country generally was very level, and most densely wooded: at one point I had to open a straight road of several miles.

I was in a desperate hurry, and after comparing our compasses and carefully allowing for their variation, I placed my assistant lieutenant, Mackaskill, of the 97th Regiment, at one end, while I took the other extremity of this straight line of dense, level forest, and we worked towards each other. Each evening, on returning to our wigwam, we mutually communicated the distance we had respectively opened up. On a given day and hour we were supposed to meet, and I became very nervous as the appointed moment for our meeting passed by. We were both equally anxious, for we could ill afford to lose the time we had expended in this experiment. I ascended the highest tree in my neighbourhood, and listened attentively for the sound of the axe of the approaching felling party. After some time, in despair I fired my gun, but no reply! The departure of half a degree by either of us from the true bearing would have separated us far from each other, and I began to fear that this was the case. I sent an intelligent native out as a scout to reconnoitre, and in two or three hours he brought me the welcome tidings that he had discovered the other party. In a short time we found ourselves working abreast of each other, with about fifty yards of forest between us. This I consider was a great triumph for the Schmalcalder compass and perambulation, the only instruments we had used, the country being too flat to render the use of the vertical angle necessary.

The quantity of game of every kind I met with daily was almost beyond description, certainly not to be believed. Sir James Emersón Tennent, in his *History of Ceylon*, gives some account of it. I should be afraid to venture into details, my subsequent experience of the district having proved to me how possible it was to nearly exterminate it in a few years.

It was difficult to restrain one's enthusiasm in advocating the capabilities of this magnificent district. Sir Robert Wilmot Horton, who was then Governor, honoured me with his confidence, and encouraged me to be unreserved in my correspondence with him. It is strange, as well as satisfactory to me, to see how my dreams for the future prosperity of this Nuwarakalawa District have at last been realised.

A few extracts from some of these letters, written in 1833, may be of some interest to those who know what the district is now:—

This country beats all my past experience of jungle; the heaviest forest is quite child's play to work through compared with these "connaughts"—a "connaught" being land on which the forest has been cleared, and several crops of dry grain taken from it, until its fertility has been exhausted, when, to renovate it, the jungle is allowed to cover it: this becomes thick and intensely thorny in proportion to the heat of the climate. In Nuwarakalawa it is a closely-matted thorny mass, which well-nigh defies the Nuwarakalawa woodsmen. Working in a narrow clearing, with high walls of this description of vegetation on either side, excluding every breath of air, and a bright, burning sun pouring down upon one, gives as lively an illustration of a tropical climate as any man need wish for. Even against such odds I find a restorative in bottles of simple decoction of tea, made icy cold by evaporation, by wrapping wet towels round the bottles. It is astonishing how soon a broiling sun can produce a cool, refreshing draught, without which the situation would simply be beyond endurance.

. . . The country, I am sorry to say, is rapidly becoming depopulated by disease and drought; it is distressing to behold the fearful objects which constantly meet the eye. By opening up the country its further deterioration may be arrested, and the Government will be redeemed from the reproach of receiving for its grain tax a commutation of 1d. a bushel. Can a greater stigma attach to any Government than that it has districts so inaccessible that their produce is almost unsaleable?

. . . Your Excellency may be pretty certain that if it could be ensured that your successors would adopt and carry out your philanthropic policy, I should not hesitate to accept your offer to become the "Regenerator of Nuwarakalawa."

This district is full of antiquarian curiosities, and abounds with game of all sorts. Every night, pretty nearly, we sleep in the centre of a herd of elephants. I hear them constantly round my wigwam. The other day Mackaskill begged me to call him when I heard one. The same night a monster was amusing himself, dismantling a leaf-shed which had just been put up. I called my friend, but took the precaution to take a gun in my hand. Mackaskill turned out very sleepy, rubbing his eyes, with nothing on but a red flannel shirt. It was not very light, and the first intimation he received of the proximity of his new acquaintance was a trumpet and a charge! I covered his retreat, and had to decide whether to try and frighten the brute away, or by shooting him have to remove our quarters half a mile further up Anarajapora High Street!!! to get away from the nuisance which the carcase would have proved. My friend no longer doubted the presence of "allias." They are very inoffensive if left alone. When tracing, if the weather is dry and fine, I sometimes do not indulge in a new wigwam, but have my curry and rice cooked under a tree, and after a long day's work am glad to stretch my bed under the same shade. My servant came to me with a long face, a little while ago, complaining that an elephant had put his foot into one of the new plates he possessed. As the servant and his plates were in tolerably close proximity, the animal could not have been much bent on mischief to have allowed us all to get off so scot-free.

The two Vellachies—Peria, or large Vellachy, and Sinna, or small Vellachy—are very curious works. The country has numerous rock inscriptions, which I hope thoroughly to investigate at some future and more leisure time. The season for working inland here is from the end of April to the middle of September. After the latter date our force should be bodily moved, either to the neighbourhood of the coast or up into the hills, to avoid the loss which would be consequent on the unhealthiness of the country, while it remains, as at present, a mass of overgrown vegetation. Even the "Chandrawankalang" or "Great North and South Street" of this city, in which I reside, is a forest, and is only defined by the wells which, centuries ago, supplied the houses with water. Some of them are very perfect. I restrain my enthusiasm as much as possible, so that you may not be disappointed when you reach the tombs of the kings and see specimens of the architecture of eight and ten centuries ago, by people who are now so feebly represented. What puzzles me beyond everything is that I can nowhere find the quarries from which the "world of stone pillars," as old Knox describes the place, have been taken.

Water, water, water, give these people water, and you may make anything of them, but without a proper, wholesome supply of it, they must die out.

The noble tanks had been injured from want of science and skill in their original projectors in not providing sufficient means of carrying off the surplus waters during the rainy seasons. I urged the Government to take active steps for the preservation of what was left of these great works, and pointed out how sadly the cultivation of rice, and the consequent health of the population, were suffering from the want of water, which in a tropical climate constitutes the vitality of the people and the wealth of the country.

Sir Robert Wilmot Horton adopted my views with eagerness, and proposed that I should become the "Regenerator of Nuwarakalawa," by devoting myself to the repair of these tanks. It would have been a work worthy of anyone's energies; but when I went into the matter with the Governor we found that the revenue of the Colony—then only £369,437—was too small to hold out any hope that the work of restoration could be carried out on a scale which would ensure success, and he agreed with me that it would be better not to touch it at all, than to begin and fail to carry it out.

It was my good fortune to proclaim in Nuwarakalawa the new charter and the abolition of compulsory labour;

an immense boon to the population of the island, of which for centuries it had been the curse. It had cost the last reigning Sovereign his throne and country, and had proved to the Chiefs a very great temptation to most cruel and unjust persecutions. I thought it unwise at the time to absolve the people entirely from any service to the Government, and suggested that a limited amount, say ten days in the year, which might be redeemed by a low rate of payment, to which all classes of the population would be liable, should be substituted for it. This measure, though on a still more moderate scale and under more favourable conditions than I had suggested, was, in 1849, brought forward and carried through the Legislature by Sir Philip Wodehouse. It limited the labour which the Government had a right to call for from every member of the population to six days, one third of which was to be appropriated to minor works and village roads, two thirds being appropriated to the principal roads of the island. This measure had the merit of extreme impartiality, as it applied to all ranks and classes, and the money commutation was so low that any man could pay it with the earnings of three days labour. The tax yielded about £50,000 a year, or in twenty-six years since it was established £1,200,000.

In 1833, while I was in charge of the works, the Peradenia bridge was completed. This is a very graceful bridge over the Mahawelliganga river, made entirely of satin wood, without a nail or bolt in it. A model of the bridge is now in the South Kensington Museum.

During the construction we had a force of twelve hundred men employed in laying and filling up the approaches. One morning, on my way to the works, I called at the bungalow of one of the married officers, and while talking to his wife, the most appalling atmospheric phenomenon occurred that I have ever witnessed. A flash of lightning and a peal of thunder broke over the bungalow, the thunder such as I had never heard before and never expect to hear again. Immediately in front of the bungalow, not a yard and a half from the thatched roof, a splendid electric ball struck the ground, sending up sprays of sparks, like beautiful fireworks, to a considerable height. Seeing that the lady was not seriously hurt, although much frightened, I rushed out of the house on to the works, to see if any mischief had been done there, but was thankful to find none. Not a single implement was in any man's hand ; the officers reported that on hearing the clap of thunder, which pealed simultaneously with the lightning flash, every man dropped his tool, and one and all, officers and men, stopped their ears, but not one of the 1,200 men was injured in the slightest degree.

About this time a Civil Engineer and Surveyor-General arrived in the Colony to form a department, and to take over the civil works from the Quarter-master-General and Royal Engineers. I was sent to initiate him into his new duties, and I travelled over the country with him, handing over to him the roads, bridges, and buildings as we reached them. His position, under any circumstances, would have been both onerous and difficult, but coming, as he did, a perfect stranger to the country, without an already organized department, it was doubly so.

The Quartermaster-General's department now being relieved from all extraneous civil duties, we undertook a military reconnaissance of the mountain zone, which I commenced under the following instructions:—

INSTRUCTIONS FOR LIEUTENANT SKINNER,
Deputy Assistant Quartermaster-General.

1. Lieutenant Skinner will be employed during the remainder of the year in examining those portions of the Great Mountain Chain surrounding the Upper Kandian Provinces which are at present most imperfectly known. Sketching its principal features and ramifications, with as much minuteness as the time to which he is limited will allow, and tracing and laying down its passes and defiles, and the roads and paths that lead through them, and which he will be required to report upon in detail at the conclusion of his work.
2. He will take as his base the line between the flag-staff in the western redoubt, and that on the Green Hill near Doregamme Vehare, in Doombera, and, reckoning it equal to 7,990 yards, which, for the purpose in view, is sufficiently near the truth, proceed at once to determine from its extremities some point near the top of the Giriagamme Pass, from whence he will carry on his triangles by Allegalle, Amboolwawa, Racksawé, Adam's Peak, Idulgasheina, and Bambroagamme to Baddoolla; filling in his sketch as he proceeds, and carefully noting down all his observations on the nature of the country, its communications and resources with reference to military operations, at the moment they occur to him, as well as the information which he may obtain from others on these important points.

He should endeavour to complete his first division of his work, namely, from Giriagamme round by Adam's Peak to

Baddoolla, by the 31st October, in order that he may have two full months to devote to the remaining segment, which, as it embraces a greater proportion of unexplored and intricate country, will necessarily occupy more of his time, supposing that equal pains is bestowed upon both. The best Theodolite belonging to the department is placed at his disposal for this service, but in a work where so much expedition is required the "Schmalcalder" compass will in most cases determine his position with sufficient accuracy, so that it is presumed he will only find it necessary to use the theodolite in fixing his principal points. When, however, he does resort to that instrument he will invariably preserve his observations, and forward copies of them from time to time to the Deputy Quartermaster-General, who must be kept regularly informed of his proceedings.

3. The annexed extracts from the code of instructions framed for the officers of the department will point out to Lieutenant Skinner the objects, generally, to which his attention should be directed, but he is more particularly referred on the present occasion to those paragraphs which are marked thus +.

4. His sketch is to be executed on a scale of two inches to a mile; but on closing his operations at Giriagamme on the 31st December next, he will prepare a reduced copy of it, on a scale of one inch to a mile, to accompany his report.

5. A requisition has been forwarded to the military secretary for a subaltern's tent for his use.

6. The instruments, tools, &c., specified in the subjoined list, are in readiness to be delivered over to him, and the annexed letter explains the means available for their conveyance as well as to assist him in his operations in the field.

7 Should he require anything further, he will lose no time in applying for it, and he will also be pleased to inform the Deputy Quartermaster-General how many Caffrees he requires in order that they may be directed to join him, there being only two in Kandy at present, who are, however, at his service to enable him to commence his operations.

8. Lieutenant Skinner will understand that he is to sketch the

general features of the whole range of mountains from Giriagamme to Baddoolla, and from Baddoolla to Giriagamme, and as much of the country to the right and left as he can conveniently lay down without materially deviating from his course, or sacrificing too much of his time, though it will be necessary for him to be more particular in the neighbourhood of passes than elsewhere.

(Signed) J. Fraser,
Deputy Quartermaster-General.

Quartermaster-General's Office,
Kandy, 16*th September*, 1833.

They were rather embarrassing instructions at first, seeing that my acquaintance with the theodolite was confined to the use of the vertical arc for determining inclines; that I had never sketched a yard of country; had never learnt the art of military sketching, and had never made a triangulation in my life. My old maxim, which I have acted on through life, came to my aid, viz., "What one man can do, any other can do equally well, if he will only apply himself with sufficient determination of purpose."

I was unfortunately too proud to acknowledge my incompetency, but gained immense strength from the faith which my old chief, Sir Edward Barnes, placed in me when he appointed me to the Quartermaster-General's department. In reply to my protest that I knew nothing of its scientific duties, he said, "Do you think I do not know that as well as you do. Will you try to qualify yourself?"

"Yes, certainly I will, Sir."

"This is quite enough, go about your business."

With the recollection of his piercing eye which went through me, his encouraging look and shake of the hand, which did so much to make a young man all that he desired him to be, I shut myself up in a room with a theodolite and *Adams on Instruments*, took it entirely to pieces, put it together again, and learnt the use of all its parts. It would have been a long and irksome day if I had not had the few words given above to cheer me. These seemed to say to me, in moments of my greatest perplexities, "Persevere; never say die!"

I next took my new friend, the theodolite, to the western extremity of my base line, and took many complete series of observations round the circle, when I found that I had gained by repeating them a certain coincidence in my angles. I sent a set to General Fraser, who had passed many days over his instrument on the same spot. Having received an encouraging acknowledgment from him, I began to grow a little more confident, but still the sketching had to be learnt and mastered. I started off to a hill near the point at which I was to commence, and tried in vain for two days to sketch something like it. I thought it would have broken my heart, so difficult did I find it to make any intelligible drawing. At the end of the second day's close application I left it, and descended to some lower and smaller features, which, after another day's trial, I managed to sketch somewhat more satisfactorily. Henceforth the sympathy between the eye and the hand improved, and became so perfect that I found no more difficulty. My triangulations were very successful, and I took an immense interest in a work which I had mastered by my own determination and without any assistance.

The one-inch sketch of the Kandian provinces and the general map of Ceylon are the result.

The total amount expended in our surveying operations, for caffrees and coolies from 1833 to 1840, came to £437 4s. 9d.* In those days of real military economy there was some pride taken in the quantity of work which could be produced with the smallest amount of public expenditure. A large portion of my pay and allowances were spent in this survey, vastly more than was drawn from the Treasury. The fact was that a given sum was allowed by the Government, and no one ever thought of reimbursement for travelling expenses or paid labour for clearing the tops of hills for stations of observation and getting from place to place. There was such a thing as the credit of the service and the department, which we thought more of than the £ s. d.

Although it was most interesting, it was precious hard work, delightful to think of in the retrospect. For six or seven months in every year I never knew the shelter of a roof from between four or five o'clock in the morning till seven in the evening, and occasionally much later. My fare, too, was often humble enough. On one occasion, going into the Wilderness of the Peak—which comprises about 500 square miles of splendid forest

* For details of General Fraser's report see Appendix, No. 2.

within its extreme boundaries—to make my reconnaisance sketch of it, my time being limited before the rains might be expected, I could not wait for the supplies which I had sent a corporal and another man down to Saffragan to purchase. I had expected some dozens of fowls for my six weeks' or two months' supply, but the men returned, after rather a lengthened absence, with only five miserable chickens, three of which had died from the rain and cold on their way up to the Peak, the other two had sentence of death passed on them immediately on their arrival; they all found their way into curries, the only dish they were fit for; those that had died on their way up the Peak did not die a natural death, having been killed by the cold instead of with a knife. This was all the animal food I had during nearly two months; I had a little salt fish, which was served out to me most sparingly, about a square inch for each meal, to give a relish to a little plain boiled rice. My people had a very knowing dodge of getting at my small stock of wine, under the plea that the bottles were broken by the men falling on the rugged rocky ground over which they had to travel. It appeared to me that though the bottles were broken, little of their contents were spilt.

These two months proved the hardest work I ever had, as hard, under the circumstances, as I believe any man could have endured. My wigwam consisted of five sheets of the tallipot leaf, stitched together with shreds of the same material. Each leaf was about six by four feet; three of these formed two sides and one end, with two others for the roof; along the top was a little ridge cap of the same material; the end which formed the door was always open. This tent of leaves contained my little camp bed, a small camp table, and chair. I think the tallipot leaves used to cost me 13½d., and generally lasted me the working season, which was six months; my lodgings, therefore, were not expensive!

I used often to see the most wonderful effects when thus camping out. On one occasion my sojourn on Adam's Peak lasted for a fortnight on the top of the cone, where I was waiting for clear weather, which I did not get, to admit of my completing my observations. One morning as the sun was rising, the shadow of the mountain was thrown across the whole land and sea to the horizon, and for a few minutes the apex was doubled, and so clearly marked that the little shed over the impression of Buddha's Foot was perfectly distinct in the shadow. Another most curious effect was when the mist had lain deep in the valley below, between the great Peak range and the opposite range of Rackwanie, it was an exact representation of the sea; the clouds rolling against the base of the mountains resembling the surf beating against the cliffs which seemed to project into the sea, the points of the hills peeping through the mist appeared like beautiful little islands.

At another time, looking down from the cone, a small white cloud, the size of a man's hand, might be seen floating upwards, about midway between the mass of vapour sea below and the top of the peak. Sometimes, under certain conditions of the atmosphere, this little bit of fleecy vapour would suddenly expand into a huge dark cloud, and come rolling up the cone, apparently lashing it as if with its utmost fury; and then suddenly envelope it with a dark mantle—a strange contrast to the clear blue atmosphere through which but a few minutes before objects might have been seen sixty or seventy miles distant.

But I must avoid all descriptions of the scenery, from the utter impossibility of my doing the most moderate justice to the tamest portions of it; much less is it possible for me to describe the grandeur of what I beheld from this singular sugar-loaf of granite, 7,000 feet above the level of the sea.

I generally pitched my camp, when I could, on the bank of a stream, as much for the convenience of making it a point of direction as for the pleasure of bathing and washing. I left my tent every morning at daybreak, and ascended one of the ranges, selecting from the highest points, and then the highest tree, on the top of which, perched like a crow waving about on its branches, I sat with my compass and drawing-board, sketching in as well as I could the various objects in the vicinity. Then I descended, crossed the valley, and mounted the next range, which had to be similarly dealt with.

The whole country being covered with dense forest, its features could only be generalized. When going over the same ground thirty-three years afterwards, when most of the forest was felled and cultivated with coffee, I was surprised to find how accurately I had succeeded in sketching in its characteristic features.

My mode of working necessarily often carried me far away from my camp, to which I did not get back till after dark, but I never lost my way although the forest was so dense; the fact was, living so much in the jungle as I did, I acquired the instincts of a woodsman.

On beginning my season's work, I found it necessary to discipline myself as to the amount of liquid I took; and for ten days or a fortnight I suffered terribly, as the exposure to the sun, with the great amount of work I had to go through, caused the most profuse perspirations, and an almost irresistible longing to put my head into every mountain stream I crossed, to quench my burning thirst. I sometimes assuaged it for a time by putting a bit of beetle-nut in my mouth, its stringency giving me temporary relief; but by persevering in this course of abstinence for a few days, I found life became more bearable. My allowance of liquid during the day was a small cup of coffee before I started in the morning; my breakfast, which, during these two months, consisted only of a bit of routé, a cake made of rice-flour and water, a cup of cold tea, which I carried in a small bottle, and a biscuit or two. In the evening my dinner was boiled rice and a small bit of salt fish, or sometimes some jungle edible roots, made into a curry; a glass of sherry mixed with an equal quantity of water; and after dinner a cup of coffee with my cigar, which I always took beside my watch-fire, which was lighted opposite the open end of my wigwam. All the liquid I took during the day did not exceed one imperial pint; this *régime* brought me into such splendid working condition that I could outrun anyone. My reputation in this respect spread throughout the country, and I often had challenges from natives, who were slow to believe that any European could rival them in activity and endurance.

One very active headman begged me to give him an opportunity of racing me up the cone of Adam's Peak, which is a steep bit of ascent. We started, and he went off at a great pace, and was out of sight in a few minutes; but half or three-quarters of a mile was sufficient to blow him. I passed him, and was on the summit forty minutes before him. In like manner I could leave all the athletes of a village behind me, who turned out to try their chance with the *Cannādé Mahotmia*, or "Instrument Gentlemen," as they called me. The advantage of this training did not cease here. To this day I never know what thirst means, although few people are so extravagant as I am in the use of salt.

The caffree soldier, or African, is supposed to be the hardiest native we had in Ceylon. I always had a certain number of them with me. Their full rations of rice, salt beef or pork, curry stuffs, and arrack, were always issued to them; and often would I have given any money for a taste of their savoury meal, but I resisted the temptation, fearing their rations might run short. They always had two or three days in camp for one day's field-work with me, except when changing the position of our quarters.

By the time I reached Newra Ellia, after having

worked through the Wilderness of the Peak, every one of my party was laid up, most of them having to go into hospital. I was the only effective one, although I was out *every* day hard at work and on such "short commons." Before the close of the season, I had to take a series of observations from the station on Pedrotallagalla—the highest point of Ceylon, and on Namone Coole, near Badoola. By the time these were accomplished a reaction took place, and, from poverty of blood, I was laid up for some time in Badoola with sore legs.

While in the wilderness I had some few adventures with elephants and other animals, but my faithful companion, a liver-coloured spaniel called "Grog," was a great protection. Before the exquisite scenery of Ceylon was destroyed by the coffee-planter's axe, the forests abounded with animals. The elephants in the wilderness were so numerous that their tracks greatly facilitated my work; they were so judiciously selected and so well trodden. The top of every ridge had its broad road, along which one could drive a carriage; from range to range one was always sure to find a cross road, which invariably led to the easiest crossing of the river in the valley. Without my dog I must always have carried a gun for my defence, but with him I felt perfectly safe. Elephants have an extraordinary aversion to dogs, and would always make a rapid retreat from "Grog," who had a special note for each description of game. I could always tell whether he was in chase of an elephant, an elk, a wild boar, a deer, a cheetah, a wild buffalo, or a jungle fowl. He would sometimes go so far in these hunts of his that his "tongue" died away until I could no longer distinguish it; and that in the stillness of the forest, where the ticking of one's watch was a disturbing noise! His range must have been a pretty wide one. At first I used to make myself very unhappy about his return; but in a short time I ceased to wait for him, finding that he always came back to me.

On one occasion, during this season's work, I spied from the summit of Adam's Peak a little open spot on the top of the ridge, which formed the southern segment of the zone range, and decided to go to it. I had sent off two intelligent men, with a week's provisions, to prepare a station for observations. I was detained longer at the Peak than I expected, waiting for clear weather—quite long enough to admit of the return of my men, about whom I began to get uneasy. At length I decided to leave, and instead of halting, as I usually did, at 10 o'clock, to admit of the men getting their breakfast, I pushed on through the forest until 3 o'clock, when we stopped at a little rivulet, and cooking commenced. I strolled away up the bed of the stream for a mile or so, a most unusual thing for me to do, inasmuch as my necessary work afforded me quite sufficient exercise without indulging in amateur walks. When away from the noise of the camp the silence of the forest was almost oppressive, and, being at an altitude of about 6,500 feet, the rarefied state of the atmosphere contributed to this stillness.

I fancied I heard human voices in the far distance, so I climbed into a tree and gave my loudest Kandian cry, which sometimes can be heard at an enormous distance; it was recognised and answered, and in half an hour I succeeded in attracting the men to me. These proved to be my own people, who had been wandering about for many days; they could give no account of themselves, beyond the fact that they had marched the whole of each day since they had left us, but had no conception how far they had been, or where they were when I found them. I conclude they had been walking, as men generally do when lost in a wood, continually in a circle. They had consumed all the provisions they had taken with them, and I could not help feeling that my thus finding these poor fellows was a merciful interposition of Providence, for they must very soon have perished from sheer exhaustion had we not thus, apparently by accident, fallen in with them.

It caused great joy in the camp when I returned with our two lost comrades. The men with me were impressed with the idea that I knew exactly where to find the others when I started from the Peak in the morning, and that I left the bivouac, when we halted, to call them. It is needless to say I had no idea whatever where the men were, nor had I the smallest hope of finding them in such a sea of forest as that which stretched out before me from the Peak.

After breakfast we prosecuted our march, which, in two days and a half, brought us to the point, on the southern segment of the zone, which I wished to reach. I took some credit to myself for having cut my way through so many miles of dark forest, over so many ranges of hills and valleys, and hitting upon the little patch of open grass land.

We reached it just after a heavy thunderstorm, which had driven all the game out of the dripping forest to graze on this open space. I counted thirteen pairs of elk on the plain—the delicate figures of the does contrasting admirably with the huge proportions of the bucks. It was tantalising to see such a profusion of fine game, while I had not a morsel of animal food to eat.

The following morning, anxious to ascend a height in time to avail myself of the clear atmosphere of sunrise for my observations, I started off by myself through the jungle, leaving orders for the men, with the surveying instruments, to follow my track by the notches which I cut in the bark of the trees. On leaving the plain I struck into a fine wide game track, which lay in my direction, and had gone perhaps half a mile from the camp, when I was startled by a slight rustling in the nilloo jungle to my right, and in another instant by the spring of a magnificent leopard, which, bounding fully eight feet over the lower brushwood, lighted within eighteen inches of the spot whereon I stood, and lay in a crouching position with his glaring eyes steadily fixed on me.

The predicament was not a pleasant one. The animal had heard me approaching, and had I been an elk, as he imagined, he would have lighted on my neck. I cannot tell how long we remained in our relative positions, but during the time we stared at each other I felt no fear.

I remembered having heard that no animal could bear the steady gaze of the human eye, and I fixed mine on his with all the intensity I could command. Had I turned or retreated, one blow from his fore-leg would have finished me, for leopards are known to kill a buffalo or an elk with one blow, and I had no weapon of defence. He turned, however, and cantered down the straight broad game track, and then I felt quite sick and faint on realising the danger from which I had escaped. Fortunately my dog was in the rear, or he would have furnished a good breakfast to my cheetah friend. A gun or pistol would have been very acceptable at that moment. I had often seen these animals in their wild state, but never before had met with so fine a specimen.

CHAPTER VIII.

On my return to head-quarters I became very intimate with our new Governor, Sir Robert Wilmot Horton, who formed an exaggerated opinion of my common sense, which he was pleased to call my sound judgment; the consequence was he consulted me on most subjects, some of which were *most confidential*, and he often sent for me to discuss complicated questions. He was very fond of doing this while pacing up and down a long verandah of the Queen's House, on which I am sure I must have walked with him hundreds of miles, for latterly it became almost a daily exercise with us. The confidence he reposed in me did me good, and it was also most flattering to be so taken by the hand as I was by a man of Sir Robert Wilmot Horton's calibre, who would have done anything for me. I was terribly honest in all my opinions, and would never "trim" for him. On one occasion I remember saying, "It is strange, Sir, that you should so consult and confide in me, who never knew that I had judgment worth a halfpenny. The only way in which I can repay you for the compliment is to be most honest and straightforward, and never allow myself to write or to say what might be agreeable to you at the expense of my judgment."

I was fortunate enough, on a later occasion, to be of some slight service to Sir Robert, and to be instrumental in saving him from the commission of one of the gravest mistakes possible for a man in his position to make, and for this service he thanked me heartily.

The unbounded confidence with which Sir Robert honoured me throughout the whole of his government made me feel that I must have possessed some of the common sense for which he gave me credit. Just before his departure from Ceylon he sent for my written opinion on two replies of his to addresses he had received from the Presidencies of India, complimenting him on the liberal spirit of his government of Ceylon. They were written in his own peculiar style. I was very ill at the time, and on returning them apologised for the weakness of my criticism, which I asked him to attribute to my physical infirmity at the moment. In reply, he told me "that whatever might be my physical suffering, my mental powers were vigorous enough to have so accurately interpreted what had given him some trouble to express, and which not one man in ten would have discovered." The fact was that the Governor did not wish to sacrifice the popularity he had obtained in the Presidencies of India, and had a special object at the time for standing well with the Honourable East

India Company, which a too liberal policy might have endangered.

In February 1834 my dear friend and patron, Sir Edward Barnes, visited Ceylon on his way home, having been recalled from the appointment of Commander-in-Chief in India in consequence of a difference of opinion with the Viceroy on the subject of the necessity for an army of exercise in the North-West Provinces during the cool season. He was dissatisfied with the want of organization and discipline that he found in the Indian army, which he considered perfectly unprepared to operate in any considerable force.

During Sir Edward Barnes's stay in India I corresponded with Churchill, his military secretary, and other members of his staff, and anything more truly prophetic than Churchill's letters eventually proved, could not be. The Sikh and China wars were fully anticipated by him, and he deplored the defects in the whole system of the Native army, which led subsequently to its mutiny. It was little matter of surprise that so true a soldier as was Sir Edward Barnes should have differed so widely and vitally from Lord William Bentinck and his councils. Could he but have got a large force of native troops together, he might have reformed the abuses which he was aware existed against discipline, and have averted that awful calamity.

The news of Sir Edward's arrival spread like lightning through the country, and caused great excitement. He was worshipped by the natives, and, when a statue of him was subsequently erected in Colombo, they would come in the night from the interior and lay offerings of flowers, rice, and money, such as they present in their temples, at the base of the pedestal, compelling us to surround the monument with a railing for protection.

In 1834 false rumours were set afloat of an intended insurrection among the people of the interior. Sir Robert Wilmot Horton had quite decided to visit the ruins of Anarajapoora, and it was about the time of his intended departure for this trip that these reports became most rife; but, with the spirit of an Englishman, he rejected all advice to postpone his plans. His suite consisted of six or eight officers, of whom I was one. We carried our guns for purposes of sport, which was, at that time, very good in Nurawakalawa, and we felt we could show a very respectable front if called upon to defend ourselves against any number of Kandians.

The road from Kandy, through Matella and Dambool, was crowded with pilgrims on their way to the sacred Bo-tree of Anarajapoora, planted there about 450 years before the Christian era.* When we reached the ruins of the old city it was perfectly alive with people, the cause of whose presence there in such numbers it was not easy to divine, as it might just as well have been for a treasonable purpose as for a religious pilgrimage. The sight of the crowd, coupled with the reports of an intended insurrection, might and

* I see in Sir J. Emerson Tennent's book that he says, "The planting of the Bo-tree took place in the 18th year of the reign of King Devenipiatissa, B.C. 288." Vol. i. p. 343.

would have made many a man nervous, but Sir Robert Horton never showed the least doubt of the loyalty of the people. We kept our eyes and ears open, but never met with the slightest interruption or discourtesy.

On our return to Kandy, however, the rumours of disaffection became more urgent. Anonymous olahs* were found suspended from trees by the roadside in every direction diverging from Kandy, and were left at the Pavilion and at the Colonial Secretary's residence. At length, with the greatest circumstantiality, the day for the rising was fixed and the chief actors were named. Molligodde, the chief Adigar, was reported to have his *walewa* (palace) fortified and full of armed men, as were also said to be the various temples.

The Council was within call all night to receive reports, and finally to act as occasion might seem to direct. Captain Atchison, of the C.R.R., and myself, were ordered to be in readiness should we be required. At 4 o'clock A.M. the Ceylon Rifles were turned out without noise. Atchison was furnished with a party to surround the Asgiri temples, and I with another party had orders to capture the Adigar and his palace full of armed men.

We were directed to take up positions which would effectually prevent any escape, and to make gun-fire the signal for our attack. I had surrounded Molligodde's *walewa* as quietly as was possible, but still felt surprise

* Leaves of the palm prepared and used for writing.

that, if the building was, as it was reputed to be, full of armed men, some watch or guard should not have been set, and that they should have allowed themselves to be so taken unawares. It was unlike Kandians, for they make up in watchfulness and caution what they are deficient of in courage.

I shall never forget my humiliation when, as the gun fired, I burst open the hall door, and instead of finding the palace bristling with men armed to the teeth, I was accosted by an old cripple, who came forward with a lantern to ask what we wanted. I ran upstairs with a sergeant and file of men to Molligodde's bedroom, where I found him asleep with his little boy. They were both, as well they might be, utterly surprised at this intrusion on their morning's repose.

My orders were to take my prisoners to the general parade, where the troops had all been turned out. I handed them over and then received orders to march my detachment back to their lines and dismiss them. I was heartily glad to get away from the scene in which I had peformed so unenviable a part. It is impossible to conceive what could have been the motive for the evidence which had been trumped up against this Chief, whom I had known from my first employment on the roads and had always believed to be a decidedly loyal subject. The Government felt obliged to bring his case before judicial investigation ; but the Supreme Court, I was happy to find, fully acquitted him and all the others who had been, I believe, maliciously reported to be implicated with him.

In 1834 and 1835 I had my last experiences of duelling, not as principal, but as friend. The first occasion was very nearly being disastrous to myself. Two very good friends of mine in Kandy had a difference of opinion about a house which one rented from the other; no written terms of agreement had been made, and it was no great marvel that a disagreement in their relative views should have existed. But it was enough that a suggestion was made that the major had put a forced construction on the terms favourable to his own interests, and the judge, who was the proprietor, was compelled to expunge the insult at the risk of his life. All I could say to Major —— would not appease him; his honour had been wounded by the insinuation that, as an officer and a gentleman, he could have tortured the terms of an agreement, though only a verbal one, a *shade* to his own advantage!

Hoping I might have arranged matters with the judge, who was also a great friend of mine, I went to him with my principal's message; but though remarkable for his coolness and impartiality on the Bench, the moment I spoke to him of his having wounded his antagonist's sense of honour by his insinuation, he voted *himself* the injured party, and I might as well have tried to oppose the principles of gravitation as to have attempted to extort from him the smallest concession.

He told me that "all solicitude on the point of 'honour' was not confined to the Army," and that the sooner I got the matter settled, without sacrificing the reputation of either party, the better: there was no use making a fuss about the thing. He said "he had perfect confidence in me. Would I act for them both? then the whole affair might be arranged that afternoon without anybody else knowing anything about it."

There seemed to be some reason in this; so that, without much consideration, I assented to the arrangement, if not objected to by my principal. I went back to tell him the result of my interview, and Major —— agreed that I should act for both, and thus avoid publicity. But I made a great mistake; it is always far better that one second should discuss such affairs with another second than with a principal. I had, however, now committed myself, and we agreed that the sooner the affair was satisfactorily arranged the better.

I appointed a meeting on a disused road, but, when I reached it, I found it was inconveniently narrow for such a purpose, being cut out of a high hill. It was, however, too late to alter, so I loaded the pistols and measured my twelve paces, then posted the belligerents opposite each other, and, handing them their weapons, explained the nature of the word of command to "Fire," which I purposely made as embarrassing to them both as I could. No sooner was this done than it was obeyed, and I heard a "fitch" cross my nose, and fancied I felt the air caused by the bullet as it passed me. I then addressed them both, and hoped they were satisfied, for that I was quite so, and explained, without letting them know from which direction the ball came, how very nearly I had received my quietus, which was quite sufficient to bring them both to their senses, and cause them to regret the folly of their misunderstanding.

I continued my work of the survey of the island until 1837, during the fine dry clear weather from about October to May, making observations from the different points I had selected for my triangulations and sketching in the features of the country, as well as superintending the drawing of the general map. I had been very fortunate in many of my triangles formed by the highest points of natural features, some proving within a few seconds of being perfectly equilateral, while some were nearly isosceles.

I became intensely interested in my work and never tired of it. There was an immense charm in working over perfectly new ground, most of which had never previously been trodden by an European, and before the axe had commenced the destruction of the finest forests, and most beautiful scenery in the world. But it was clearly too gigantic an undertaking for a department so under-officered as ours was. What could one assistant do in an island as large as Ireland, in which a single triangle had never been laid and an angle never taken? I look at the map of Ceylon and the reconnaisance of the Mountain Zone with surprise at the temerity of my noble old chief, General Fraser, in having had the pluck to undertake such a work with such means, and I look also with considerable satisfaction at the result and cost thereof.

In 1836 Sir Robert Wilmot Horton was kind enough to send me the copy of a letter he had written to Lord Hill, dated 25th April of that year, with extracts from the minutes of the Executive Council to which he referred.

Colombo, 25th April 1836.

My Dear Lord Hill,

A vacancy has lately occurred among the captains of the Ceylon Regiment to which as the senior of his rank Lieut. Skinner hopes to succeed. I am aware that Major-General Sir John Wilson has strongly applied in favour of that Officer, and I might have ventured to mention him to your Lordship on the grounds of the personal regard which I bear towards Mr. Skinner, but I really feel it as a sort of duty to him to beg you to read the testimony paid to his merits in certain "minutes," on the subject of military reductions here by the Governor and Executive Council, in special reference to his services as Deputy Assistant Quartermaster-General, which minutes have lately been transmitted officially to the Secretary of State.

I remain, my dear Lord,
Most faithfully yours,
(Signed) R. W. Horton.

The Right Hon. Gen. Lord Hill, &c. &c. &c.

Extract from the Minutes by the Governor transmitted in a Despatch to the Secretary of State, bearing date the 19*th November* 1835.

In reference to the Services of Lieut. Skinner, *Ceylon Rifle Regiment, Deputy Assistant Quartermaster-General.*

I am bound to state my opinion that notwithstanding the high and conclusive testimony which has been given to the efficient merits and indefatigable zeal of Mr. Skinner which he so amply deserves, &c. &c.

Extract from the Minute by Major-General Sir John Wilson, 21*st October* 1835.

Do. Do. Do.

The Deputy Assistant has of late been employed in sketching the Great Mountain Chain which surrounds the Upper Kandian Provinces, and that Officer has proved how much may be effected by diligence and perseverance, &c.

Extract from the Minute of the Colonial Secretary, the HON. P. ANSTRUTHER, ESQ., *24th September* 1835.

The Deputy Assistant Quartermaster-General has recently been employed in Surveying, with a view to perfecting the Map of the Island; it is not possible for a single Officer to carry on such a duty to any great extent. The highly meritorious Officer so employed has, by incredible diligence and activity, added to extreme good fortune in the preservation of his health, done more than could have been anticipated, &c.

[True Copies.]
(Signed) W. T. STANNUS,
A.D.C. and Private Secretary.

Sir John Wilson, commanding the Forces, sent me at the same time a copy of his recommendation of me to Lord Fitzroy Somerset, on the occasion of a vacancy occurring in my regiment:—

Extract from Major-General SIR JOHN WILSON'S *Despatch to* LORD FITZROY SOMERSET, *dated Ceylon, Colombo, April 4th,* 1836.

I beg to recommend the claims of Lieut. T. Skinner, and 2nd Lieut. W. Hardisty, the senior Officers of their respective ranks in the Ceylon Rifle Regiment, for promotion to the favourable consideration of Lord Hill. Lieut. Skinner (who has served seventeen years as Subaltern) has recommended himself more particularly to my notice, by the zeal and activity he has displayed in the discharge of the duties of Deputy Assistant Quartermaster-General, and by the great utility which, in a military point of view, the Colony has derived from his services. He has been principally employed in the field duties, and the useful topographical information we are now acquiring of this Island is due almost exclusively to the indefatigable exertions of this Officer.

[True Extract.] Signed by E. MACREADY,
Assistant Military Secretary.

This vacancy was caused by the death of Captain Fretz, whose case, a most extraordinary one, I will quote from Sir James Emerson Tennent's account of it :—

Amongst extraordinary recoveries from desperate wounds, I venture to record here an instance which occured in Ceylon to an Officer while engaged in the chase of elephants, and which, I apprehend, has few parallels in pathological experience. Lieutenant Gerard Fretz, of the Ceylon Rifle Regiment, whilst firing at an elephant in the vicinity of Fort MacDonald, in Ouvah, was wounded in the face by the bursting of his fowling-piece, on the 22nd of January 1828. He was then about thirty-two years of age. On raising him, it was found that part of the breech of the gun and about two inches of the barrel had been driven through the frontal sinus at the junction of the nose and forehead. It had sunk almost perpendicularly till the iron plate called "the tail-pin," by which the barrel is made fast to the stock by a screw, had descended through the palate, carrying with it the screw, one extremity, of which had forced itself into the right nostril, where it was discernible externally, whilst the headed end lay in contact with his tongue. To extract the jagged mass of iron thus sunk in the ethmoidal and sphenoidal cells was found hopelessly impracticable ; but strange to tell, after the inflammation subsided, Mr. Fretz recovered rapidly, his general health was unimpaired, and he returned to his regiment with his singular appendage firmly embedded behind the bones of his face. He took his turn of duty as usual, attained the command of his company, participated in all the enjoyments of the mess-room, and died *eight years afterwards* on the 1st of April 1836, not from any consequences of this fearful wound, but from fever and inflammation brought on by other causes.

So little was he apparently inconvenienced by the presence of the strange body in his palate, that he was accustomed with his finger partially to undo the screw, which but for its extreme length he might altogether have withdrawn. To enable this to be done, and possibly to assist by this means the extraction of the breech itself through the original orifice (which never entirely closed), an attempt was made in 1835 to take off a portion of the screw with a file ; but after having cut it three parts through the operation was interrupted, chiefly owing to the carelessness and indifference of Captain Fretz, whose death occurred before the attempt could be resumed. The piece of iron, on being removed after his decease, was found to measure two and three-quarter inches in length, and weighed two scruples more than two ounces and three quarters. A cast of the breech and screw now forms No. 2790 amongst the deposits of the Medical Museum of Chatham.—*The Wild Elephant*, by Sir James Emerson Tennent, page 90.

Thus after serving seventeen years as a subaltern, I succeeded to my company. This would be considered an unendurable hardship in these days.

CHAPTER IX.

In 1837 Sir John Wilson sent for me and informed me that the Government had intimated to him that the Surveyor-General and Civil Engineer's Department had got into such inextricable confusion, and had become so demoralised, that my services were required to take over the duties of the department, if I could be spared. He said the offer was a very complimentary one to me, and that he left it entirely to my own decision to accept the appointment or not, but advised me to have nothing to do with it.

As a member of the Government, he of course knew more than I could know, and he warned me that there would be extreme danger in identifying myself in any way with the concern. I told him I would rather the appointment had not been offered to me, for I had become aware of much that was objectionable and wrong in the practice of the department; but that having been called upon to act, I could not show any unwillingness to assist the Government, nor allow it to be inferred that I was afraid of the responsibility. If the difficulties proved to be great, I hoped I should gain the greater credit if I succeeded.

This, I maintain, is the principle which should influence every young officer, to *court* rather than to shun, difficulties and responsibilities. That I succeeded in a most ungracious and very unsatisfactory task the Right Honourable Stewart Mackenzie bore testimony to in 1839 and 1840.

Copy of the 21*st Paragraph of the Hon. the Acting Colonial Secretary's Letter to* CAPTAIN SKINNER, *the Acting Civil Engineer and Surveyor General, dated* 15*th January* 1839.

In conclusion, I am directed to convey to you the Governor's entire approval of the zeal, discretion, and ability with which, under most irksome and least satisfactory circumstances, you have conducted the department over which you preside; and His Excellency looks with confidence to your carrying into effect the modifications now decided on with firmness and decision.

Extract from the Address of His Excellency the Governor the RIGHT HON. STEWART MACKENZIE, *to the Legislative Council, in January* 1840.

His presence* alone prevents me from bearing testimony to the unwearied activity of the Acting Surveyor General, to the entire inadequacy of his means to overtake all that under the names of Surveyor General and Civil Engineer would be expected from him. That he has performed a most ungracious, and a very unsatisfactory work, during his tenure of these combined offices, most zealously, I can bear most ample testimony were it necessary.

The Right Honourable Stewart Mackenzie assumed the government on the 7th November 1837, Sir Robert Wilmot Horton having left Ceylon on the 15th Novem-

---

* NOTE.—Captain Skinner being a Member of the Council.

ber of that year. In him I lost a much-valued, but, I fear, a very partial friend. Before he left he planned a most delightful trip for me to England, where I was to stay with him and have the use of his stables; indeed, he seemed to think he could never do enough for me. Shortly after his return to England he wrote to Lord Hill a letter about me, of which he sent me a copy. It is a strong proof of the goodness of his heart.

From the RIGHT HON. SIR R. W. HORTON, BART., *to* LORD HILL, *Commander-in-Chief. Copy forwarded by the former to* CAPT. SKINNER, *after his (Sir R. W. H.'s) retirement from the Government of Ceylon.*

Cavendish Square, 7th June 1838.

MY DEAR LORD HILL,

Forgive my requesting you to read my enclosure, which is a letter sent to me the day I left Ceylon, by Capt. Skinner, of the Ceylon Rifle Regiment; he has been acting for some time as Deputy Assistant Quartermaster-General. He was a great friend and favourite of my predecessor, Sir Edward Barnes, as he was of mine. His patron has unfortunately closed his brilliant career. I am more encouraged, therefore, to record that I, who know him well, have the highest opinion of Captain Skinner's heart, head, and attainments, and if he had the opportunity of distinguishing himself in his profession, I think, unless checked by a bullet, his success might be warranted. He is now acting for the absent Civil Engineer and Surveyor General. My object in writing this letter to your Lordship, is to put my opinion of Capt. Skinner on record with you; begging you to remember that there is such an Officer who will, in my judgment, do honour to any promotion which he may obtain, or to any position in which he may be placed.

Believe me, my dear Lord,
Yours, &c.,
(Signed) R. W. HORTON.

During 1838-9 I had, as may be inferred, very hard work, but am most thankful to add I found time to marry. My wife was a daughter of General Burrell.

* * * * * * *

In August 1839 I was directed to accompany the Governor, the Right Honourable Stewart Mackenzie, on a tour to the Eastern Provinces, and, to my surprise, found I was to be His Excellency's only attendant. We drove the first stage to Matella, and next morning, the 5th August, we started in our saddles for Nalande; breakfasted there, and in the afternoon, or about mid-day, left that station for Dambool. The heat was something terrible; had we galloped through it, it would have been much less overpowering than the walk to which the Governor chose to confine his pace. I do not know that I ever experienced a much more trying day. At about 2 o'clock, when nearly mid-way between the two stations, the Governor half fell, half slid from his horse on to the road, where he lay in the burning heat of the sun. There was no shade near to which I could remove him, but there was, fortunately, a little rivulet crossing our path, beside which I placed him; bathed his head and kept him quiet for an hour or two; but how I was to get him over the other seven miles of our journey, or what was to happen when we reached Dambool, were matters of painful uncertainty. It seemed even doubtful if I should be able to get him into the saddle again. It was rather a "fix," for the country was most desolate, the road being practically only a bridle path, and the nearest European resident twenty-one miles off!

To sleep out at night in our condition would to a certainty have given us both fever, and it was evident Mr. Stewart Mackenzie was suffering from a *coup de soleil,* the effect of which who could foretell? I kept him quiet as long as I thought it safe; but, at length, when I proposed to start for Dambool, the question arose as to how far he was capable of riding. We got him on his horse with some little difficulty, and our two horse-keepers walked one on either side supporting him. We reached Dambool in the cool of the evening a little after dark, and, as the sun set and the temperature fell, His Excellency seemed to rally. I got him at once to bed, and administered a cooling draft. He slept very fairly during the night, and, when I awoke him between three and four in the morning, being anxious to proceed on our journey before the sun was very high and the heat oppressive, he seemed much better, and was bent on pushing on to Galle Oya, which was 23½ miles further.

I was rejoiced to find the Governor capable of accelerating his pace a little; but, unfortunately, it was too apparent that his brain was affected by the sunstroke, for he talked occasionally very incoherently. In three days after this event we reached Trincomalie, where I was glad to find my father-in-law, Colonel Burrell, commanding the 18th Royal Irish, and a relative, Sir Frederick Maitland, who was stationed there with his flag-ship, H.M.S. *Wellesley.*

I dreaded my return journey with His Excellency to Kandy, but knowing that he was tied to time, having to attend an important meeting of Council within a few days, I managed to get him home on the fifth day, glad enough to be relieved of the responsibility.

Amongst my old papers I have found a copy of a letter addressed to Mr. Stewart Mackenzie, dated 11th August 1840. It is so prophetic of events to be realised in due course of time that I shall insert it here.

Ambagamuwa.

MY DEAR SIR, 11th August, 1840.

I am very sorry that your Excellency's letter of the 1st instant has remained so long unanswered. I received it on the eve of my departure from Colombo, and being destined for this place, as there are points in it that I could only reply to by information which I expected to receive here, I ventured to defer the acknowledgment of it till now. On my arrival here on the 7th, I found that both the Surveyors, Mr. Bagenall and Mr. Sargent, from whom I made inquiries as to the lands which had already been appropriated in this vicinity, had gone down to Palampettia with Captain Lillie, and it was only last evening that I met them. He gave me such a sweeping list of lots applied for, that I feel it would be quite hopeless my attempting to describe them to you. I will therefore request Mr. Norris to send your Excellency a copy of the general sketch of the whole, which I understand he has, and by which you will perceive that the margin of the Great Wilderness of the Peak (in this particular direction) is tolerably well allotted.

I am sorry that Anstruther and Wodehouse are so late in the field, for I should have preferred seeing them in this neighbourhood, instead of either of the two, for which the latter has such a predilection, viz. Ballangoddi and on the ascent to the Peak from

Ratnapura. I fear they will both (and all the south-western falls of the great mountain zone) be too much exposed to the violence of the south-west monsoon winds, and at the elevation they would require for coffee would be subject to continued fogs for seven or eight months out of the twelve.

Ballangoddi has the additional disadvantage that it is thirty miles from water carriage by a most impracticable native path along which a loaded bullock could not travel, and the lands they might select may possibly be ten or twelve miles off this road. This is a grave matter, selecting a site for an estate on which parties seem determined to go ahead, at the pace A. and W. seem bent on. Mr. Turnour's land here is that piece which your Excellency went over after a five o'clock breakfast on the banks of the Attella Oya, where you may remember was a pretty little waterfall. It is described by all who have seen it as the finest piece of land in all this neighbourhood. I suspect we saw the worst portions of it on that occasion. Mr. Carr's and my land is the sloping forest on the right bank (within the elbow) of the Mahavilla Ganga, the villages of Ambegamoa being our northern boundary; but as regards relative positions of this and other estates (! ! !) Mr. Norris's surveying sketch will explain them better than I can. I have asked him to send you a copy of it.

With all these purchases and applications, the demand for land appears to be just as insatiable as ever, while the general cry is "Where shall we go to look for land?" In vain I proclaim that there is a choice of between 200,000 and 300,000 acres of the finest forest land in Ceylon within the Wilderness of the Peak, possessing in the most eminent degree every requisite of soil and climate, far above anything to be found on these outskirts of it.

"How are we to get at it?" is the not unnatural sequence, for although I have spent many dreary months in it, and there is not a valley I have not traversed, nor a feature, from the highest point of which, and from the top of the highest tree to be found on it, I have not attempted to sketch in my reconnaisance, I know that many a man might dive into the depth of 500 square miles of unbroken pathless forest, who would never find his way out of it again.

Will you, Sir, just open your map and look at the distance between Kotmalie Valley and Ballangoddi, and consider that by opening a bridle path, and building two small temporary Rest Houses between those places, you would open out a country such as has not yet been presented to the capitalist; a large area of land with a climate more like that of Southern Europe than a region within 7° or 8° of the equator, and in which I believe may be produced most European vegetation.

I respectfully urge upon your Excellency that the object is well worthy of the trifling outlay it will cost. I leave out of the question the great advantage which would result from establishing a direct communication between the central and southern provinces of the island. Instead of, as is now the case, a traveller being compelled to go round the base of the mountains, descending from Kandy to Pallapany, thence by Ruwanwella and Ballangoddi, or if by the eastward, then over the highest mountains of the country Nuwara Elliya, and thence by one of the three following passes, viz. Gallagamwa, Idulgashenia, or between that and Allipot.

I feel pretty confident that I might offer to open a 5-feet path, build and furnish the two Rest Houses, from the proceeds of the sale of land along the line during the first six months after it was opened. I trust your Excellency will excuse me if I am permitting myself to address you too freely on this subject: I feel intensely interested in it. Who can view this exquisite scenery, enjoy this perfect climate (at present the thermometer is between 67° and 68°) without feeling that it would be conferring a blessing upon humanity to be the means of removing some 20,000 of the panting, half-famished creatures from the burning, sandy plains of Southern India to such (comparative) paradise; benefiting not only them, the colony, the individual by means of whose capital they would be brought here, but also our own native Singhalese people inhabiting the margin of this wilderness, living as they now are like monkeys, for safety compelled to hide in places scarcely accessible to man, to render their dwelling inaccessible to elephants. Many totally unable to cultivate a grain of paddy, or to procure a morsel of salt, would find themselves attracted to a new centre within this, at present, trackless wilderness, which (although I have often been jeered at for stating it), I advisedly repeat, is destined ere long to become the garden of Ceylon, such a garden as has not entered into the mind of us Pioneers to conceive—a garden of European as well as of tropical productions, peopled with European as with Asiatic faces.

To facilitate this desirable end, I plead for a bridle path as the first requisite.

Hard work and privation have endeared the Wilderness of the Peak to me. I have often had rough work in it, crossing flooded rivers, and living on edible roots and plants, which the Singhalese, familiar with forests, alone could have selected; but my last two months and a half work in it were the most trying, from continued insufficiency of food. I reached Adam's Peak as light of baggage as could be, hoping to be able to get some fowls up from Ratnapura. My messengers returned with only five; three died on their journey up, from cold and wet, the remaining two had to be killed on arrival to "save" their lives. They all in due course found their way into curries, and I could not discover which had yielded to the sharpness of cold, or which to that of steel.

They constituted the only animal food I had during the ten weeks when, working every hour against time, I accomplished my task, having worked up to the top of Pedrotallagalle before the monsoon burst, and I have thought well of the sustaining properties of boiled rice ever since.

I hope, when you next visit Colombo, Sir, you will be so kind as to spare us half an hour or an hour of your time to preside at a meeting of the subscribers of the Barnes Testimonial: we have sent home £610, and have £150 now. If you will be so kind as to let me know when it will be convenient to you to meet the subscribers, the committee will call a meeting. It is a fact of some importance that during the late season of almost unparalleled sickness and mortality in other parts of the island, this district has been quite healthy.

I remain your Excellency's faithful servant,

(Signed) T. Skinner.

CHAPTER X.

In 1840 the Surveyor General returned to the colony and resumed his office. I therefore rejoined my own department, and was happy to take the field again. During the years I had been doing duty for the Surveyor General, my friend, Captain Philip Payne Gallwey, of the 90th Regiment, had acted most efficiently for me, and did a great deal in the way of field work and triangulation.

Our work was professedly rough. Our instruments were old and rickety, and it was only by repeating our angles almost indefinitely and taking their mean that we could neutralise their errors. When, however, Gallwey and I connected our work, his from the north by the eastern coast, and mine from the central provinces, in a triangle of sides of upwards of sixty miles, our intersections at Hambantotte were so near that the error could only be just appreciated with the fine point of the bow compass. For all practical purposes surely this was near enough!

When the Surveyor General's Department, with the advantage of numerous first-rate scientific assistants, with the best modern instruments, and unfettered in regard of expense, re-measured our base of verification upwards of five miles in the Kadarame Gardens, they found their computation of its length differed from ours only in the 5th decimal of the logarithm, showing a variation of but a few inches.

In 1840 the officers of the public service ran wild *in re* coffee-planting. As pioneers they were encouraged, to the ruin of many; for though one or two had been very successful, others lost heavily by embarking in an enterprise of which they were perfectly ignorant. Sir W. O. Carr, the chief justice, and myself went into partnership. Our estate had only just come into bearing when the protective duties in Ceylon were removed, and the price our produce realised fell from upwards of 100s. the cwt. to 45s., the latter sum being the cost of production on the estate.

In 1841 the unfortunate Civil Engineer and Surveyor General's Department again became disorganized, and I was requested by the Governor to take over charge of the roads and bridges of the colony, in the keeping up of which by far the largest amount of expenditure of the department occurred. My appointment was confirmed by the Secretary of State, and I henceforward became a civilian, though it was not till six years later that I finally left the military service.

In 1845 I applied for an increase of salary, finding £800 a year inadequate recompense for the labour and responsibility of my office. My request was backed by the Governor and granted by the Secretary of State in rather flattering terms.

Extract from a Despatch from His Excellency SIR COLIN CAMPBELL, *to the Right Hon. the Secretary of State, No.* 164, *of August* 14, 1845.

Captain Skinner's Memorial deserves my warmest support. The labour and responsibility which attach to the office of Commissioner of Roads are very great, and hourly on the increase, from the number of new roads now required to be opened and the increased traffic on the old lines. To Capt. Skinner personally the Colony is much indebted for his indefatigable exertions; and I am happy to add my testimony to those already borne by my predecessors to his merits.

Colonial Secretary's Office, Colombo, 2nd February, 1846.

SIR,

I am directed to acquaint you that the Governor has received from the Secretary of State authority to increase your salary from £800 to £1,000 per annum, and that this augmentation will take place from 1st February, 1846. I am at the same time directed to acquaint you that this augmentation was recommended by his Excellency, and conferred by his Lordship, as a special recognition of the zeal and fidelity with which you have, for so many years, discharged the duties of your office; and that it is not to be continued to your successor.

I have the honour to be, Sir,
Your most obedient Servant,

Captain T. Skinner. J. EMERSON TENNENT.

Extract from a Despatch from His Excellency SIR COLIN CAMPBELL, *to the Right Hon. the Secretary of State, No.* 71, *April* 13, 1847.

I have to communicate to your Lordship the retirement of Major Skinner from the Rifle Corps of Ceylon, by the sale of his Commission, after twenty-eight years' service. This step has been taken by him with my ready concurrence, in order to secure a continuance of his services as Commissioner of Roads, of which the Colony was on the point of being deprived by the removal of his regiment to Hong Kong.

He has filled that office entirely to my satisfaction ever since its formation in September, 1841; and previously he had been employed for upwards of twenty years in the construction of roads, and the prosecution of surveys, and similar scientific operations throughout every district of the Island. His knowledge of the Colony, therefore, and his experience in his own department are so extensive, that in the event of his departure it would have been impossible for me to have found an Officer in the Colony adequate to undertake and discharge his duties with efficiency. His appointment as Commissioner of Roads was approved of by the Secretary of State in January 1842, and his salary fixed at £800 per annum, which was subsequently increased to £1,000, in consideration of the zeal, fidelity, and ability with which he has conducted his duties.

I applied for leave to visit England in 1848, after twenty-three years service. During a good deal of that time my work had been of the most laborious and exposed character. On leaving the island my friends—the principal native chiefs—presented me with the following most kind address :—

Address from the MAHA MODELAIR, MODELAIRS *of the* GOVERNOR'S GATE, *and of the* ATTEPATTOO,* &c., *to* Major SKINNER, *Ceylon Civil Service, on his departure from Ceylon on leave of absence.*

SIR, Colombo, 6th May, 1848.

We the undersigned cannot suffer you to leave this Island, though temporarily, without embracing this opportunity to evince our high sense of your worth, and to express our feelings of regret at your departure from among us.

---

* The Maha Modelair is the highest Native Authority in Ceylon. Modelairs of the Governor's Gate are the next in rank to the Maha Modelair. Modelairs of the Attepatto are the third Grade, being Chiefs of Provinces and Districts, after whom follow Mohottears, Mohandrums, and many other subordinate ranks.

Various, indeed, have been the occasions on which we experienced your truly liberal and friendly offices towards us; and, when we consider that you commenced your career amongst us under the auspices of the late lamented Sir Edward Barnes, it is consolatory to reflect upon the past, and, as the result of such reflections, to state that in your intercourse with us you have always, after the example set by that distinguished personage, taken the warmest interest in the welfare of the Singalese community, in which we have been some among the many who received incontrovertible proofs of that liberality of sentiment which has characterized you at all times; and the anxious solicitude for our welfare, which you have manifested both in your public and private capacity.

It is unnecessary on our part to say one word regarding your public services—there is, and can be, but one opinion as regards the immense public benefits which you have conferred upon the inhabitants of this Island, by the zealous performance of your duties. Suffice it, however, to say, that having at heart the welfare of the native population of this Island, you have, in the prosecution of those duties, ever been anxious to promote our interests.

Permit us, then, to express our grateful and heartfelt thanks to you, and also a sincere hope that we shall, ere long, have the felicity to welcome you and your family's return, with renovated health for renewed exertions, to a scene of truly useful and invaluable labours in this Island.

Wishing you a happy voyage to your native land, and from thence back to Ceylon,

We beg to subscribe ourselves, Sir,

Your most obliged and obedient Servants,

(Signed)

E. D. Saram, Maha Modelair.

J. L. Perera, Modelair of the Governor's Gate.

Don Solomon Dias Bandaranaycke, Modelair of the Governor's Gate.

S. De Livera, Modelair of the Governor's Gate, and of the Hewagam Corle.

J. L. Pieris, Attepattoo Modelair of the Western Province.

D. D. Alwis, Modelair of His Excellency's Gate, and First Interpreter of the Supreme Court.
J. G. Perera, Modelair of the Salpetty Corle.
T. G. C. Pieris, Mohandrum of the Attepattoo.
J. A. Perera, Mohottear of the Attepattoo.
David De Alwis, Modelair of the Rygam, Corle, and Caltura District.
Jas. De Alwis, Proctor of the Supreme Court.
L. De Lewera, First Modelair of the Attepattoo.
H. Perera, Modelair of Pasdom Corle.
D. B. F. Obeyesekera, Modelair of Talpay Pattoo.
D. C. H. Bandaranaike, Mohandrum of His Excellency's Gate.
D. D. D'Lewera, Modelair of the Governor's Gate.
Thos. Dias, Mohandrum of the Government Agent's Office.
Franciscus De Lewera, Mohandrum of the Attepattoo.
D. J. D'Silva, Modelair of the Attepattoo.
V. D. Saram, Modelair of His Excellency's Gate.
D. H. Dassenaike, Modelair of the Adicary, and Medepattoo of the Sina Corle, and Modelair of the Attepattoo.
J. D. Silva, Mohandrum of His Excellency's Gate.
H. D'Alwis, Modelair.
J. H. Pieries, Modelair.
P. M. W. Pieries.
J. A. Perera.
J. H. Perera.
D. C. P. Dias, Interpreter of the Court of Requests, Colombo.
D. J. Dias, Mohandrum of His Excellency's Gate.
C. M. D. Sivena, Mohandrum of the Government Agent's Department, Colombo.

I had not been long in England before the news arrived of an insurrection having broken out in Ceylon. I was at the time living in Northumberland, not far from Howick, and Lord Grey, who was then Secretary of State for the Colonies, wrote to inform me of the intelligence he had received, and asked me if I had had any letters on the subject. I replied that I had not; but that I was not at all surprised to hear such news, inasmuch as I had, nearly twelve months before, warned Lord Torrington, the then Governor, and the members of his executive, that a revolt was imminent.

I told Lord Grey that the scene of disaffection must be in the districts of the Seven Korles and Matella, where, before I left Ceylon, I had predicted it was pretty certain to occur, owing to the misgovernment of those districts. In my periodical visits there I had witnessed a rapidly-increasing discontent amongst the natives; but I was not supposed to be as well informed of the internal state of the country as the presiding local judicial and revenue authorities were. Many of the chiefs, however, who had known me for years, were far more communicative with me than they were with their own immediate superiors.

My warnings had been disregarded, and this outbreak was the unfortunate result. A long Parliamentary inquiry was the consequence, which ended in Lord Torrington's recall, and the removal from the colony of Sir James Emerson Tennent and Sir Philip Wodehouse; but Lord Torrington, who had arrived in the Colony only in 1847, could hardly be held responsible for a social disorganization which had its origin at a date long antecedent to his assuming the Government.

It was fortunate that Tennent and Wodehouse were emancipated from the contracted sphere of their services in Ceylon to broader fields for ambition. A more able and independent administrator than Sir Philip

Wodehouse I do not believe the Colonial or Indian Office bear upon their rolls.

MEMORANDUM with reference to the past and present Social Condition of the Native Population of Ceylon. By Major Skinner, *and referred to in his Evidence, before a Select Committee of the House of Commons.—July* 1849.

The coast of Ceylon has been more or less in the possession of European powers for the last three centuries; their permanent authority, however, scarcely ever extended beyond a few miles from the sea-shore until 1815, when the Kandian territory fell to our arms. The rebellion of 1817 and 1818 kept the country in so unsettled a condition, that we cannot be said to lay claim to the uninterrupted possession of the whole island for more than the last thirty-one years.

In endeavouring to trace the effect of our government on this interesting country and its population, I will divide this period of thirty years into three eras, during which, respectively, I have observed the most marked changes in the social condition of the people.

The following Officers have administered the Government during this period:—

—	—	—	Years.	Months.	Days.
First Era, 6 years	To Feb. 1820	Sir Robert Brownrigg*	2	–	–
	,, ,, 1822	Sir Edward Barnes .	2	–	–
	,, Nov. 1822	Sir Edward Paget .	–	9	–
	,, Jan. 1824	Sir James Campbell .	1	2	–
Second Era, 14 years	,, Oct. 1831	Sir Edward Barnes .	7	9	–
	,, ,, 1831	Sir J. Wilson . .	–	–	10
	,, Nov. 1837	Sir Robert Horton .	6	–	–
Third Era, 11½ years	,, April 1841	Mr. Stewart Mackenzie	3	5	–
	,, ,, 1847	Sir Colin Campbell .	6	–	–
	,, May 1847	Sir J. E. Tennent .	–	1	–
	,, ,, 1849	Lord Torrington .	2	–	–

* Government commenced in 1812; whole period eight years.

Sir Robert Brownrigg's attention, for the two years from the suppression of the rebellion of 1818 to the date of his handing over the government to Sir Edward Barnes, was sufficiently occupied in the restoration of order and in systematizing the machinery of government for the recently conquered provinces, the population of many districts of which had been reduced to a condition of extreme wretchedness by their prolonged struggle to expel us from their mountain fastnesses.

The task of organization had, however, been sufficiently accomplished by the date of Sir Robert Browrigg's departure, to admit of Sir Edward Barnes at once proceeding with those works which his judgment pronounced to be the first and most necessary step to secure our possession of the country, and to remove from the minds of its inhabitants any idea which the disaffected might be encouraged to entertain of their ability to drive us from it, and, above all, for the development of the resources of our newly acquired possessions.

So inaccessible were the interior districts at this time that Kandy was only approachable by narrow jungle paths, so steep and rugged as to be quite impassable for any description of vehicle, and often dangerous as a bridle path. Commissariat supplies, and ammunition, &c., &c., were from necessity carried, to the capital and numerous outposts of the interior, on men's backs.

With such energy and judgment, however, did Sir Edward Barnes proceed, that within twelve months from the date of the order for surveying and tracing his new roads, one line of eighty-four miles, from Colombo, through the principal grain district, to Kandy, was so far opened, and his transport department so complete, that his supplies for troops and his post were conveyed by wheels to Kandy with ease and celerity.

The means employed in the construction of the first 200 miles of road by Sir Edward Barnes were a splendid body of pioneers which he raised, such of the native troops as could be spared for and were adapted to the work, and the gratuitous labour of the inhabitants, which, according to their own laws, they were compelled to render to the State.

The machinery of the native executive in the interior, established on the suppression of the native government, was composed generally of the headmen who served under their late king; and, no doubt, in calling out the regulated quota of the population for the public works, the same partiality and bribery prevailed which was known to have existed under their own government; every pains were, however, taken to guard against abuses, and the works were prosecuted with such vigour that the period during which there existed the greatest demand for compulsory labour was of short duration, while the effective result of the labour, in the benefit it conferred on the country, compensated, as much as anything could do, for the exercise of so arbitrary a power. Although those roads of Sir Edward Barnes were surveyed, traced, and opened, through a closely wooded, mountainous country, with a rapidity which allowed no time for the correction of errors, they fortunately exhibit no mistakes; they have mainly contributed to raise the colony to the importance she has attained, and on them she is still dependent.

After administering the government for two years, in February 1822, Sir Edward Barnes handed it over to Sir Edward Paget; who, in November of the same year, gave it over to Sir J. Campbell, by whom it was retained until Sir Edward Barnes's return, in January 1824. During the absence of the latter from the Colony, every effort was made by the two officers who held the government in the interval to advance the works which had been commenced in 1820; during the progress of these operations, with our comparatively imperfect knowledge of the country, and with a people too timid, and too recently overawed by the force of arms, to offer resistance, much injustice and oppression may have been endured. The cholera and small-pox made their first visitation to the country about the year 1820, and swept off great numbers in the interior; they were considered as the visitations of Providence for their treachery to our government. All things, in fact, combined to make these first six years, from 1818 to 1823 inclusive, a period of great depression and suffering to the Singhalese population.

Within what I have denominated the second era of my acquaintance with Ceylon are comprised the second government of Sir Edward Barnes and that of Sir Robert Horton, from January 1824 to October 1837, nearly fourteen years, during the first ten of which nothing could exceed the contented, happy condition of the people. The native population, sensible of the benefits he had conferred on their country, hailed with joy Sir Edward Barnes's return to resume the government; he continued progressively to perfect the several works which in 1820 (when Lieutenant-governor) he had commenced. Rajakara, or the gratuitous services of the people, he availed himself of with moderation, particularly in those districts wherein the greatest efforts had been made by its means since 1820. His personal intercourse with the official headmen and chiefs, and their families, was frequent; his conduct towards them was kind and encouraging, evincing an interest even in their private and domestic affairs, all tending to uphold their respectability and influence, while his knowledge of every district, and his frequent progresses through them, induced every member of his government, whether in the metropolitan or rural districts, to exercise the same line of conduct towards the natives, and compelled them to acquire the most intimate knowledge of the country, to prevent their appearing less informed than he was himself; he had no fears that the authority and influence of the native chiefs would be exercised prejudicially, and by protecting and upholding it, strengthened his own government and preserved order in all classes of society. His government was characterized by its decision and great energy; during the early part of it, he was compelled to exact much gratuitous service from the people, still he won the affections of all classes to his person, and their attachment to his government; his name is honoured throughout the land, as well by peasant as by chief. A handsome statue has been erected at Colombo to his memory, although, owing to delays in England, it was not sent out until seventeen years after he had ceased to exercise authority in the country. On its erection natives from all districts flocked to it; during the night, offerings were so frequently left at its base that we were obliged to enclose it with a railing to prevent its being converted into an idol. I mention this fact, as evidence that there is not that deficiency of gratitude and want of feeling, on the part of the natives, of which they are sometimes accused.

The first supposed interruption to the contentment and loyalty of the Kandian population occurred in 1834, towards the close of which reports of disaffection in some of the districts were made to Government, with such precision and minuteness of detail as regarded the time and mode, and such exaggeration as regarded the means of an intended attack, that on the night on which it was said the preparations were completed by the rebels in Kandy, and on the eve of the supposed insurrection, the troops were turned out in silence, and at a given signal before daylight certain officers, of whom I was one, were told off for the apprehension of the most influential chiefs and priests. Government supposing, from the information it had received, that the temples and houses of the the chiefs were prepared for resistance; each officer was provided with a military party. My own inglorious office was the seizure of the first adigar, "Molligodde," in whose walawa (or palace) there was such an entire absence of preparation, either offensive or defensive, that the martial array by which we were supported (suggested by the false and exaggerated information on which Government had acted) gave to the whole affair, when daylight dawned upon it, a character of extreme burlesque.

Molligodde, however (with certain others), was tried for high treason; was acquitted; he has since died from the effects of intemperance, a vice acquired in his European intercourse. His son, a fine youth of about 21 years of age, has fallen a victim to the same propensity, and the name of a once high and powerful family is now extinct.

My own impressions have been that the reports of this intended insurrection were wilfully exaggerated by informers, who hoped by their zeal and the importance of their information to ingratiate themselves with Government. The result of the State trials, at the beginning of 1835, was seriously to impair the influence and authority of Government in the minds and affections of the people.

With the exception of this supposed intended insurrectionary movement, things went on very prosperously. Government gave many substantial proofs of the liberality of its policy.

It abolished its right to exact compulsory gratuitous labour, or Rajakara, from the people. A new charter of justice was proclaimed. Newly organized councils (executive and legislative) were established; savings banks opened; entire liberty conceded to the press; while liberal means were assigned for and great encouragement given to the education of the natives; so that, altogether, the fourteen years between 1824 and 1837 inclusive may be said to have been looked upon as an era of prosperity and happiness to the people.

There was, however, a marked difference between the paternal character of Sir Edward Barnes's Government and that of Sir Robert Horton's, and with each succeeding Government that character has, unfortunately, been more widely departed from. Sir E. B. saw in the position of a newly conquered, jealous people, and in the character of the varied population of the country, a necessity for winning the affections of the people, and of gaining their attachment to our institutions by kindness and conciliation, and by evincing, what in truth he felt, a personal interest in the individual and collective prosperity of the various classes of society.

The third era or division of the period I am glancing over embraces the eleven years from 1838 to 1848 inclusive. Mr. Stewart Mackenzie governed the colony for three and a half years, Sir Colin Campbell for six years, and Lord Torrington for two years.

During these eleven years a great change has occurred in the whole aspect of the affairs of the colony; the social condition of its people has been no less affected by it than has been its commercial importance.

While granting some of these changes are doubtless of a salutary nature, it is a subject of humiliating regret that on the mass of society they have had a contrary and demoralizing tendency. Amongst the causes which have led to this result must be enumerated the vice of intemperance, into which the people have been led, the demoralizing effects of the sudden influx of enormous capital, and the encouragement to indulge in the most litigious spirit which ever afflicted the taste of a people. While these evils have been operating on the social condition of the people, unfortunately the authority of the Government and native executive has been exerting but very feeble counteracting influences.

That the vice of intemperance has become an enormous evil, and that it is rapidly gaining ground, there is left no room for doubt. A revenue of between £50,000 and £60,000 a year is derived from the sale of arrack farms. Renters purchase from Government the monopoly of the taverns of a district; the conditions requiring the renter not to sell his spirits under 4s. a gallon, he purchasing it from the distillers at an average of 1s. 2d. a gallon. The competition for these arrack farms is so great that they are seldom sold much under their value. It is, of course, the object of the renter to sub-let as many of these taverns as possible; they are established in every district, almost in every village of any size throughout the interior, often to the great annoyance of the inhabitants, and in opposition to the headmen. To give the people a taste for the use of spirits, it is often, at first, necessary to distribute it gratuitously, the tavern-keepers well knowing that, with the use, the abuse of the indulgence follows as a certainty. I have known districts, of the population of which, some years ago, not one in a hundred could be induced to taste spirits, where drunkenness now prevails to such an extent that villagers have been known to pawn their crops upon the ground to tavern-keepers for arrack. We know the train of evils which are the inevitable consequences of intemperance in the most highly civilized societies; but deprive the poor uncivilized, uneducated native of his great redeeming virtue of sobriety, and you cast him adrift at once, an unresisting victim to all the vices of humanity.

Government, by the tempting item of its revenue derivable from the arrack farms, has been induced tacitly to allow, if it has not, through its agents, positively encouraged the use of spirits throughout the land; it justifies itself by the (intended) restrictive price, under which rate it forbids it to be sold by retail. It would have been more consistent with the duty of a paternal Government to have limited the number of taverns in the rural districts, or, at least, not to have allowed them to be forced upon the people against their wish.

It is during the last eleven years that the influx of European capital, and the extensive cultivation of coffee, has thrown a large amount of specie into circulation in the interior; I think it is estimated at three millions sterling. As a very large portion of the money has been paid in specie for labour, it followed that temptations to, and examples of intemperance, and vice of every kind were rife; the most profligate of the low country Singhalese flocked from the maritime provinces into the interior, and spread far and wide their contaminating influences over a previously sober, orderly, honest race. Robberies and bloodshed became familiar to the Kandyan, in districts where a few years before any amount of property would have been perfectly safe in the open air.

The Superintendent of Police, a very shrewd observer, whose official duties afforded him the means of possessing the best information on the subject, not long since assured me, that what with law, proctors, and intemperance, there would not, ere long, unless the present state of things was changed, be a respectable Kandyan family left in the country. My own observations for years past had, long before the date of this communication, brought me to something of the same painful conclusion.

Probably in no people in the world does there exist so great a love of litigation as in the Singhalese. It is much encouraged by, if it does not altogether owe its existence, to the state of their law of inheritance, by the result of which property has become so subdivided that the 120th share of a field, or the 99th share of a small garden (containing perhaps not half-a-dozen trees), becomes the fruitful source of legal contention. With their own government, the result of an appeal to law depended less upon the merits of the case in dispute than upon the relative means and inclination of the parties to pay for a favourable decision; hence a lawsuit was too frequently the corrupt instrument of revenge in the hands of the rich and powerful, where no better means of indulging a vindictive spirit of animosity or tyranny presented itself. Witnesses can, even in these days, be obtained for evidence of any character. Perjury is made so complete a business, that cases are as regularly rehearsed in all their various scenes by the professional perjurer as a dramatic piece is at a theatre. So long as the courts of the colony were more those of equity than law, and were unclogged by quibbles and delays, this litigious spirit appeared to be on the decline; the presiding judge sifted his own evidence, and if he possessed a knowledge of the character of the people, a fictitious case was less easily "got up" than it can be now.

The prevailing system of our little district courts admits of the proctors feeding upon their clients for years. I have repeatedly, at uncertain intervals, been summoned to attend a district court as a witness in a case which had been before the court ten or eleven years. On my appearing in obedience to my summons to give evidence, I have been told that the case was again postponed; and so I conclude it will continue to be deferred, until by the death or departure from the country of the most important of the defendant's witnesses it may be found expedient to press for a decision of the case.

I have seen instances wherein the judicial stamps have far

exceeded the value of the case under adjudication, and which by numberless vexatious postponements have been protracted over a period of many years, to the ruin of both plaintiff and defendant; the proctors by their fees, and the Government by the sale of judicial stamps, being the only gainers.

If private individuals have suffered from the nature and system of our law courts, Government has been no less victimised; their cases are postponed for years, and the unsuccessful issue of their suits is proverbial.

A tabular abstract of the business of the several district courts of Ceylon, under the following heads, for the last five years, would exhibit curious results:—

Case, when instituted.

Case, when decided.

Value of case under litigation.

Cost of stamps.

Number of postponements.

Number of cases on the books of the court.

These evils may, I hope, be in some degree mitigated; I shall hereafter refer to the means by which I think it may be accomplished.

While the foregoing demoralizing influences have been operating on the social condition of the people, the authority and moral influence, both of European public servants and of the native chiefs, have been sadly on the decline in too many of the districts.

With the introduction of the supposed endless stream of capital which poured into the colony, simultaneously came a number of European settlers of every grade and age, in the various capacities of capitalists, planters, agents, superintendents, overseers, &c., &c. Amongst these were not a few whose habits and conduct tended much to diminish the respect in which the English character had previously been held by the natives; while a most fatal error committed by Government, in allowing its public servants to embark in the seductive speculation of coffee, by placing too many of them in the general category of "planters," weakened the moral influence and authority which they previously possessed, no less than it tended to circumscribe their pecuniary means of independence and usefulness, and finally, in too many instances, ruined their finances. It also placed their interests in rivalry with their duty, which in Ceylon (where so much depends on the individual example, influence, and energy of the public functionary) demands, and had previously received, their undivided attention and time.

During the feverish excesses of this delusive speculation, little could be thought of but the wealth and prosperity to which, by its means, and the instrumentality of European capital, the colony was to be raised. Money was abundant; for a time the price of coffee was remunerative. Trade was brisk, and the revenue flourishing. It was no matter of surprise that, under these circumstances, few were to be found with sufficient boldness and calculating foresight to predict anything like a doubt of the boundless elasticity of our colonial prosperity.

As European capital was to accomplish such prodigies, it was but a natural consequence that European interests should gain the ascendency.

The natives, who had previously had comparatively little acquaintance with the precious metal, during the last ten or eleven years found it, in the coffee districts, pouring into the deep recesses of their forests with a kind of Californian superfluity, and too frequently accompanied with its attendant evils; the cultivation of the staple article of food of the country (rice) declined; large tracts of land were thrown out of cultivation, while in one province alone was there to be seen any attempt to increase the means of irrigation, or to extend or improve the cultivation of native productions. Intercourse between the European local public functionaries and the natives had become less frequent, while the native chiefs were placed in a position anomalous and invidious for some years past. A vague idea has prevailed that their influence and authority has been too great, and under an impression that it was necessarily subversive of the stability and efficiency of our own authority, the policy has been to allow it to decline, and without any avowed determination to destroy it we have practically discouraged and undermined it.

The authority and influence of the European over the native, to be as general, effective, and beneficial as it ought to be, must necessarily descend, railway-like, in an unbroken gradient from the governing through the various grades of the governed, rather than by abrupt leaps and disjointed falls. Masses of the machinery of the social order cannot be cast off and heedlessly strewed in the way without danger; but we have placed the chiefs and headmen (a most important fraction of that machinery) in a position in which they are in various degrees calculated to impede, rather than to facilitate, the progress of good Government; we have rendered them discontented, their respectability, and influence (for good) with the mass of the people is generally impaired, and they are becoming alienated in feeling from the Government.

Under these circumstances, Society in its various, but especially in the lower, grades has been (for the last ten or eleven years) becoming demoralized, and so palpably so of late that it required no great power of discrimination to predict, twelve months before it manifested itself in open revolt, the anarchy to which some of the districts were approaching.

In brief recapitulation, then, it may be said of the last thirty-one years, that the first six were to the native population a period of trial and depression; the next fourteen of contentment and prosperity; the last eleven of a fictitious prosperity, as transient as it was locally partial, of eventual bankruptcy to European capitalists, and as regards the natives, of demoralization more or less in most, ending in anarchy in some districts.

While the causes I have referred to were hastening the native population into various degrees of disorganization, want of intercourse with, knowledge of, and sympathy in the people, kept many of the local European functionaries so completely in the dark as regarded their (the people's) social condition, that the warning which I gave (twelve months before the late insurrection broke out) of the state of anarchy to which the two rebellious districts (Seven Korles and Matella) were approaching was disregarded, if not disbelieved.

The same want of knowledge of the real state of public feeling in the country appears to me to have excited exaggerated fears in the Government when disorders overtook it, and prevented its rightly distinguishing between the feelings which prompted the people to meet in large, but orderly and peaceable assemblages, to obtain information of the intentions and objects of Government (the necessity for which explanation it was the duty of the local officers to have anticipated), and those feelings which in other districts urged the disaffected to open rebellion.

Had there existed less ignorance of the social condition of the people, the late troubles might easily have been averted, even at the eleventh hour; while to that ignorance is to be attributed the (in my humble judgment) exaggerated view taken of the nature and extent of the disaffection, and the consequent severity of the punishments inflicted on those implicated in the revolt. Although amongst the latter were to be found headmen and priests, there was that, in the nature of the whole affair, and in the character of its ringleaders, to stamp it as the result of disorganization, and inefficiency in the system and machinery of our executive Government, rather than as originating from any general and serious disaffection of the people. Had the higher classes been the authors of it, they would not have condescended to select as their leaders a set of low country vagabonds, of inferior caste, for whom they entertain the greatest possible repugnance and contempt.

I have known the Districts of Seven Korles and Matella, when such was the deference and respect for the authority of Government, and for its agents, that the mere suggestion of a wish, on the part of the latter, would ensure the readiest and most cheerful obedience from the entire population; but unfortunately our authority and influence have been most wantonly frittered away.

A year or two ago I visited the Seven Korles on a tour of duty, when I found one of the principal headmen of the district obliged to abandon his own village, and compelled to reside in the bazaar of Kornegalle (the revenue, judicial, and police head-quarters of the district), a mile beyond the precincts of which he dared not ride, unless armed and protected by an European gentleman; ruffians, who had escaped from gaol, or had evaded the law, and for whose apprehension rewards were advertised by Government, had fortified the huts in which they were living at a short distance from Kornegalle, and defied alike the Government agent, fiscal, and native headmen, to capture them; but a few years since, the authority of an unarmed messenger would have sufficed for that, or any other fiscal duty.

No stronger illustration need be adduced of the extent to which, by local mismanagement and apathy, we have destroyed the prestige of our own authority, and the influence of the native chiefs.

But for the great sacrifice of life, liberty, and property which have resulted from the late insurrection, it might be regarded as a fortunate event, if by its means the Government has been aroused to a sense of the defective system which produced it, and which would finally have resulted in still more general anarchy, had not the state of disorganization thus early developed itself.

Lord Torrington has been blamed as the cause of the late insurrection; but with the general disorganization, which alone led to the outbreak, his Lordship had no more to do than had any other Peer of the Realm. It was on the first month of his Lordship's arrival in Ceylon, that on my return to the seat of Government, from a long tour made by order of his predecessor, on a special duty, as I have before stated, I pointed out the state of anarchy to which I foresaw the Seven Korles and Matella districts were approaching, and represented the general disorganization which I thought would result from a perseverance in our existing system of internal Government.

The nature of my duties compelling me to visit the various provinces and districts occasionally, almost periodically, the retrograde movement in the good feeling and order of the natives, in most of the districts, has perhaps appeared to me, after intervals of absence, in stronger relief than it may have done to the resident civil functionary; but if those evils and dangers which I foresaw were unobserved, or unrepresented by the local authorities, surely his Lordship (a perfect stranger to the country) must stand excused that he should not have been inspired with an instinctive knowledge of the true condition and feeling of a people amongst whom he had but just arrived.

The mischief done has been too progressive for the last ten or twelve years to admit of degrees of responsibility for the result, attachable to any particular Government, being defined; the errors of omission have been as productive of evil, if not more so, than those of commission.

The population of Ceylon amounts, it is conjectured (we have no accurate census), to 1,500,000; its area to about 24,000 square miles, of which I should conjecturally estimate 18,000 are inhabited, 6,000 uninhabited.

There are six provinces of unequal area and population.

To each province there is a Government Agent (political and

revenue), with, on an average, three Assistants; the staff of native officials is numerous.

One-eighth area of the Island is mountainous; one-eighth hilly; three-fourths comparatively flat. The whole covered either with heavy forests or dense jungles, except in occasional open plains, and in those comparatively small patches cleared for cultivation.

Vegetation is so rank and rapid that a piece of ground cleared for cultivation will in three years, if neglected, be covered with thorny impenetrable jungle; the country is much intersected with rivers, the higher portions beautifully watered, and commanding the means of irrigation, if properly managed, at all elevations; the villages are imbedded in these close jungles or forests, and, except where they lie contiguous to a main road, are very inaccessible.

There are no large native towns, except those of the principal military and civil stations; the largest villages may number from 100 to 150 houses; but on an average they may be rated at from twelve to fifteen.

The head-quarters of the civil, political, and revenue officer is, in five cases out of six, situated on the border of his province, and not unfrequently at a remote corner of it; he is the representative of the Government, and for executive detail is dependent on the various grades of native officials, who receive their "acts" or "commissions" of appointment from Government: they are numerous, and the functions of the respective grades, in all their minuteness, are well understood by themselves; their authority and efficiency depends far more upon the moral influence and respect which they command from, and which is generally yielded to them by, their countrymen, than from any legal recognition of their powers.

The population being so generally diffused in small and secluded villages over an (at present) inaccessible country, it follows that the order, good government, and general improvement of the people in the rural districts, no less than the authority and influence of the Government, must very materially depend on the efficiency of the headmen. To have upheld their respectability, and to have supported, while we directed within proper limits, their legitimate influence and authority, ought to have been our policy; but, unfortunately, a vague and, I humbly conceive, most erroneous impression has prevailed, that, consistently with the maintenance of our own authority, it has been inexpedient to uphold that of the higher classes of natives, which, as I have before stated, has in some parts of the country declined to an inconvenient extent, weakening our own control over the people, and leaving large sections of the rural districts with a mere nominal Government, without any sufficient restraint on the vicious and disorderly of the lower classes.

These remarks, though they are of too general, are fortunately not of universal application; there is one special, bright, and encouraging exception to the rule (as there are other minor ones) in the Northern Province, where the converse of what I have just described prevails, and where the progressive improvement, general good order, respectability of the higher classes, and deference to authority (both European and native), mark the happy result of the wise and benevolent policy of the man whose enlightened government of that prosperous province has raised it to its present condition.

One of the principal objects assigned as a reason for desiring to diminish the influence of the higher orders of natives, has been a desire to destroy the distinctions and prejudices of castes; but nothing, in my opinion, has been more exaggerated than the supposed evils resulting from it in its very modified form in Ceylon. The common acceptation of the term in Ceylon differs from that which it signifies in India, where, I believe, the distinctions of castes are more of a religious than a secular character.

In Ceylon a high-caste family means one of ancient and aristocratic descent, and is as well applied to Christians as to heathens; it no doubt also applies to professions, trades, and occupations, but in this respect it is fast dying away. Nothing is so much calculated to retard its extinction as attempts to forcibly suppress it; nothing being so certain to excite the opposition of those who fancy they have anything to lose by it, as an open invasion of so old a national prejudice. Members of some of the highest families in Ceylon have assured me of their willingness to allow these prejudices and distinctions to die off gradually, while they complain bitterly of the precipitancy evinced in the desire to suppress them.

Education and civilisation are the only sure and legitimate means of eradicating it, by elevating the native character above the consideration of caste, rather than by (in effect) lowering the higher orders in the estimation of the inferior classes.

It is also urged that the lower classes are kept in a state of bondage to the hereditary chiefs, to whom they yield more readily allegiance than to Government. I have known the country from its first emancipation from the oppressive tyranny of its native Government; my duties have kept me in frequent intercourse with every province and almost every district for many years, enabling me to observe the transitions of the natives from their state of feudal vassalage to their present condition of perfect independence. The lower classes have shown anything but an insensibility to the advantages of the privileges granted to them, and are now as well aware as Europeans are, of the inability of the Government, or the chiefs, legally to call upon them for any service whatever, and are very little disposed to submit tamely to exactions of any kind.

Respect, approaching to veneration, for aristocracy, in a pure, ancient, and unblemished family descent, pervades every class; their fastidiousness with respect to it in their family alliances is one of their strongest characteristics. An ancient family may be reduced in circumstances, and denuded of all official rank and authority, but we cannot deprive it of the large amount of consideration and influence which will be rendered to its members by their countrymen; and why should we deprecate or desire to subvert this element of social order? We may rest assured that any sudden attempt to do so will only recoil, and deservedly so, on ourselves. Whenever there is reason to complain of the chiefs (this term applies to men of family and property, whether in office or not) possessing too much influence, or exercising an undue authority, it is conclusive evidence of the culpable absence of the directing and controlling authority of Government, arising from the want of energy, ability, or zeal of its representative.

No one will, I presume, contend that the country can be governed without the instrumentality of native subordinate officials; and if practicable, would it be just to desire it? Admitting that in justice the natives ought, and from necessity they must, participate in the executive of the country, who should the Government so reasonably look to for assistance, and who would the people so naturally desire to see placed in authority, as members of families they respect, and who hold the largest stake in the country? I do not mean to say that office should be held by them to the exclusion of merit in other grades, but maintain that rank, wealth, and ancestry should be no disqualification; we cannot prevent their commanding consideration and influence, which we may easily turn to the advantage of Government, and benefit of society, failing in which, they may perchance prove antagonistic to both.

The experience of Indian Government, where some of the large collectorates are little inferior either in area or population to the whole Island of Ceylon, proves what may be done by properly controlled and well-directed native authority; and why should the natives of Ceylon be considered less worthy of confidence and authority? It is said the whole policy of our Government, and the nature of its institutions, are dissimilar to those of India, and that despotism and corruption are so characteristic of the Ceylonese, that he is unfitted for carrying out our liberal system, which strikes at the root of all his predispositions; but this my experience enables me to deny. Supposing, however, it were true, will a remedy to the evil be found in still further depressing the native gentleman in his own, as well as in the estimation of others? We have no alternative but to use the native as a means for carrying out our Government, and the higher he stands in his own esteem, and in the respect of others, the more effective instrument shall we find him.

My confidence in the integrity, and intelligence of the native gentleman, has induced me to raise many of them in my own department to appointments of equality, in responsibility and trust, with European officers; the expenditure of very large sums has been intrusted to them, and I am happy to say, that in no single instance have I had to complain of misappropriation of funds, or other irregularities, but of which there were unfortunate instances amongst my European assistants, who both by birth and education were gentlemen.

To Ceylonese occupying positions on the bench, at the bar, and in the church, we may with great satisfaction and security, refer for proof that there is no deficiency of integrity, intelligence, or independence in the native character.

The peculiar facilities which I have enjoyed of judging of the practical results to the Colony generally of the administration of the various Governors who have presided over it for the last thirty years, enable me to state that from nothing has it suffered more than from a want of personal knowledge of the country in the head, and often in many of the leading members of the Government.

The population, soil, climate, productions, wants, interests, character, and circumstances of the various provinces and districts differ so materially from each other, that it is impossible to legislate for the whole, with impartiality and good effect, without a practical knowledge of them.

A Governor, whose experience and knowledge of the country is confined to Galle, Colombo, Kandy, and Newera Ellia, and to the carriage roads connecting those places, can but coldly and indifferently enter into the propositions and plans (be they ever so able) of an agent for the improvement of the remoter districts, if they are at all at variance (which they constantly may be) with the preconceived views of the Governor, founded on his limited experience; while the latter is unable to initiate any design for local improvement, or to take much interest in those which, after a long and discouraging advocacy on the part of the agent, he (the Governor) may at length have reluctantly sanctioned. No more effectual "drag" can be applied to the improvement of a colony, than a Governor who contents himself with presiding at his office table from year's end to year's end, to be mystified with a confused jumble of unpronounceable proper names which he can rarely identify or apply.

A greater interest is necessarily felt for things with which we are acquainted than for those of which we are ignorant, while the interests of the absent are but too frequently sacrificed to that of those who are present. So it is in Ceylon; with a very limited knowledge of, and interest in, the remoter districts on the part of the majority of the executive Government, the means available, whether for general improvement, for educational, or other purposes, are doled out with a penurious frugality to the remoter districts, while comparatively they are lavishly expended in the metropolitan districts. For this reason, I conceive it would be much for the general benefit of the colony if every province were represented in the Legislative Council by its proper Government Agent;

while they should also have a voice in the central Educational Commission, for in no department is advocacy of the interests of the remote and rural districts more needed : in Colombo, and at some of the other principal stations, comparatively large sums are expended in affording to the population means of education far more profound than the position in life and ultimate destinies of the majority of the recipients require, while in other districts educational means are culpably deficient.

Much has been said of the advantages to be anticipated from a representative form of Government for Ceylon ; but such cannot be seriously advocated by parties possessing a knowledge of the country, which is utterly deficient of the requisite elements for such a system ; the only effect of any attempt at which, for years to come, would be to give European interests a more preponderating influence than they already possess. A paternal form of Govern- is the only one at present suited to the country ; the rights and interests of the Natives being under the special care and support of the Government.

The most enlightened policy of the Imperial Government and the best efforts of the local legislature will alike fall short of, or be tardily productive of, their intended benefits to the secluded population of the interior of Ceylon, unless properly carried out under the supervision of energetic Government Agents and their assistants, on whom must necessarily mainly depend the improvement of the country. In the case of the Northern Province we have an example of the extent to which the good effect of an agent's influence may be made to pervade every class and portion of a province ; how the general improvement and good order of a people may be made to progress by the influence of one individual ; but to obtain influence, there must be intercourse with, and knowledge of the people, and it is to a want of both these requisites, I repeat, that we have to attribute the retrograde or stationary condition of the native community generally for some years past. But if there be any justice in the charge which has been made, of a decline in that active interest which the agents and their assistants ought to take in their provinces and districts, and of an absence in many of the latter of any evidences of improvement for some years past, it should be stated, in extenuation, that those officers for several years, instead of receiving that encouragement which would awaken or keep alive an ardent zeal for the advancement of their districts, have, in the absence of any local means for improvements, and in their dependence on the Government, which was ill able to provide them, had everything to discourage them.

So unable, indeed, has the Government been to meet the appeals made to it for local improvements, and, I fear, in too many instances so unable, from want of sufficient local knowledge of its chief officers, to discriminate between the relative importance of the numerous applications from various districts, that in many instances officers are deterred from suggesting improvements to Government, from the improbability of their being sanctioned; where the merit of a Government Agent in the charge of a Province consists (as I have known it to be estimated) in his giving no trouble, in being rarely heard of or from at head-quarters, where conscience will justify, policy will not unfrequently dictate, while the enervating effects of climate (when given way to) may confirm habits of passive indifference to all beyond ordinary routine in the public functionary, who is, or ought to be, the main-spring of the social order over which he presides; but in such case the source of the evil is in a higher quarter than the Government Agent or his assistants.

The Labour Ordinance, by giving to every district means of internal improvement proportionate to its population, and by bringing the Government Agents and their assistants more continually in contact with the people, will give to all parties (if properly managed) a great common interest in, and a grand stimulus to improvements. No year ought henceforth to pass without a decided advance in a well-devised systematic plan of improvement in each district; but the local plan should be well considered, and recorded long in anticipation of the means which will annually be available for their execution. If the labour of a district is squandered away on ill-organized unprofitable works, it will soon disgust the people, who would, on the contrary, rejoice in the result of its proper application.

I have adverted to the possibility of checking the ruinous and demoralizing tendency of the indulgence of the natives in their love of litigation. There is no local magistracy in Ceylon corresponding with the country magistrates in England; there are justices of the peace, but they have only the power of committal, and have no collective judicial power; the District Courts, Police Courts, and Courts of Requests (all expensive appendages of the of the Government) are situated, in some instances, 40 or 50 miles and upwards from portions of the population. One individual for a trifling suit may, in instances, if he chooses, withdraw from their village and necessary occupations one-half of its population as witnesses. The journey to and fro, and attendance at court, occupy perhaps not less than a week or ten days; and it is uncertain how often this expense and annoyance may be repeated, while the prevailing system of postponements and procrastination in our courts is permitted.

In the native government existed a primitive and very simple institution, termed "Gangsaib," or "Gamsaib," whether of Indian or Ceylon origin I am uncertain; the first syllable of the word being the Singhalese for "village"; the second, the Hindoostanee for "lord or master." The institution appears to have long existed in the north of India, as we hear of its having formed a highly-prized portion of the system of the ancient government of the Punjaub.

These gangsaibs were composed of three or five elders, of one large, or of a convenient number of contiguous small villages; they were elected by the people, and held their meetings, transacting their business, under the wide-spreading branches of the venerable village tree, under which the villagers are wont to congregate for public discussions, &c., &c.

I do not know the exact powers these gangsaibs may formerly have been invested with, but am convinced that their re-establishment in the rural districts, if merely for adjustment of petty disputes by arbitration and advice, under the mutual agreement and application of parties requiring such intervention, and for their own little municipal arrangements, would be productive of an infinity of good to the people. Quarrels and disputes would be inquired into on the spot, where the circumstances would be generally so well known to the community as to prevent an attempt at gross, premeditated perjury being resorted to; and in nine cases out of ten, I should anticipate that parties would be contented with the opinion and advice of the gangsaib. It should, however, in all cases, be eligible for the parties to appeal to higher tribunals; but when such an alternative is resorted to, the fact of the evidence having been previously rehearsed before the elders of the village would, in most cases, deter parties from bringing forward false witnesses.

The want of this (I may almost term it indigenous institution) has been very frequently represented to me by natives. I have known many headmen who, at the request of the inhabitants, individually perform the functions of the gangsaib, while one (a most respected friend), who is justly esteemed for his high integrity and uncompromising honour, is obliged to devote nearly the whole of his time to this benevolent purpose. His "wallawa" (palace) is usually thronged with people from the surrounding districts, who, having a wholesome dread of the consequences of being drawn within the vortex of our law courts, agree to submit their cases to this good man; he hears all that is to be urged on either side, and with a short summary of the evidence, from which he draws his conclusions, gives his opinion or judgment.

I once asked him if he had the satisfaction of knowing that his pains were rewarded by their being preventive of ulterior litigation, or if it frequently occurred that the defeated parties took their cases to courts after his hearing. He said, when he first commenced his system of arbitration, there were two or three instances of parties who, dissatisfied with his opinion, resorted to court; but the evidence having been rehearsed, as it were, in public before him and an audience whose local information prevented any attempt at gross perjury, it could not afterwards be much adulterated before the District Court; consequently, after repeated attendances, protracted, vexatious, and expensive law proceedings, the same decisions were legally pronounced, with this difference, that both parties were nearly ruined, and in some cases the defeated ones quite so. Of late, he said, parties rarely appealed from his decisions or advice.

The quarrels and disputes which lead to, and are both aggravated and perpetuated by these protracted law proceedings, might, in nine cases out of ten, be amicably settled had the parties ready means of seeking the intervention of any recognised referee. It becomes a point of honour with an Asiatic, that his supposed grievance should be investigated. Give but a patient hearing to the most exasperated parties, listen to what they have to say, and you may depend on their adherence to your award, and most generally the adjustment of the apparently most irreconcileable animosities.

Now, while the gangsaibs would accomplish this object with peculiar efficiency, they might be made to supply the present want of anything like municipal institutions, of which, in fact, they would form the basis. Arrangements regarding qualifications, elections, and functions might be easily made.

Simultaneously with the foregoing, let the number, duties, and powers of the headmen of each province, district, and village, after careful consideration, be revised and legally recognised. Give to the agents of Government and their assistants, as justices of the peace (which they are), a limited criminal jurisdiction while making their progress through their districts (something of the kind they formerly possessed), in conjunction with the gangsaibs or elders of villages, as assessors; this jurisdiction might even extend to punishment for cattle-stealing, which is carried on as a business by a set of lawless migratory thieves, and we should soon find crime and drunkenness yield to order and good government, to both of which nothing can be more prejudicial than too suddenly engrafting on society, in its most primitive state, institutions adapted to the highest existing state of civilisation.

The people of Ceylon are shrewd, clever, and yet tractable; they are quick and accurate observers, and will readily confide in, and may easily be guided by, men who they perceive really feel an interest in their welfare, and are capable of advancing it. It is only for the European to give himself the trouble of knowing, and allowing himself to be known (presuming him to be worth knowing) by the native, and the sympathies of either are pretty sure to be reciprocated, the former finding that complexion is not the surest test of virtue, and that often in the at first despised "black fellow" is to be found one of nature's perfect gentlemen.

Ceylon is a vast field of raw material awaiting and inviting the manufacturer, who, with a moderately skilful head, but with an honest and benevolent heart, may mould it to his will; preserve her from the indolent apathetic placeman (who in a luxurious climate stagnates almost to corruption), and with active rulers she may be made to the British Crown a "gem" indeed. Such are the convictions of thirty years' experience.

T. SKINNER.

Devonport, 9th June 1849.

I resumed my duties in Ceylon at the end of 1849. Lord Torrington was still at the head of the Government; his recall was not announced until September, when he was succeeded by Sir George Anderson, till then Governor of the Mauritius. On his arrival I waited on him as a matter of course, when he was pleased to recognise me as a connection, and invited me as such to special confidential communication with him, having, he said, heard much of my "sound judgment, and of my extended knowledge of the island."

In 1850 the Civil Engineer's Department again fell into disorder, and I received a very brief peremptory order to "take it over" and "incorporate it with my own." From that time up to my resigning the service in 1867 I conducted the entire public works of the colony.

From the "Colombo Observer," August 12, 1854.

Amongst the passengers who go home by the present steamer is Major Skinner, the Commissioner of Roads. We cannot allow the departure without a word of notice of one who has worked hard in and for the Colony for the best years of his life—from 14 to 50—the sole survivor of the band who, under the directing and contagious energy of Sir Edward Barnes, opened the magnificent Kandy Road, and whose name is closely associated with every line of communication opened in the Colony from 1819 to 1854, the result being a network of roads which, however we may consider them insufficient for the growing wants of an advancing commerce, render us the envy of the neighbouring continent with its teeming populations and immense revenues. Very interesting must the reminiscences of this able and untiring active officer be. He could tell of his patron, General Barnes, with Mamoty in hand, pioneering the operations on the Kandy Road with the same zeal and earnestness with which he fought his country's battles in the Peninsula and at Waterloo. He could also tell of a time when the forests of the interior, which now teem with the results of European industry, were unpenetrated and unknown until he and his co-labourers in the great survey of the Island traversed them in the course of triangulations extending from Colombo to Batticaloa, and from Hambantotte to Trincomalie. The difficulties of such a work, in the times in which most of it was performed, can be but slightly appreciated in these days of comparative civilisation. The mode in which it was performed, resulting in a vast fund of topographical information at a slight expense, secured for those engaged in it the gratitude of the Government they served; Major Skinner especially receiving the highest possible testimonials from all the authorities, civil and military, under whom he served. Whenever the survey or road-making operations of the Colony went at all wrong, Major Skinner was invariably called in to extricate the tangled skein; and, at length, when the interests of the Island, which he had seen advance from a mere garrison to a great commercial emporium, required the creation of a special department, Major Skinner was at once fixed on as the fittest man to be its head, the allowances in his case being raised from £800 to £1,000, as a special token of approval by Government and the Secretary of State of his long, arduous, and beneficial public services. The able document which we recently published shows how earnestly Major Skinner advocates the formation of railways, and what large views he takes of the improvements, material and moral, that might result to the Colony from energetic action in this direction; while of all those who advocate attention to the capabilities of Ceylon to grow the staple article of food, none has felt or spoken more strongly on the restoration of old irrigation works, and the formation of new ones, than Major Skinner. Indeed, it is within the scope of our knowledge, that one of the Governors of Ceylon contemplated the special devotion of his services to the regeneration of Newera Kalawa. Nothing but an iron frame, and the most temperate habits, could have enabled Major Skinner to survive his exertion in, and on behalf of, the Colony. Believing that, with all allowances for matters of detail, there is not a man in Ceylon to whom the Colony owes so much in the way of material improvement, on which moral advancement so closely depends, we feel bound to yield him this parting tribute of gratitude which he has so well earned.

In 1858, when Mr. Gibson, the Auditor-General, was at home on leave, and submitted his resignation to the Secretary of State, I applied for his appointment, and Lord Stanley, now Lord Derby, approved and confirmed my application; but subsequently Mr. Gibson waited at the Colonial Office in London, and asked if there would be any objection to his withdrawing his resignation, as he had changed his mind and wished to resume his duties in the colony. He was informed that the only person who was likely to object would be Major Skinner, to whom the Audit Office had been promised by the Secretary of State.

Mr. Gibson's return was, of course, a disappointment to me, for after thirty-nine years hard work in the colony I naturally thought myself entitled to an office which would ensure me a little rest. On Sir Charles MacCarthy's going home on leave Mr. Gibson was appointed to act for him as Colonial Secretary, when, on consideration of my having been last year given the appointment by the Secretary of State, I asked Sir Henry Ward to allow me to act for Mr. Gibson, and this he was pleased to approve. Sir Henry had then been in the Government between three and four years. As Commissioner of Public Works I had constant personal communication with him, and found him one of the largest-minded public men I had yet met with.

The very first day I waited upon him on my return

from leave of absence in 1856 I took with me plans of iron bridges, of which the colony was in desperate need, and urged him to have a dozen out at once, telling him I had ordered out one of 100 feet span on my own private account, hoping that he would take it off my hands, which he said he would do, and then laughingly observed :

"This is a pleasant prospect, when the first day of my acquaintance with my Commissioner of Public Works he coolly commits me to an expenditure of £12,000 or £15,000 for bridges, with about as much more to pay for their erection."

Fortunately Sir Henry had been an intelligent observer of the wants of the country, and was but too ready to grasp at the idea of supplying a very serious deficiency. For three years we worked most harmoniously together : he gave me all the money he could possibly afford for the works, and I spared no pains to use it to the best possible advantage.

About this time the necessity for a railway between Colombo and Kandy came under discussion. There was not a man in the colony who did not earnestly desire the railway, and as long as the estimates of the cost were kept within £1,200,000 nobody demurred; but at the opening of the Session of the Legislative Council on the 18th July 1859, it was stated that "the results of the survey just completed proved that it was impossible to construct a line between Colombo and Kandy for anything like the amount indicated by the two previous surveys. The cost, as estimated by the

Company's engineers being £2,214,000, in lieu of £856,556 as estimated by Captain Moorsom."

On examination of the Company's estimates by the sub-Committee of Council, I took exception to the rates of cost, for during my long identification with the public works of the Colony I had kept accurate records of the expense of every description of work, and in the mere matter of earth-work, which was charged for at 11d. a yard, I proved, or rather asserted, that it had cost me for all descriptions of such work an average of 3½d. a yard. I subsequently heard that sub-contractors were making a profit on the line, taking jobs of earth-work at 2½d. a cubic yard. In every other particular the charges were, in my opinion, equally excessive.

A few days before the debate in the Legislative Council took place I had occasion to wait on the Governor to solicit a personal favour from him, which in his usual kind manner he promised to confer. When this subject was concluded, he started the railway argument. We had been discussing it very warmly when the bell rang to announce luncheon, which we disregarded, and I afterwards expressed to Lady Ward my regret that she should have been "deprived of the Governor's company at tiffin;" but I added, "the fault is entirely His Excellency's; I wanted to retreat when the tiffin bell rang, but he would not let me."

At this moment Sir Henry entered the corridor from another direction, joined the party with his hearty

English laugh, and proposed that I should go in and refresh myself after the contest. He said: "I knew perfectly well that I could do nothing with you, after you put on a certain expression of countenance which is always an indication of your obstinacy!"

We parted as good friends as we had ever been, but certainly with no doubt on His Excellency's mind as to the course I should pursue in the railway debate.

This action I have never regretted, although it resulted in my being superseded in the Audit Office by a young civilian from England and therefore obliged to forfeit my seat in the Councils and in the Government. These individual sacrifices were of small moment in comparison with the enormous public advantages I helped to secure for the Colony, which was now no longer to be made the victim of an unscrupulous railway company's jobbery.

A railway has now been completed of seventy-four miles, between Colombo and Kandy, at a cost, not of £2,214,000 as approximately estimated by the Ceylon Railway Company, but for the sum of £1,285,000.

The *Ceylon Directory* for 1875, page 264*d*, states that "At present we pay an annual consolidated sum for interest and sinking fund of £62,000, and last year the railway not only provided this but gave to the general revenue £90,000 more. In a few years the last of the debentures for the main line will be redeemed, and all the profit will then be so much gain for the Revenue."

My friends in Ceylon have never been fully aware of the penalty I paid for my defence of its interests on the 15th of September, 1859. The continued prosperity of the railway, year after year, has been my reward and my justification for the course I took.

CHAPTER XI.

In October 1860 Sir Charles MacCarthy arrived in Ceylon from England and assumed the Government, and from him I received every mark of consideration. I was fortunate enough also to enjoy his confidence, a matter of no small importance to the Colony after I resumed my duties as Commissioner of Public Works, as I required all the influence I could command to overcome the niggardly cheese-paring policy which was constantly being pressed upon the Governor.

The enterprise of coffee-planters could not be checked, and the demand for roads was excessively urgent in order to prevent the loss of much of the capital they had invested. During Sir Henry Ward's Government he exercised a will of his own, and it required no great persuasion to convince him of these wants; but now the expenditure was not considered with reference to the increased facilities given to the planters, but to the additional charge likely to be entailed upon the revenue for additional annual expenses. The Happootella district, a group of probably the finest estates in the Colony, furnished a painfully striking example of the need of roads. I had long foreseen the strait to which the proprietors were inevitably drifting. Their rice and other provisions could be carried to the estates by manual labour, but directly the coffee tree was old enough to yield a crop the consequences were palpable. I had long been struggling to open a road for wheel traffic from the highest navigable port of the Caltura River to the Port of Colombo, at Ratnapora through Saffragam to Ouvah, and had got as far as Pallamadula, twelve miles above Ratnapora. There still remained at least thirty-eight miles of the most execrable native mountain path, ever traversed and intercepted by rapid torrents, only fordable in dry weather. Over this path the planters sent down their maiden crops, which were always small and light, on men's shoulders.

I urged upon the Government that it had a far greater stake in the success of a whole district than any planter had in the prosperity of his individual estate, and pointed out that unless the Happootella district were at once supplied with a road of access the planters would grow coffee only to rot in their stores, and at last I induced the Government to sanction my submitting an estimate for continuing the carriage road from Pallamadulla to Ballangodde, a distance of fifteen miles.

Anticipating that Government could not much longer withhold this boon, I had had two estimates furnished for the work. One of them amounted to £30,000, which of course I rejected at once and sent another officer, pointing out to him the absurdity of framing so unreasonable a document, and requiring him to reduce the charge. He professed to have taken a great deal of pains, and claimed credit for reducing the amount to £25,000.

This estimate was still so excessive that I could not subject it to Government. I therefore sent one of the most experienced officers in the Department, warning him against the extravagance of his two predecessors. I cautioned him that if he made too low an estimate, I should send him up to direct the execution of the work himself; if I thought it too high, that I should carry it out under my own directions and make it a test of accuracy. The only officer of my Department whose testimony was called for, who supported me in my view of the cost of work, was Mr. Evatt, who by his systematic arrangement and strict adherence to principles of economy must have saved the Colony an enormous sum of money. He had been a subaltern in the 90th Light Infantry, never was a civil engineer, and yet was of more value to me than many highly scientific men.

I feel assured the officer to whom I finally entrusted the framing of this third estimate was painstaking and conscientious, and I know he was an able man; but he, like many of my assistants, held an exaggerated view of what the cost of work should be, and his estimate was between £18,000 and £19,000. Feeling convinced that the fifteen miles of road could be opened for less money, I submitted the estimate to Government, but placed two divisions of pioneers on it, under two good native officers, who reported to and corresponded with me direct. Instead of the work costing between £18,000 and £19,000, the amount of the sanctioned estimate, the expenditure was only £9,163.

Directly the road was opened, I drove Sir Charles MacCarthy up to Ballangodde. He was enchanted with the work, and I showed him that we had saved 57 per cent. of the estimate, and volunteered to complete another section of equal distance for the surplus money if he would authorize the expenditure. I pointed out to him what poor encouragement it would be to the Department, if money thus saved should go back to the Treasury. To this assertion he agreed, and I had the satisfaction of making my way up to Happootella, and of saving that district from almost total ruin.

If this story is ever read by the Public Works Department of Ceylon, it may help to show the value of a little care and system, and what can be done by departmentally trained natives. This work, and the reduction from the railway company's estimate of £2,214,000 to a contract for £873,039, ought to teach people how needful is strict and conscientious inquiry. Although I was sensible of the great increase in the price of labour, I felt satisfied that I had been right on the railway question.

In March 1861, I was superseded in the Audit Office by Mr. Pennefather from England, and resumed my charge of the Public Works Department.

When visiting the Batticaloa district in May 1862, I

received an express, informing me that my old friend and chief, General Fraser, was very seriously ill at Kandy, and of his urgent request that I should return immediately. I lost no time in obeying his summons; but my progress was limited by the inability of my travelling establishment to advance quickly.

Day after day, fresh expresses reached me with bulletins of my friend's state. Before I reached Newera Ellia, however, to my great grief I received the sad tidings of his death, which occurred much sooner than was expected, and I had the mortification of hearing that during the last few days of his life he constantly inquired when I might be expected. He must have had a presentiment of his death, for during several previous months he always begged me not to go away, if I could avoid it, to any great distance from him.

He was a splendid soldier, and probably one of the most accomplished general officers in the Service. He had fought with the late Sir Charles Napier, was a great friend and correspondent of his, and not very unlike him in character. Instead of identifying himself so completely with Ceylon, had he returned to England after the completion of his famous Paredenia Bridge, his great abilities and soldier-like qualities were such that they must have placed him in a position in his profession which, we all thought, would have led to a peerage. It is a drawback in the Colonial Service that an officer is tempted and beguiled to remain on, from year to year, until his interest in a new country, in which he is made useful, overcomes the ardour of his zeal for his profession, which he is thus often induced to leave.

In March 1865, Sir Hercules Robinson arrived as Governor, and the month after his landing gave earnest of the interest he intended taking in the welfare of the island by starting on a tour through Happootella and Saffragam. The Colony was much to be congratulated on the advent of such a Governor, the most painstaking, hardworking man I have ever met in his position. An extraordinary love of justice was his most peculiar characteristic, and I have seen frequent instances of this when travelling with him; he would not decide any claim on a superficial view of the case, but would insist upon receiving the most minute details before giving an opinion.

He astonished me on one occasion, when, on a very remote journey, he called me into his temporary office, and said, "At last I have got to the bottom of that case of yours *in re* Modelair Fonceka."

This was a man who had been in my department for upwards of thirty years, and was most efficient and economical. In a revision of the establishment of my department, I had recommended this faithful old servant for a higher class of pay; but the Colonial Secretary refused me on the plea that eight or nine years before he had given false evidence in a court of law prejudicial to the interests of the Government. I admitted that at one time I had entertained a similar impression of the man's conduct, but that circumstances had occurred which had completely exonerated him; and I stated that, had not this been the case, it would have been my duty to have represented his conduct and to have recommended Government to dismiss him, and that the Government itself, if convinced of his having played it false, would not have been justified in keeping him in its service. The fact of the Government retaining his services for eight or nine years subsequently, showed that his former supposed delinquencies were condoned. The subject had been laid before the Government three or four months previously; but the papers had been repeatedly referred backwards and forwards to the Supreme Court, to the Queen's advocate, and to my office. At last, while in a temporary resting-place in a remote out-of-the-way jungle, Sir Hercules investigated a mass of correspondence and judgments in Court, showing that Sir Henry Ward, the judge, and the Queen's advocate had all exonerated this man; and His Excellency had the satisfaction of unravelling Modelair Fonceka's case, and of giving him the increase of pay which he so thoroughly deserved, and for which he had been recommended.

In travelling with Sir Hercules, he would often discuss subjects of the kind with me, and never would he allow the humblest person to rest under a sense of injustice; he would require, to be satisfied, that every real grievance should be thoroughly investigated. This is a beautiful trait in the character of a public man; but it requires a very peculiar temperament to carry it to the extent to which Sir Hercules Robinson did.

In August 1865 my old friend General Studholm Hodgson arrived, as Commander of the Forces. The last time we had met we were both of us in the first rank in the Army, and were about the wildest subalterns in it. He was an ensign in the 45th Regiment. In my old family papers I find that General Hodgson's grandfather and my great-grandfather, General William Skinner, Chief Engineer of Great Britain, were associated together in the taking of Belle Isle in 1766.

In September 1865, Mr. Pennefather, the Auditor-General, having died, Sir Hercules Robinson sent for me and asked me to accept the acting appointment, as he had no one else he could appoint President of a Royal Commission to determine the amount of military force required for the internal preservation of peace, and to decide the amount to be paid by the Colony for that force.

The following papers refer to the constitution of the Commission. The evidence and report were published by order of the Government in December 1865.

COMMISSION.

In the Name of Her Majesty VICTORIA, of the United Kingdom of Great Britain and Ireland, Queen, Defender of the Faith.

By His Excellency Sir HERCULES GEORGE ROBERT ROBINSON, Knight, Governor and Commander-in-Chief in and over the Island of Ceylon, with the Dependencies thereof.

HERCULES G. R. ROBINSON

To the Honorable *Richard Theodore Pennefather*, Auditor-General and Member of the Executive Council; *Charles Peter Layard*, Esquire, Government Agent for the Western Province and

Member of the Legislative Council; *William John MacCarthy*, Esquire, Registrar-General of Lands; Deputy Inspector-General of Hospitals *John Fraser*, Doctor of Medicine and Companion of the Bath; Colonel *Robert Michael Laffan*, of the Royal Engineers; Deputy Commissary-General *Edward Barrington De Fonblanque*; Lieutenant-Colonel *Henry Charles Byrde*; *Alfred Wise*, Esquire, and *Christopher Barker Smith*, Esquire, greeting:

Whereas it hath been agreed between Her Majesty's Government and the Government of this Island that a full and detailed investigation should take place into every part of the Military Expenditure of the Colony, with the view to settle a definite scale of Military Force and Military Works and Buildings to be chargeable to the Colony in time of peace, and also to determine how far the administration and detailed payment of the service should rest or not with the Colonial Government, and what should be the amount and mode of payment, whether by fixed sums or by capitation rates on the Troops employed or assessment for services undertaken by the Imperial Authorities; and whereas We the said Governor have been instructed, authorized and empowered by Her Majesty through Her Secretary of State for the Colonies, to nominate, constitute, and appoint certain persons to be Commissioners for the purpose of making such investigation,

Now know ye, that We, reposing great Trust and Confidence in your Zeal, Discretion, and Ability, have authorized and appointed, and do by these presents authorize and appoint you the said *Richard Theodore Pennefather*, *Charles Peter-Layard*, *William John MacCarthy*, *John Fraser*, *Robert Michael Laffan*, *Edward Barrington De Fonblanque*, *Henry Charles Byrde*, *Alfred Wise*, *Christopher Barker Smith*, to be Our Commissioners for the purposes aforesaid.

And We do hereby authorise and empower you, Our said Commissioners, to enquire into the said matters, and particularly into the following points of detail:

(1). The total strength of Force, in Rank and File, to be fixed as the Peace Establishment for Ceylon in Infantry and and Artillery, European and Native.

(2). The organization in Officers and Men of the Native Troops, and the source or sources from which they should be recruited.

(3). The Establishment, as precisely as possible, of Staff and Engineer officers, and of Clerks, Attendants and other Civilians to be attached to the Force and Military Departments.

(4). The Stations through which the Force should be distributed, and the strength of the Detachments to be placed at each, having due regard to sanitary as well as political considerations.

(5). The Barracks and Hospitals, Forts and Batteries, and other Military Buildings or Works to be required at each Station, and the order of any new constructions, with plans and estimates (in as full detail as possible).

(6). The mode of administering the several Services, whether by Imperial or by Colonial Agency, especially as regards Commissariat and Works and Buildings.

(7). The amount and mode of Payment, whether by fixed sums or capitation rates for services undertaken by the Imperial Government, and the amount and form of Ordinance appropriations for Military purposes, in substitution for the Ordinance No. 16 of 1864 enacted by the Governor of Ceylon with the advice and consent of the Legislative Council thereof.

And all other matters or things in any wise relating to the subject generally or to any of the points in detail.

And we do hereby authorize and empower you, Our said Commissioners, or any four or more of you, to obtain information thereupon by the Examination of all persons most competent by reason of their knowledge, habits or experience to afford it, and also by calling for all Documents, Papers or Records, which may appear to you, or any four or more of you, calculated to assist your researches, and to promote the formation of a sound judgment on the subject of this Inquiry.

And We do hereby command and require you, *Richard Theodore Pennefather*, to preside over and to conduct throughout the Inquiry herein referred to.

And for your further assistance in the execution of these presents, We do hereby authorize and empower *John Frederick Dickson*, Esquire, to be Secretary to this Our Commission, whose services and assistance We require you to use from time to time as occasion may require.

And We do hereby reserve to Ourselves full power and authority to submit for your investigation and report further points of detail and matters of Inquiry, bearing on the subject of the present Inquiry, from time to time as occasion may require.

And We do hereby command and require you, or any four or more of you, to report to Us under your Hands and Seals, with all convenient speed, your Opinion on the several Matters hereby referred to you for your Consideration.

Given at the Pavilion, Kandy, in the said Island of Ceylon, this Fifteenth day of June, in the year of Our Lord One thousand Eight hundred and Sixty-five.

By His Excellency's Command,

WM. CHS. GIBSON,
Colonial Secretary.

SUPPLEMENTARY COMMISSION.

In the Name of Her Majesty VICTORIA, of the United Kingdom of Great Britain and Ireland, Queen, Defender of the Faith.

By His Excellency Sir HERCULES GEORGE ROBERT ROBINSON, Knight, Governor and Commander-in-Chief in and over the Island of Ceylon, with the Dependencies thereof.

HERCULES G. R. ROBINSON

To the Honourable *Thomas Skinner*, Acting Auditor-General and Member of the Executive Council.

Whereas by Our Commission being dated the Fifteenth day of June in the present year of Our Lord One thousand Eight hundred and Sixty-five, We appointed the late Honorable *Richard Theodore Pennefather* and others therein named to be Our Commissioners for the purposes of making the Investigation in the said Commission specified, and We further commanded and required the said *Richard Theodore Pennefather* to preside over and to conduct throughout the Inquiry therein referred to: And whereas, owing to the demise of the said *Richard Theodore Pennefather*, it has become necessary to appoint another in his place,

Now know ye, that We, reposing Great Trust and Confidence in your Zeal, Discretion and Ability, have authorized and appointed, and do by these presents authorize and appoint you the said *Thomas Skinner* to be Our Commissioner for and in the place of the said *Richard Theodore Pennefather* to make the Investigation in the said Commission specified, and We do further command and require you to preside over, and to conduct the Inquiry therein referred to, and to exercise the powers and perform the Duties therein conferred and imposed as fully and as effectually as if your name was inserted in the said Commission so issued by us.

Given at Queen's House, Colombo, in the Island of Ceylon, this Third day of October, in the year of Our Lord One thousand Eight hundred and Sixty-five,

By His Excellency's Command,

WM. CHS. GIBSON,
Colonial Secretary.

Colombo, 5th December 1865.

YOUR EXCELLENCY,

I have the honour to submit the report of the Commission on Military Expenditure, of which your Excellency did me the honour to appoint me President on the death of the late lamented Mr. Pennefather, whose loss to the Colony, to society in general and especially to themselves, the Commission have to deplore.

I am requested by the Commission to express to your Excellency their grateful thanks for the assistance you have been kind enough to render them on every occasion.

I am requested to thank your Excellency for the fortunate selection of the gentleman who has officiated as Secretary to the Commission and to convey to your Excellency the sense the Commission entertain of the great ability and zeal with which Mr. Dickson has performed his difficult and trying duties; the Commissioners have heard with great satisfaction that your Excellency had been pleased to grant him a pecuniary recompense, and they trust that you may be pleased hereafter to confer upon him some further mark of your favour.

The Commission has been happy to learn that your Excellency has been pleased to reward Mr. Askey, the clerk of the Commission, whose duties have been performed with much assiduity.

I am requested to bring to your Excellency's notice, the great advantage the Commission has derived from the promptitude and care with which the printed evidence has been rendered day by day as it has been required. This the Commission thinks has been the more creditable to the Superintendent of the Government Printing Office, as the service was rendered under circumstances of great pressure, consequent upon the sitting of the Legislative Council during the period of the Inquiry, and as the work of the Commission has necessarily thrown upon the Superintendent of the Government Press a larger amount of additional labour, I am requested to express the hope that your Excellency may be pleased to grant to Mr. Herbert some compensation for the extra work which he has rendered so willingly and efficiently.

I have the honour to be, &c. &c.

(Signed) T. SKINNER.

To His Excellency, Sir Hercules Robinson, Knt.
Governor and Commander-in-Chief, Ceylon.

Colonial Secretary's Office, Colombo, 8th December, 1865.

SIR,

I am directed by the Governor to acknowledge the receipt of your letter of the 5th inst., addressed to His Excellency, submitting the report of the Commission on Military Expenditure, and I am to convey to you the expression of His Excellency's high sense of the very efficient manner in which the Commission have conducted the important Inquiry entrusted to them.

I am also to state that the Governor has directed, in accordance with the recommendation of the Commission, that a gratuity of Fifty Pounds be granted to the Government Printer.

I have the honour to be, &c. &c.

(Signed) WM. C. GIBSON.

The Hon. T. Skinner,
President of the Military Commission.

Owing to my wife's serious illness and subsequent death, in 1866, I proceeded home on leave, but had to return to Ceylon as soon as possible to prepare the estimates of the Colony for the Legislative Council.

During my stay in London, I waited on Lord Carnarvon, Secretary of State for the Colonies. He very kindly invited me to his seat at High Clere, and I was much gratified by this visit. His Lordship questioned me very closely on various topics of engrossing interest connected with Ceylon, and listened to my views before he gave expression to his own. This was most considerate and judicious, and relieved me of all embarrassment, for, not knowing what his opinions were, I was enabled to give my own freely and honestly. I could not have believed that any man in his Lordship's position could have been so thoroughly and rightly informed on various topics concerning a distant Colony as he was. He told me that when Under-Secretary of State for the Colonies he had been much interested in Ceylon, and had then expressed very fully his ideas in writing in regard to the several subjects we had discussed. I do not hesitate to assert that Lord Carnarvon's knowledge of Ceylon surpassed that of several members of the Local Government. I know I felt myself very fortunate in being so well up in the affairs of the Colony before so intelligent and well-informed an inquirer, and I enjoyed my visit to High Clere exceedingly.

On my return to Ceylon my time was very much occupied with preparing for the Supply Bill, and in arranging for the works to be taken in hand immediately after the beginning of the new year.

I had made my preparations for a final visit to all the districts and works in the interior of the island. This involved the laying-in of supplies of every description for myself and officers while travelling—corn for my horses, oilman's stores, wines, groceries, together with clothes and books, for several months' use. I had started off two railway-trucks full of luggage of every conceivable description, to the value of £300; but on the evening of the day they left Colombo, I had the annoyance of receiving a telegram to the effect that the railway-trucks had caught fire, and that the whole of my property had been destroyed. Having only just spent £600 on my voyage and expenses to and from England, this proved a most untoward loss. I was advised to apply to Government for reimbursement, as it was argued "Government was responsible for the safety of the goods it took charge of, as ordinary carriers"; besides which, I was travelling on duty. But my appeal met with a decided rejection, and I thought it unadvisable, at the closing scene of my long service to the Government, to enter an action for damages against it.

My last few months in Ceylon were spent in travelling through the districts with Sir Hercules Robinson. I felt very sad when reflecting that it was to be my last visit to places in which I had spent so many years of hard work.

My long sojourn in the island brought me into pleasant contact with many interesting and distinguished persons, and the remembrance of these chance meetings are amongst my most pleasant reminiscences. When the present King of the Belgians visited the country I had the honour of his acquaintance, and found him one of the most intelligent and agreeable men that it had ever been my privilege to know.

Another, the Baron Eugène de Ransonnet, was a charming companion and likewise a talented artist. His book of *Sketches in Ceylon* is well known, and includes some most interesting submarine drawings taken while in a diving-bell, as well as others of scenery along the coast. There are many more whose names one would like to mention, but time and space will not permit one to linger too long amongst these happy bygone scenes.

Mr. Molesworth, my successor, begged me to remain in office another year; but I had promised my children I would return home within that time, and could not disappoint them.

The following extracts from the *Colombo Observer* of the 29th of June 1867, on my retirement, must be read as the production of a partial critic :—

Retirement of Major Skinner.

From the "Colombo Observer," June 29th, 1867.

The absorbing topic to which we have to address ourselves on this occasion is the final departure from the Colony of the oldest, and we may safely say the most useful member of the Public Service. Whatever general objections may be offered to the practice of presenting addresses to public servants on their retirement, we feel that a case so exceptional as Major Skinner's calls for an exceptional expression of opinion on the part of those whom his life-long labours have benefited so largely. We are, therefore, glad to learn that the Natives have in this manner shown their appreciation of Major Skinner's character and services. From the Seven Korles; from Kandy and the Ouvah Districts; Saffragam, the Southern, and from other districts within reach—the people of the land came forward to say a kind parting word to the man who has done so much for them and their country.

We are equally glad to learn that the European Merchants, Planters, and others have made a fitting demonstration in the shape of a Memorial to the Secretary of State, praying that an enhanced pension may be granted to the veteran road-maker. As tax-payers, and most of them extensively interested in the Commercial and Agricultural enterprise of Ceylon, those who join in the Memorial assure the Secretary of State that it would be grateful to their feelings to learn that the Government, Major Skinner has so long and so faithfully served, had consented to reward his special services with a special pension of £1,000 per annum. A case so remarkable as his has never come before the Government of Ceylon, and no similar case is likely to recur. From the time when as a young officer of fifteen "Tom Skinner" was chosen by Governor Sir Edward Barnes to aid in opening the Kandian Provinces for Military operations and general intercourse by the great road up the Kaduganava Pass, until now that the grey hairs of three score and four warn him to seek repose in the bosom of his family for the evening of life, he has been incessantly employed in the construction of those means of communication to which Ceylon owes most of whatever material progress she has made; with much of the intellectual and moral improvement which here as elsewhere ever follow increased facilities of intercourse. The latest portion of his career has not been the least creditable to him or the least useful to the Colony. Incited by the encouragement afforded him by an appreciative Ruler, he put forth all the energy for which his youth and manhood were distinguished, in efforts (largely successful, we are happy to know) to bring his Department into such a position as regards numbers and efficiency as will render comparatively easy the task which remains for his successor; to continue that comprehensive scheme of communications which, many years ago, Major Skinner planned, and which, when finally completed, will make this Island the best roaded Colony in the British Empire.

Without a trained body of workmen to rely upon for good, steady and continuous work, such results would never have been attained as Major Skinner has lived to accomplish, and the point in respect of which his determination of purpose—or, as some have called it, his obstinacy—has beyond all calculation served the public is the Pioneer question. We well remember that about 1854 there was a very strong desire on the part of Sir Geo. Anderson's Government, including Messrs. Macarthy and Gibson, to reduce the Pioneer Force. Indeed, long before then it had at times been proposed, and nothing but Major Skinner's persevering and strenuous opposition to so suicidal a measure prevented its being carried out. When he proposed, or rather insisted on, the Establishment of a Pension Fund for the Pioneer Force he met with nothing but discouragement on all sides. Happily he persevered, and to the existence of that fund, which has now, without the cost of one shilling to the public, a Capital of about £22,000 and an income of upwards of £3,000 a year, we owe it that during the progress of the Railway, and when the demand for skilled labour has been so great that a pensioned Pioneer can earn from 3s. to 4s. a day, the Public Works Department was enabled to keep its force together, and from it to form the nucleus of the present force of nearly 4,000 men. What would Ceylon have been without this force? As roadless as many parts of the Continent of India still are. The Pioneer Force is now in a high state of discipline and efficiency and is equal to any things the Colony can require of it. Major Skinner has been in the habit of inspecting and recording in his inspection rolls the characters of every man in the force, at least once a year, but every half-year when he could devote the time to it. The result has been most happy in imbuing the men with an *esprit de corps* which leads them to be proud of their position and anxious to earn the good opinion of their Officers, and those substantial records in the shape of higher rank and better pay which the semi-military character of the organization secures.

The character of the Pioneer Force and the value of its services to the Colony were so well and forcibly described in a Memorial presented to Sir George Grey when Secretary of State for the Colonies in January 1855, that we cannot do better than quote a few passages. Referring to the recommendations of the Committee of Council on the Establishment of the Colony, the Memorialists wrote:—

"By one of their resolutions the Committee propose to strike off from the Fixed Expenditure of the Colony the Pioneer Establishment of the Department of Public Works, a measure which would infallibly break up the Pioneer Corps, perhaps the best organized Civil Force to be found in our Eastern Empire, and without which it would have been impossible to have carried out the great Works which have been executed in Ceylon during the last ten or twelve years; and it is much to be feared that the Department of Public Works would thus be so crippled that it would be found impossible to keep up the Roads in an efficient state.

"The subject involves so many considerations that we could not venture, in a letter, to take up your time with all the details requisite to lay it fairly before you; but we may call to your attention the fact that in 1833 the same measure was adopted, from economical views, with regard to the then equally efficient corps of Pioneers, and an attempt was made to carry out Public Works with occasional hired labour; but the results were so unsatisfactory that it was soon found necessary, with great trouble and expense, to organize the present Pioneer force, under the former system, placing it on the Fixed Expenditure; and at the same time, Major Skinner adopted such measures to form a Pension Fund as made the service a highly desirable one, and placed at the command of the Roads Department the very best class of Malabar labour that can be obtained.

"During the disturbances of 1848 the Pioneers were, to a certain extent, armed and drilled, and were found a most valuable and efficient body of men, quite capable of affording important aid to the Military, and far superior to the Native Police.

"The climate of Ceylon, the nature of the country, the apathetic character of the Cingalese labourers, and the difficulty of getting Public Works performed efficiently and with good faith by contract, are amongst the causes inherent in the Colony which render a force of skilled and experienced labourers absolutely essential to the making and upkeep of roads. But it is not to be expected that the fine body of men now permanently settled in the Colony under the Roads Department will remain there if deprived of regular wages and of the Pension Fund, which are to them strong inducements to good conduct; and upon neither of them could they depend for the future, if their employment is to be contingent only on the carrying out of such estimates as may be, from Session to Session, sanctioned by the Governor and Legislative Council.

"We consider that the proposed alteration would be found extremely prejudicial to the effective working of the Department of Public Works, and most detrimental to our interests as proprietors of land in Ceylon; and we beg to reiterate the request we have so recently made to you to examine Major Skinner himself (who is now in England) on this most important topic, and we cannot doubt that his evidence will bear out our belief that the measure proposed would be a most imprudent one, and would in the end lead to a great increase of expenditure.

"We are the more disposed respectfully to press our views on this matter, as we have had, for several years, unusual opportunities of watching the working of the present system in the Kandian Province; while the members of the Legislative Council, though doubtless individually anxious for the welfare of the Colony, have, with one or two exceptions, been for many years placed in such circumstances as have unavoidably debarred them from the advantage of personal experience on the subject."

We only trust no future attempt will be made to reduce or dispense with the Pioneer Force, until that distant period when it can be said that Ceylon needs no more roads, bridges, or canals. The last word reminds us of a system of communication to which the British Government in Ceylon has as yet paid but too little attention, and in regard to which Major Skinner has had to fight almost as many battles for the interests of the Colony as in the case of the Pioneers.

One of the greatest difficulties he had to contend with was the opposition of the present Colonial Secretary and others to all his propositions and efforts to restore the efficiency of the Inland Navigation. In 1851 it was destroyed at Natande and Negombo, and other parts of it impeded, so that it cost the boatmen from £4 to £5 to cart their salt and other produce past these obstructions, boats only plying between them. Major Skinner was constantly told that any attempt to restore the Navigation would result in the total waste of the money expended on it. He was obliged, in 1851, after (with Mr. Norris' Department) the Canals were handed over to him, to commence the work of restoration "on the sly," in places where he could not be observed—at Periamulle. north of

Negombo, where he built his first revetment walls, after clearing out the canal which had filled in with sand four or five feet above the level of what should have been high water. The effect of that work has been that not a spoonful of stuff has been taken out of the canal since, its depth having for upwards of fifteen years been preserved by the scour of the water. The system has been extended; the Natande *impossibility* has never once been obstructed since re-opened by Mr. Campbell, and the tolls have risen in proportion. If, however, Major Skinner had realised the predictions of his opponents by failure, they would have infallibly crushed him for his obstinacy. Sir H. Ward took much interest in this work. Sir H. Robinson came down the line from Putlam to Mutwall in April of this year, and was, we hear, so pleased with it that he is prepared to carry out Major Skinner's suggestions for its further improvement for, as it is hoped at no distant date, Steam Navigation.

In Major Skinner's Ceylon career of not far short of half a century the Island has changed from a purely Military possession into one of much commercial importance. When he arrived in 1819 it was to find the flames of a great Rebellion scarcely yet quenched in the recently-acquired Kandian Provinces; the British forces having suffered far more from the absolute want of roads than from any resistance offered by the mountaineers. Indeed, in the Maritime Provinces, which had been in British occupation since the closing years of the last century, there were practically no made roads beyond the limits of the principal towns, while permanent bridges were absolutely unknown. The first work in which Major, then Ensign, Skinner took part was one which rendered further resistance on the part of the Kandians impossible by the facilities afforded to the movements of British troops; and impossible in the higher and better sense of converting enemies into loyal and attached friends by the protection to life and property which became possible to the British Government, and by the benefits which European enterprise brought in its train. He has lived to see the ancient inhabitants, the European Planters, and the Immigrant labourers from the coast of Coromandel all living and labouring peacefully side by side. He has survived to see a magnificent net-work of roads spread over the country from the sea-level to the passes of our highest mountain ranges; and instead of dangerous fords and ferries, where property often suffered, and life was too frequently sacrificed, he has lived to see every principal stream in the Island substantially bridged or about to be spanned by structures of stone or iron. A few years before he came to the Island, a writer on Ceylon was compelled in the interests of truth to state that "strictly speaking there are no roads in the Island."

He has lived and laboured to see this reproach wiped away, and a contrast so great established that Ceylon, with an area of 25,000 miles, can now count nearly 3,000 miles of made roads, one-fifth of which consists of first-class metalled roads, and another fifth of excellent gravelled highways. What a favourable contrast this state of things presents to the following picture of one of the richest and most important portions of the Empire of Hindustan, including, as the tract adverted to does, the Valley of the Indus. The passage occurs in an able minute by Sir Bartle Frere, lately Governor of Bombay, and now Member of the Council of the Secretary of State for India, advocating the formation of a Railway to run from the Punjab through Scinde to Kurrachee:—

"Let us consider how far the great quadilateral formed by lines joining Lahore, Allahabad, Bombay, and Kurrachee is provided with means of communication. The sides of the quadrilateral are given in the annexed diagram, in round numbers and in direct distance, and the included area cannot be less than 400,000 square miles. Perhaps a better idea of its magnitude may be obtained from the other sketch map marked B, on which France and Germany, Great Britain and Ireland are projected to scale within the space of North-Western India, of which I am speaking. Let us consider this vast space, compared with which Germany and France seem so small and compact. How is it furnished with means of transit and intercommunication? Throughout this space, a line drawn north and south from Jumna north of Agra to the sea, say 600 or 700 miles, or about twice the distance from London to Edinburgh, will, till it reaches the Baroda railway, close to the sea coast, touch no railway nor navigable river nor canal, nor even a common cart road 100 miles in length. A line drawn east and west, say from Kurrachee to the Allahabad and Jubbulpoor road, will, in like manner, in a course of more than 900 miles, or about as far as from London to Rome, cross neither railway nor navigable canal, and only one cart road, that from

Agra to Mhow. Even that is still unbridged and unmetalled, incomplete, and not available for continuous cart traffic, though it has been more or less under construction for at least 30 years. The whole of this vast space, so full of large cities, fertile districts, and promising wastes, is in fact furnished with no better appliances for facilitating transit than the natural surface of the country affords and has afforded for centuries past. Here and there, no doubt, a few short lines of made road may be found, but I believe I speak within compass when I say that in no part of this immense territory could a cart find (except on the incomplete Agra and Mhow line above noticed) 100 miles of ordinary bridged and metalled road traversable by wheeled carriages for the whole year round, nor 200 continuous miles of made road, however imperfect, in any part of the area."

With the advent of Railway travelling, we shall be too apt to forget the great change for the better introduced when a fully bridged and well metalled road *first* connected Colombo with Kandy. A writer on Ceylon, whose book was published so lately as 1841, is amusing from the enthusiasm with which he contrasts the ease and comfort of coach and carriage travelling in Ceylon with the primitive Indian mode of conveyance by palanquins, in which the traveller was carried over hot and trackless wastes on the shoulders of o'er-wearied men.

So different is the case with Ceylon that a Map in which all the roads are prominently filled in looks as chequered as a draught-board; and although more roads are still wanted, yet the difference between Ceylon and India is, that while she has yet to make the feeders for her great Railway Lines, our system of feeders to a large extent is ready to our hands: thanks to the race of Road-makers which commenced with Barnes as its Chief, and whose last representative is leaving us just as the great Kandy Road is about to be superseded by the Railway. On that road, let us never forget, ran the first Mail Coach ever started in Asia; while we may here recall to our readers' recollection the figures representing tolls and cart traffic which Major Skinner framed a few months ago.

From the Colombo Observer, Feb. 26th, 1867.

As Major Skinner took part in the formation of the great Kandy Road, so he has lived to see it about to be all but entirely superseded by a Railway. On the eve of this event the Commissioner of Roads has opportunely put together the figures which constitute the history of the main artery of the Colony's commerce for the quarter of a century commencing with 1842 and ending with 1866. In the five-and-twenty years the toll revenue of the road has been £572,362, while the expenditure was only £422,915. The net profit, therefore, has been £149,447. For the whole period £264 were expended per mile per annum against £341 collected.

From a note we learn that there was established on the line of road in June 1865, 2,300 Dwelling houses, occupied by 9,114 inhabitants, and 707 Halting Stations for the accommodation of Carts and Bullocks traversing the road.

So that the halting places were 10 to each mile. In a second table Major Skinner adds 16 per cent. for expenses of collections, and brings the whole yield in tolls of the Kandy Road up to £663,940. The carts equivalent to these tolls Major Skinner puts down at

Loaded	2,140,920
Unloaded	237,870

So that at least $2\frac{1}{4}$ millions of carts traversed the great Kandy Road in the quarter-century. [By the time the Railway is opened we may make the number 2,400,000 at the very least.]

With the formation of nearly every mile of road, and the erection of every bridge in the country, Major Skinner has been more or less intimately connected either as subordinate or Chief of the Public Works Department; while we cannot forget that simultaneously he laboured, amidst expósure and privation of which present explorers of the Kandian Provinces can have but the faintest idea, in surveying and fixing the topographical features of the country he was opening up; the result being seen in the beautiful and useful Map of the Colony, and especially that of the Mountain Zone, with which his name, in conjunction with those of Fraser and Gallwey, will be ever honourably associated.

As the result to a great extent of the improved communications, especially by their affording easy access on the part of Coffee Planters to the forests of the hill country, the commerce of

Ceylon has increased from a few hundreds of thousands per annum to an aggregate of ten millions sterling; the export of Coffee alone having risen from a value of about £10,000 to close on three millions. The revenue has increased in proportion until we have seen half a million sterling voted for the Public Works Department in one year.

Any record of Major Skinner's public services would be incomplete which did not include honourable mention of his efforts to secure for the Colony, by his knowledge of work and prices, a contract at a moderate rate for the construction of a Railway—an undertaking which no one in the Colony has been more anxious to see completed than himself; from the feeling he so readily avowed, that the advancing commerce of the Colony rendered the iron highway absolutely necessary as the supplement and superseder of the great road on which his first efforts were put forth under the eye of the eminent Governor who had genius enough to anticipate, and energy to provide for, that future of Ceylon which the worthiest and most devoted of his disciples has lived to see. Finally, we cannot forget Major Skinner's recent services to the Colony, as President of the Commission appointed to report on the proportion of Military expenditure fairly chargeable to this Island in time of peace.

Having thus expressed our sense of Major Skinner's valuable public services (not at greater length and not more warmly than we conscientiously feel the case demands), and having indicated our hope that services so unparalleled may be especially rewarded, it remains that we should testify our respect for the rectitude of this great worker's private life, and wish him, as we cordially do (speaking, we believe, in the name of the great majority of the people of Ceylon), all possible happiness in the calm of the closing years of a career so honourably laborious, and to this Colony so useful. Though once, in the early part of his career, at the point of death from fever contracted in the Valley of the Maha Oya—so fatal to many of his brother officers and multitudes of the labourers they directed—Major Skinner at the age of sixty-four seems so hale and hearty that we cannot look at him without thinking of the description of another great worker of whom it was said in his old age that "his eye was not dim, nor his natural force abated." But sixty-four is only six years short of the term allotted to man, and if, as we hope, Major Skinner is destined long to outlive that period in vigour of intellect and strength of body, we feel sure that never will the lengthened enjoyment be grudged to him of the largest rewards which a just Government at the voice of a grateful country can confer.

Major Skinner's Services.

The following succinct statement made by Major Skinner before the Committee of Council on Public Works in 1864 will show what his services have been :—

"I was first employed on the roads of the Colony in 1820, in the opening of the two lines to Kandy, one by the Kaduganava Pass, the other through the Seven Korles, and have been more or less identified with them since; for though employed for a short time on the Garrison Staff, I was even then detached to trace roads, and when in the Quartermaster-General's Department, I had the charge and direction of them. In 1833, when the Public Works of the Colony were transferred to the Civil Authorities, I was selected to induct the newly-appointed Surveyor-General and Civil Engineer, and for a time to assist him in setting his Departments in working order. In 1837, the Departments having got into confusion, I was requested to take charge of them. Having, to the satisfaction of Government, restored them to order, I handed them over to the Surveyor-General and Civil Engineer in 1840. In 1841 I was again offered charge of the roads of the Colony, with the appointment of Commissioner of Roads, which was confirmed by the Secretary of State and the Lords of the Treasury. In 1850 I was ordered to take over the Civil Engineer's Department, and to incorporate it with my own. In 1859 I was appointed to act as Auditor-General. In June, 1861, I returned to the charge of the Public Works."

In his evidence before the Military Commission Major Skinner stated:—"I came out to join the Navy, but was placed in the Army. At the age of between fourteen and fifteen I was ordered to march in command of a small detachment of the 19th, 83rd, and Ceylon Rifle Regiments across from Trincomalie to Colombo by the jungle paths then existing. In 1820 (when still but a boy)

I was ordered to take charge of a party of 200 Kandians with a proportion of Headmen to be employed in opening roads."

We may add that in 1865 Major Skinner again acted as Auditor-General, in which capacity he succeeded the late Mr. Pennefather as President of the Military Commission. On both occasions of acting in the Executive he showed rare administrative talents, with that independence of character for which he was ever distinguished. As member of the Legislative Council he brought his great local knowledge to bear on the discussions, especially in a masterly speech on the Northern Province.

Major Skinner may be said to have been born in the Army, being the son of a field officer and having received his Commission before the age of fifteen. The effect of early military training has been beneficially evident in the organization and training of the Pioneers.

It was only just as Major Skinner was on the eve of retiring that his salary was raised to the point at which it ought to have been fixed many years previously. That the remuneration of the office should, during Major Skinner's incumbency, have been so inadequate is an additional reason why he should be liberally dealt with in the matter of pension.

Sir Emerson Tennent's Testimony.

The extent to which Major Skinner traversed Ceylon and the use he made of his opportunities for observing the physical peculiarities of the country, its people, its natural history, productions and ancient monuments, are evident from the frequent references to him in Tennent's exhaustive work on Ceylon. In Ichthyology and Conchology Major Skinner's name is honourably known, his collections of sea and freshwater shells being about as complete as any in existence. Sir Emerson Tennent gracefully acknowledged his literary obligations by dedicating his work on the Elephant to Major Skinner, while in his work on Ceylon he thus refers to that Officer's labours in triangulating the Island and covering it with roads:—

"When the British took possession of Ceylon, and for many years afterwards, nothing deserving the name of a road was in existence, to unite these important positions.* Travellers were borne along the shore in palanquins, by pathways under the trees; troops on the march dragged their guns with infinite toil over the sand; and stores, supplies and ammunition were carried on men's shoulders through the jungle. Since then, not only has a high-way unsurpassed in construction been completed to Colombo, but continued through the mountains to the central capital at Kandy, and thence higher still to Neuera-ellia, at an elevation of six thousand feet above the sea. Nor is this all; every town of importance in the island is now connected with the two principal cities, by roads either wholly or partially macadamised. One continuous line, seven hundred and sixty-nine miles in length, has been formed round the entire circuit of the coast, adapted for carriages where it approaches the principal places, and nearly everywhere available for horsemen and wayfarers.

"No portion of British India can bear comparison with Ceylon, either in the extent or the excellence of its means of communication; and for this enviable pre-eminence the colony is mainly indebted to the genius of one eminent man, and the energy and perseverance of another. Sir Edward Barnes, on assuming the government in 1820, had the penetration to perceive that the sums annually wasted on hill-forts and garrisons in the midst of wild forests, might, with judicious expenditure, be made to open the whole country by military roads, contributing at once to its security and its enrichment. Before the close of his administration he had the happiness of witnessing the realisation of his policy; and of leaving every radius of the diverging lines, which he had planned, either wholly or partially completed. One officer who had been associated with the enterprise from its origin, and with every stage of its progress, remained behind him to consummate his plans. That officer was Major Skinner, the present Commissioner of Roads in Ceylon. To him more than to any living man the colony is

---

* *Percival*, p. 145. An idea of the toil of travelling this road in the year 1800 may be collected from the number of attendants which the Governor was forced to take on his journey from Colombo to Galle when starting on a tour round the island; one hundred and sixty palanquin bearers, four hundred coolies to carry the baggage, two elephants, six horses, and fifty lascars to take care of the tents.—*Cordiner*, ch. vi. p. 168.

indebted for its present prosperity; and in after years, when the interior shall have attained the full development of its productive resources, and derived all the advantages of facile communications with the coast, the name of this meritorious public servant will be gratefully honoured in close association with that of his illustrious chief."

"Down to a very recent period no British colony was more imperfectly surveyed and mapped than Ceylon; but since the recent publication by Arrowsmith of the great map by General Fraser the reproach has been withdrawn, and no dependency of the Crown is now more richly provided in this particular. In the map of Schneider, the Government engineer in 1813, two-thirds of the Kandian Kingdom are a blank; and in that of the Society for the Diffusion of Knowledge, republished so late as 1852, the rich districts of Neuera-kalawa and the Wanny, in which there are innumerable villages (and scarcely a hill), are marked as an "*unknown mountainous region.*" General Fraser, after the devotion of a lifetime to the labour, has produced a survey which, in extent and minuteness of detail, stands unrivalled. In this great work he had the co-operation of Major Skinner and of Captain Gallwey, and to these two gentlemen the public are indebted for the greater portion of the field-work and the trigonometrical operations. To judge of the difficulties which beset such an undertaking, it must be borne in mind that till very recently travelling in the interior was all but impracticable, in a country unopened even by bridle-paths, across unbridged rivers, over mountains never trod by the foot of an European, and amidst precipices inaccessible to all but the most courageous and prudent. Add to this that the country is densely covered by forests and jungle, with trees a hundred feet high, from which here and there the branches had to be cleared to obtain a sight of the signal stations. The triangulation was carried on amidst privations, discomfort and pestilence, which frequently prostrated the whole party, and forced their attendants to desert them rather than encounter such hardships and peril. The materials collected by the colleagues of General Fraser under these discouragements have been worked up by him with consummate skill and perseverance. The base line, five and a quarter miles in length, was measured in 1845 in the cinnamon plantation at Kaderani, to the north of Colombo, and its extremities are still marked by two towers, which it was necessary to raise to the height of one hundred feet to enable them to be discerned above the surrounding forests. These, it is to be hoped, will be carefully kept from decay, as they may again be called into requisition hereafter.

MEMORIAL FOR ENHANCED PENSION TO MAJOR SKINNER.

The following is the Memorial signed, to which we have alluded :—

To His Grace the Duke of Buckingham, the Right Honourable the Secretary of State for the Colonies.

YOUR GRACE,

We, the undersigned Colonists, Merchants, Planters and others unconnected with the Government, cannot allow Major Thomas Skinner to retire from this Colony, after forty-eight years of almost uninterrupted service, without expressing a hope that your Grace may be pleased to take into your consideration, as a special favour in his case, an extension of the Pension to which he is entitled under the existing rules of the Service. Major Skinner has for many years been at the head of one of the most important Departments of this Government, the arduous duties of which are attended with constant toil and anxiety. He has performed all these duties cheerfully and successfully, and has overcome every difficulty which stood in his way, by his untiring energy and perseverance.

The Colonists are deeply indebted to Major Skinner for his long and zealous services on behalf of the Colony; and the undersigned feel confident that the entire community, both Native and European, would be much gratified if your Grace were pleased to extend Major Skinner's Pension to £1,000 per annum. The larger Pension would add much to his comfort in the decline of life, and would bear witness to the good-will of his fellow Colonists, and to their appreciation of his unwearied exertions in the development of the resources of the island.

Hoping that this humble expression of our feeling towards Major Skinner will meet with your Grace's approval,

We have the honour to be your Grace's
Most obedient and humble Servants.

[Signed by the Merchants and principal residents of Colombo Kandy and Galle, besides those up country and along the coast.]

Presentation of an Address to Major Skinner from Native Chiefs, &c., of the Island.

This took place at the office of the Commissioner of Roads yesterday (the 28th instant), when a deputation waited on Major Skinner, who had previously declined to accede to the request that he should be treated to a public banquet, expressing a wish rather that any public notice of his departure might be made as simple as possible. Mr. James Alwis was the spokesman on the occasion, and he did his part feelingly and well, as follows :—

" Sir,

" Twenty years ago it was my privilege, as it is now, to read to you an Address from the Native Chiefs of the Western, Southern and Central Provinces. Though within that interval of time a generation has passed away, and you do not now see many of the hoary heads which you saw on the first deputation in this very hall—and you yourself have lost the dear help-mate of your life—it is nevertheless satisfactory to you to know that the children of those with whom you commenced your official career, before we were born, appreciate the good which you have done for their country during forty-nine long years ; and that you leave amongst us a son, who, if he follow the footsteps of his father, will not fail to be endeared to us all. I know, Sir, as do many of the gentlemen here present, that you have done signal service to the Singhalese. Imbued with all the liberal principles which prompted the good rule of Sir Edward Barnes's administration ; knowing, as you do, the great respect and esteem in which he held the higher classes of the Singhalese, you have ever been their friend, and have, to my own certain knowledge, pleaded their cause here as elsewhere. I know, too, from various causes, that you have got right, and not the erroneous notions which the Government of this country have entertained of the Natives and their agricultural operations; and I have no hesitation in saying that the result of your just representations on Agriculture, combined with the Roads which you have opened in this island, will be productive of incalculable benefit to the Singhalese, and the Government which you have served.

"As regards Roads, the main cause for the growing prosperity of this island, allow me to read an extract from a Lecture which I delivered in 1864:—

"'Where fifty years ago a man from Colombo had to trudge six weeks before he could reach Kandy, and that, too, with great personal inconvenience, over scraggy rocks, precipices and ravines, he is now able to make the same distance in less than ten hours. A country which had 'no roads' in 1807, and where 'wheeled carriages could only be used in the neighbourhood of the large European settlements on the sea-coasts,' is now intersected with *bandy** roads in every direction—eleven lines of which traverse through its length and breadth. Besides several mail coaches between small towns, a mail coach now runs every day to and from Kandy, and likewise from Galle. The good-will of the Colombo and Kandy coach was recently sold for £3,000, and the revenue derived from the two coaches is alone estimated at £7,000 per annum. Where half a century since, in travelling, footpaths were only discernible, but never any broad beaten way, regularly formed, marked with the tracks of wheels, and bounded with walls or ditches, we now have an infinite number of carriage roads, upon the repairs alone of which no less than a sum of £189,138 is annually expended. Where 10 years ago the line of travelling led over natural meadows, sometimes over rugged strata of clay, sometimes through beds of deep and heavy sand, there are now upwards of 2,550 miles of road, highly finished and well metalled, of which nearly 800 miles have been opened during the last 15 years. And the means of conveyance in the Colony, calculated upon other wants and other times, is "about to be made to keep pace with the immense development of its producing powers" by the opening of a railroad.

* *Bandy*—a small carriage.

"These are, Sir, some of the reasons which induce us to address you—not with a view to seek favour, for you are going to leave us, but in grateful remembrance of what you have done, both publicly and privately, to promote the true interests of the Singhalese. Before reading the Address, I have only to add that this same Address, which is very largely signed by people of several districts, has not yet arrived in Colombo from a neglect on our part to let them know the exact date of your departure; but that the same will be forwarded to you to England in a few days by the Maha Modliar."

"*To Major T. Skinner, Civil Engineer and Commissioner of Roads, Ceylon.*

"Dear Sir,

"We, the undersigned Native Chiefs and other inhabitants of the Maritime and Central Provinces of Ceylon, impelled by a grateful sense of the valuable services you have rendered to this Colony during your official connection with it for the last 49 years, and the kind interest you have ever taken in encouraging native talent and upholding native merit, are anxious to testify our highest respect and esteem for you, and the regret with which we contemplate your final departure from this country.

"To speak of the manner in which you have executed the important public duties confided to you would be presumptuous in us; still, we should be doing violence to the warmth and sincerity of our feelings if we forbore all expression of the admiration with which we look back upon your long career of public usefulness. In taking a glance at your long and useful public life in this Colony, we cannot help noticing the fact that you were one of those selected by the late Sir Edward Barnes to carry out that great work, the road from Colombo to Kandy, a work which will ever be remembered by all well-wishers of our country with gratitude.

"The high state of efficiency in which this great road has been maintained ever since your appointment to the head of the Roads Department, will alone entitle you to our gratitude; but your energy and zeal did not rest here, your name is associated with several other acts, which it becomes our pleasing duty to record. We allude, amongst others, to the organization of the Pioneer

Corps, the liberal provision made for this useful body of men by means of a Pension Fund; the encouragement held out to native talent by the admission of young men into the Government Factory as apprentices, with a view to qualify them as practical Engineers, and the warm interest which you have always taken in promoting works connected with Inland navigation.

"These are but a few of the many works of permanent usefulness in which you have taken an active part.

"We cannot forget that when you began public life in this Colony, nearly half a century ago, the interior of the country was almost inaccessible, and that roads and other means of communication were then almost unknown. Much as there is yet to be done, it must be admitted that the Colony now possesses a network of roads, such as few Colonies can boast of, and we should be unjust if we did not acknowledge the fact that this state of things is in no small degree attributable to your indefatigable zeal and energy.

"Private enterprise has doubtless given a great impetus to works of this kind now-a-days, but we cannot forget that to your early labours in this Department we are indebted for much of that private enterprise which we are glad to observe is adding greatly to the general prosperity of the Colony.

"It will doubtless be a pleasing memory which will accompany you in your retirement to your native country, that Ceylon, which on your first arrival was almost an inaccessible jungle, without a road or bridge to boast of, was intersected by a series of the finest roads, bridges and canals, when you left her in the year 1867.

"You are one of the few Europeans who have laboured among us so long. Many of us were not born when you came to this country; and we assure you that the great esteem in which you were held by our fathers has not in the slightest degree diminished in their sons, and our own personal knowledge of your worth enables us to endorse that high opinion which our ancestors have always entertained of your public and private character.

"Though we cannot grudge you that rest and retirement which you have so fairly earned after your long service, we cannot but feel the loss which we would sustain by your absence from the

Councils of the Government, where your extensive knowledge of the country and its wants would have been of the highest service. Be assured, Sir, that your memory will be cherished, and your absence felt by all who have known you, while by such of us in particular as have had the privilege of your personal acquaintance and friendship your name must ever be most gratefully dwelt upon.

"Farewell, Dear Sir,—Our sincere prayers shall be offered up for your welfare, and we earnestly trust that, restored to your native country, you may, through God's grace, long enjoy, amidst relatives and friends, the blessings of health and happiness.

"We remain, Dear Sir, with much respect,
"Your attached humble servants,
"H. Dias; J. A. Perera; J. Alwis;
"And 1,593 Signatures of Singhalese
"Chiefs and others in the Mari-
"time Province, Saffragam,
"Kandy and Kornegalle."

Major Skinner (who was much affected) said, in reply,—"I am quite unprepared, and totally unable to say how much I value the kind and flattering terms in which Mr. Alwis has introduced the subject for which I have been invited to meet you, and for the feeling manner in which he has referred to his having conferred a similar favour on me years gone by—he must only imagine my feelings, which are far too full to admit of their finding utterance; and to you generally, my dear friends, it is impossible that I can adequately express the feelings which agitate me, whilst endeavouring to thank you for this most disinterested, and to me invaluable proof of the kind regard and esteem expressed in the Address which you have just done me the honour of presenting to me. It is indeed a gratification and a reward which I little dreamt of receiving; it is, I feel, one of the highest honours which could be conferred upon one who has lived amongst and worked for you, from a date to which few of you can trace back your memories. In referring to my long services, you reviewed them in the same kind and partial spirit which has characterized the conduct and intercourse of the Natives of this country towards me, from the day I was first launched upon public life, when, not fifteen years old, I marched in command of a detachment of troops from east to west through your beautiful country; from that time, throughout my life, to this day, I have not forgotten the impression made upon my mind by the extraordinary kindness I then (a mere boy) received at the hands of every Native with whom I was brought in contact, and who could afford me any service or attention. And it is with the greatest gratitude I am now enabled to state that that most kind and friendly spirit, though in an immeasurably greater degree, has been continued to me in an unbroken chain to this day, on which you now give me this much valued proof of the unimpaired existence still of the mutual feeling of kindness and affection which had its origin with a past generation.

"This tribute is the more highly prized by me because it cannot be the result of personal benefit or advantage I have been able to confer on any. I have never held office which could have given me the means of advancing your individual interests; but, on the contrary, in every district into which my duties have directed me I have at all times been the recipient of your kindness, and have been laid under obligations by your fathers and yourselves for favours for which I have scarcely ever been able to make the smallest return. For a country so beautiful, and for a people so generous and kind, it would have been as impossible as unnatural not to have felt the deep interest I have entertained for their welfare—it would have been extraordinary if I could have shown indifference or want of zeal in the performance of my im-important and most interesting duties. Oh, no! I am thankful to say that has never been; my work has been my pleasure, almost my life, and although I leave much yet to be done, it is to me a most gratifying retrospect to compare the Ceylon of 1819 with her condition in 1867, and to feel that I have been a humble instrument of an enlightened Government in effecting the great change. Had its power and means been equal to its will, we might have had still greater cause for congratulation; but I am most thankful to receive the assurance of the chiefs and people that they are satisfied with my efforts in the humble position I have been privileged to occupy in the good work.

"There are one or two subjects in respect of which (as materially affecting the welfare of the people and the prosperity of the country) I shall take a great and anxious interest as long as my life is spared—I allude to education, specially of the females in the rural districts; to the improvement and extension of works of irrigation as the means of extending cultivation and to the strengthening of that which has somewhat declined of late years, the proper, legitimate influence of the chiefs and country gentlemen in the provinces. I dare not enlarge on any one of these topics; each would need an essay. The matter of agriculture is, I am happy to know, occupying the serious attention of the native gentry, who cannot, I believe, devote their intelligence and energy to a higher or more important subject.

"Here, now nearly twenty years since, on the occasion of my proceeding home on leave, I received, from many who are now present, and from others who are now at rest, an affectionate address which I now hold in my hand. It is painful in the extreme to observe how many of the most esteemed and valued friends of my youth, and still nearer and dearer ties to many of you, have since then been taken from us: let this remind us, my friends, that our time cannot be very long; that *that* of some must in the course of nature be very short; that we each have yet much to do, and at the best but an uncertain time to do it in. I part from you to-day with the feeling that in reality I am going *from*, rather than *to* my home. I shall never cease to be grateful for all the kindness and affection I have received at your hands and those of your countrymen for whose prosperity and that of your lovely isle I shall ever feel the greatest and most anxious interest. May God's blessing attend you.

"T. Skinner."

The kindness and affection of my friends, and especially of the natives, shown on my approaching departure, surpassed anything I could have expected. Headmen came in from all parts of the country to see me and bid me farewell; some of them, who had travelled considerable distances, and found on their arrival at Colombo that I had left for Galle, drove those additional seventy-two miles to say "Good-bye."

My time at the last was so precious that I could ill spare much of it on interviews. It was no uncommon occurrence, on my rising at 5 o'clock in the morning, to find several native gentlemen waiting outside the door to take advantage of the opportunity of seeing me before I had entered on my engagements of the day. Is it surprising that for such a people I should have conceived a deep attachment?

This was the second generation of men for whom I had felt the warmest possible affection; for with their fathers I had long lived on the most intimate terms, and they were specimens of nature's truest gentlemen. It was a source of pride and pleasure to me to witness so many of their sons worthily inheriting the virtues of their sires. I value intensely every little memento I hold from those dear people, and shall do so to the day of my death.

Let only good and just government be continued to Ceylon, as it happily has existed, with rare exceptions, during the long period since I first knew the country in 1818. Let the missionaries enjoy ordinary facilities in extending vernacular education, so that the population may be able intelligently to comprehend Christianity, and the pure and simple Gospel will have its desired effect in enlightening and expanding the minds of the natives, who are susceptible of the highest mental cultivation, and are behind no other races in their reciprocation of disinterested and kindly feeling.

The effect of education, and the extraordinary social progress which has, within my knowledge and personal observation, taken place in Ceylon, ought to encourage every well-wisher of the country in their hope and expectation of its future. And let it never be forgotten that *much*, very much of that progress and improvement is due to the persevering efforts of the various missionary societies in the island. I am not intending to go into the matter at the length I should wish, but I cannot resist making a feeble record of the strong conviction I have for many years entertained of the enormous good these missionaries have been quietly and unostentatiously working out, not only amongst the natives but amongst our own people.

Most of the native gentlemen who are in Holy Orders received their education from missionaries. Sir Richard Morgan and many other members of the Bench and Bar received their earliest tuition from them. Several most useful native officers, in whom I placed the same confidence as I did in my European assistants, had been the pupils of missionaries; they were entrusted by me with very large expenditure, and I am happy and thankful to say I never was disappointed in one of them.

The American Mission was established at Jaffna in 1816. A medical college, several boys' schools, and a first-rate girls' school were started, presided over by "Father Spaulding," as he was affectionately termed. When first opened, it was so difficult to induce the higher caste natives to send their daughters to the school, that Mr. and Mrs. Spaulding received girls of the lowest classes only. During my last visit to Oodooville Mr. Spaulding informed me that by the time the first batch of children were educated, the school became so popular as to be always full of children of the highest castes. Brahmins had stated to him that so highly did they prize the moral training and education given, that they were all willing to risk, for these advantages, the chances of their daughters being converted to Christianity.

I asked Mr. Spaulding if he followed up the history of his pupils after they left school. He replied in the affirmative, that they took much pains in tracing the characters of their pupils in after life, and so far as they had been able to ascertain, that only in three instances, of all those who had passed through their school, had they to regret departures from the Christian faith, or transgressions in morals. Many of these girls married high caste native officers, clerks, and non-commissioned officers in my own department, and their characters proved exemplary. In many cases they formed schools for the education of the children by whom they were surrounded, and they exhibited an amount of energy, neatness, and cleanliness in their houses which had a most civilizing and beneficial influence on all who saw them.

When a member of the Councils in Ceylon I had held a seat at the Central Board of Education, or School Commission, and had felt much dissatisfied with the progress of vernacular education in the rural districts, more especially amongst the female part of the population. I knew from personal observation to what an unlimited extent this advantage could be carried in the missionary districts if the means could be found; but the conditions of the school commission were so stringent in reference to restrictions in religious teaching, that only one Mission, and that not a Church Missionary school, could feel itself justified in accepting the grant offered. Whenever I advocated a more liberal policy, I was always in a small minority. I proposed that grants should only be made to Mission schools containing a given number of pupils—that the Inspector of Schools should satisfy himself that a proper amount of secular education was imparted in it before any grant in aid was made, and, as a proof that no violent proselytism was carried on in that school, that the grant should be withheld when the number of pupils fell below a minimum, to be determined by the School Commission.

In 1864 Government expended £15,331 12s. 3¾d. on the education of the country, of which £14,528 12s. 3¾d. were spent on Government schools, and £803 on private and mission schools.

In 1864 there were in the island 125 schools under Government inspection and direction, inclusive of 17 private and mission schools. Of the 17 aided schools 10 were private and 7 were missionary; the latter, containing 347 pupils, received aid to the amount of £178 2s. 6d., or on an average £25 9s. for each school, or 10s. 3d. for each pupil.

In 108 Government schools in 1864 there were 4,463 boys, 796 girls, making a total 5,259. Four years further back, in 1860, when I collected returns from five Protestant missions, there were 10,162 boys, 3,411 girls, making a total of 13,573.

In the 108 Government schools 5,259 pupils cost 55s. 6d. each; 17 private and mission schools 1,268 pupils cost 12s. 6d. each.

Up to the year 1860 three of the five Protestant missions alone had educated 92,249 children, and between 1860 and 1864 it may be assumed that 12,000 more were educated by those three missions; for in returns furnished to me, it appeared that these missions educated on an average annually 1,000 children each, the limitation to those numbers having been caused by want of means only, which the rules of the School Commission prevented their receiving.

Does this statement, I ask, prove that there has been shown by the natives any distrust of missionary teaching? The examination of their schools by Government inspectors was not objected to by the missionaries, who properly declined the restriction to their religious training which was an inevitable condition of their accepting any aid from the Government; and I hope that all who may become acquainted with these facts will honour the missionaries, as I do, for their consistency and fidelity to the principles on which they were sent out; and I am thankful to be able to record that they were ultimately rewarded, by the Government yielding to their conscientious scruples, and to the interests of the people.

Education was most urgently needed for one of the most benighted populations in the Queen's dominions, and especially so for the female portion of it; and who but the missionaries could effectually impart it, to the extent required, at a cost which the Colony could afford. We were for a long while injuring the social condition of the people by educating the men far too highly in many cases, and neglecting the women, because they would not generally attend our Government vernacular schools, which, as a rule, were inefficient in the rural districts.

I have often been much pained by hearing missionaries and mission work spoken of disparagingly by thoughtless persons, who seemed to me to adopt that course as a kind of justification for their not aiding the cause, and in utter ignorance of a work, the importance of which to a whole people it is scarcely possible to exaggerate, but in respect of which these declaimers were perfectly indifferent.

It is impossible to remember those good men and their work without a feeling of the greatest honour and respect for both.

A very influential Buddhist, the Basnaika Nillemy, having responsible charge of all the temporalities of one of the most sacred districts in the island, has frequently expressed to me his conviction that, in the course of fifty years, a very large majority of the population of Ceylon will have become Christian.

God grant that this prophecy may be realised, and that professing Christians may, by their blameless lives, the integrity of their dealings, and the sobriety of their habits, commend the religion they desire to impart to their fellow-subjects in Ceylon !

CHAPTER XII.

How strange were my feelings on the day of my embarkation at Galle, after a long life of extreme tension and of hard work, though truly it was, throughout, a "labour of love" in a beautiful country, and amongst a kind, affectionate people, by whom my most enthusiastic sympathies had been called forth; for, from the time of my first arrival in Ceylon, I was impressed with its great capabilities and enraptured with the exquisite beauty of its scenery.

My embarkation from the jetty at Galle was a step of cruel severance from scenes and associations, toils and responsibilities, in which I had borne my part. I had found scenes and associations of the purest and most elevating sort among the beauties of nature and the friendship of valued friends; the toils and responsibilities I had, I hope, borne cheerfully; and I had endeavoured to act rightly, according to my judgment, in matters of importance. Now all was to cease, and I was to be parted from *all*, to which I had clung with so much devotion, and from the officers of my department, to whom I was deeply indebted for their zealous energetic activity, and for the economy with which they carried out their work.

In an hour this country, which had been my home for so many years, and where the energies of my whole manhood had been spent, would be for ever lost to sight, and I was to wake in the morning with the sense of having nothing further to do. Henceforth mine was to be a life of "idleness," and an entire absence of public responsibility! Who that has taken a similar step will not have felt as I have done?

* * * * *

When in London, in 1869, I received the following letter from the Duke of Buckingham and Chandos:—

Chancery of the Order of Saint Michael and Saint George.

Colonial Office, Downing Street,
24th February, 1869.

Sir,

I have the honour to acquaint you that the Queen has been graciously pleased to appoint you to be a Companion of the most distinguished Order of Saint Michael and Saint George, and to transmit to you Her Majesty's grant of that dignity, together with the insignia thereof, a copy of the statutes of the Order and a blank form of covenant for the restoration of the insignia, which document you will be so good as to sign and return to me when duly attested.

I have the honour to be, Sir,
Your most obedient Servant,
(Signed) Gordon Gairdner,
Secretary and Registrar.

Thomas Skinner, Esq., C.M.G.

Grant of the Dignity of a Companion of the Most Distinguished Order of Saint Michael and Saint George, to Thomas Skinner, Esq.

Victoria by the Grace of God of the United Kingdom of Great Britain and Ireland Queen, Defender of the Faith, Sovereign and Chief of the Most Distinguished Order of Saint Michael and Saint George, to our trusty and well-beloved Thomas Skinner, Esquire, late Civil Engineer and Commissioner of Roads for Our Island of Ceylon, Greeting: Whereas, we have thought fit to nominate and appoint you to be a Member of the Third Class or Companions of Our Most Distinguished Order of Saint Michael and Saint George: We do by these presents Grant unto you the Dignity of a Companion of Our said Most Distinguished Order: And We do hereby authorise you to Have, Hold and Enjoy the said Dignity as a Member of the Third Class or Companions of Our said Most Distinguished Order, together with all and singular the privileges thereunto belonging or appertaining.

Given at Our Court at Osborne House, Isle of Wight, under Our Sign Manual and the Seal of the said Order this Eighteenth day of February 1869, in the Thirty-second year of Our Reign.

By the Sovereign's command,

(Signed) George,
Grand Master.

(Signed) Victoria, R.G.

Sir Hercules Robinson being at home on leave from Ceylon, I called on him, in London, to ask him if it was to his kind offices I was indebted for this mark of approval of the manner in which I had accomplished my duties in Ceylon. He replied:

"No; a few days ago I received an intimation from the Secretary of State that he wished to see me. On my arrival at his office he said:

"'I have sent for you to ascertain if there is any

officer under your Government you think specially deserving of a mark of the Sovereign's approbation for the manner in which he has performed his duties, and on whom you would wish to confer the Order of Saint Michael and Saint George, it being the intention to enlarge it.'

"I replied: 'There is an officer who has lately retired from the service, whom it would be a discredit to the Government to allow to retire into private life without rewarding him with some mark of his Sovereign's favour and approbation of his services.'

"'Who is that officer?' asked the Secretary of State.

"I named you.

"'Oh!' said the Duke of Buckingham, 'I have already put Major Skinner's name down for the Order.'

"'What Class of the Order has your Grace intended for Major Skinner?'

"'The Third Class,' replied the Duke.

"I answered: 'I could never think of offering it to him as a recognition or reward for his services to the colony of Ceylon. The only advantage it will be to him will be that in the direction of his letters there will be the addition of "C.M.G." after his name.'

"The Secretary of State said that, if you were abroad, to be invested with the Second Class of the Order would be a heavy expense.

"I replied that you were not abroad, but actually in London.

"His Grace desired me to confer with you on the subject."

I told Sir Hercules that I was very grateful to him for his kind advocacy of my interests, and begged him to offer my respectful thanks to the Secretary of State for so kindly wishing me to be consulted, and to state that I was too poor to covet the title of the Second Class; that I was gratified with the expression of approval of my services from my Sovereign, and should be quite satisfied with the Third Class of the Order, which His Grace had sent me, and which reached me this morning.

It proved a disappointment to my children and friends that I had refused the distinction which had been offered to me; but, on the whole, if I erred, I hope it was on the right side.

* * * * * * *

CONCLUDING CHAPTER.

The concluding act of my father's life, alluded to in the last chapter, was quite in keeping with the rest of his life and character. His life was the most consistent, humble, unselfish one, that can be imagined.

When the Duke of Edinburgh visited Ceylon and India, my father was invited by the Ceylon Government to go out and help to entertain the Duke—to show him the beauties and sport in the island—the Ceylon Government offering to pay all expenses.

The Secretary of State sanctioned the proposal, but the Lords of the Treasury objected to the expense of sending anyone from England for the purpose.

The following extract from the *Ceylon Observer* shows the feeling of the island on the subject:—

"With reference to what will be the first visit of a member of the Royal Family to Ceylon, a suggestion has been made, to which we should think there can be here but a united and cordial response, that the man who knows more about Ceylon, and all of interest connected with it, than any other living—Major Skinner—should attend His Royal Highness through the island."

On the occasion of the Prince of Wales going to Ceylon my father was consulted as to the best time of year to visit the island, and also about the elephant-shooting, as H.R.H. was anxious to have some sport.

My father was very fond of conchology, and had one of the finest collections in England. He used to tell the story of how he fell a victim to this "hobby." He was travelling through the island with some friends who were keen conchologists, and their eagerness over the discovery of some, to his unpractised eye, insignificant shell, caused him much amusement. To revenge this insult to their favourite science, they determined to make my father a convert to it; so they agreed to ask him if he *should* happen to find a shell they would be glad if he would give it to them.

They then took care to place a few where he was likely to find them, and on his showing them the shells they exclaimed with delight that they were very rare specimens and a great addition to their collection! This pleased my father, and he began looking for more with the same result till they convinced him that he had a special "eye for shells." They even bribed the natives to bring him some, which he bought, finding it afforded his friends pleasure. By the end of this trip my father found there was "something" in conchology after all; and his friends were satisfied in their revenge, having secured another enthusiast!

Some shells my father discovered were previously unknown to conchologists, and were called after him. He has told me that many hours were thus beguiled when he was alone in Ceylon, my mother being in England, and that without this "hobby" the separation would have been unbearable. He never did anything "by halves," and, notwithstanding all his hard work, he was not content until he made his collection as perfect as possible.

He retained his love for fishing to the end, and every spring and autumn found him by the river-side, either in Cumberland, Ireland, or Scotland fishing for trout or salmon. There were few who could beat him at that sport, as in former years there were few who rivalled him with the gun in Ceylon. Most of the rivers were known to him, and the lovely scenery through which they flowed was an endless delight.

The pleasure he took in everything connected with nature was beautiful to see; but his principal delight was in contributing to the happiness of others. Children loved him, and everyone was glad to welcome him. I think his heart remained young to the end, and the entire absence of self made him the delightful companion he was to young and old alike.

It was my privilege to be with him during the last few years of his life, which he spent principally in visiting old friends and travelling, the latter being always a special pleasure to him. He felt his work was done, and he was just waiting for his call Home. It is not for me to add to the record he has left of what that work was; I can only speak of the brightness of the eventide, which seemed to shine more brilliantly as the end drew near. One day, looking up, he said, "My child, all, *all* is bright; there is not a single cloud anywhere."

On the 24th July 1877 he passed peacefully away to the Home he was so longing for, and I felt the promise was fulfilled that

"At evening time it shall be light."

ANNIE SKINNER.

Guildford, 20th June 1890.

THE END.

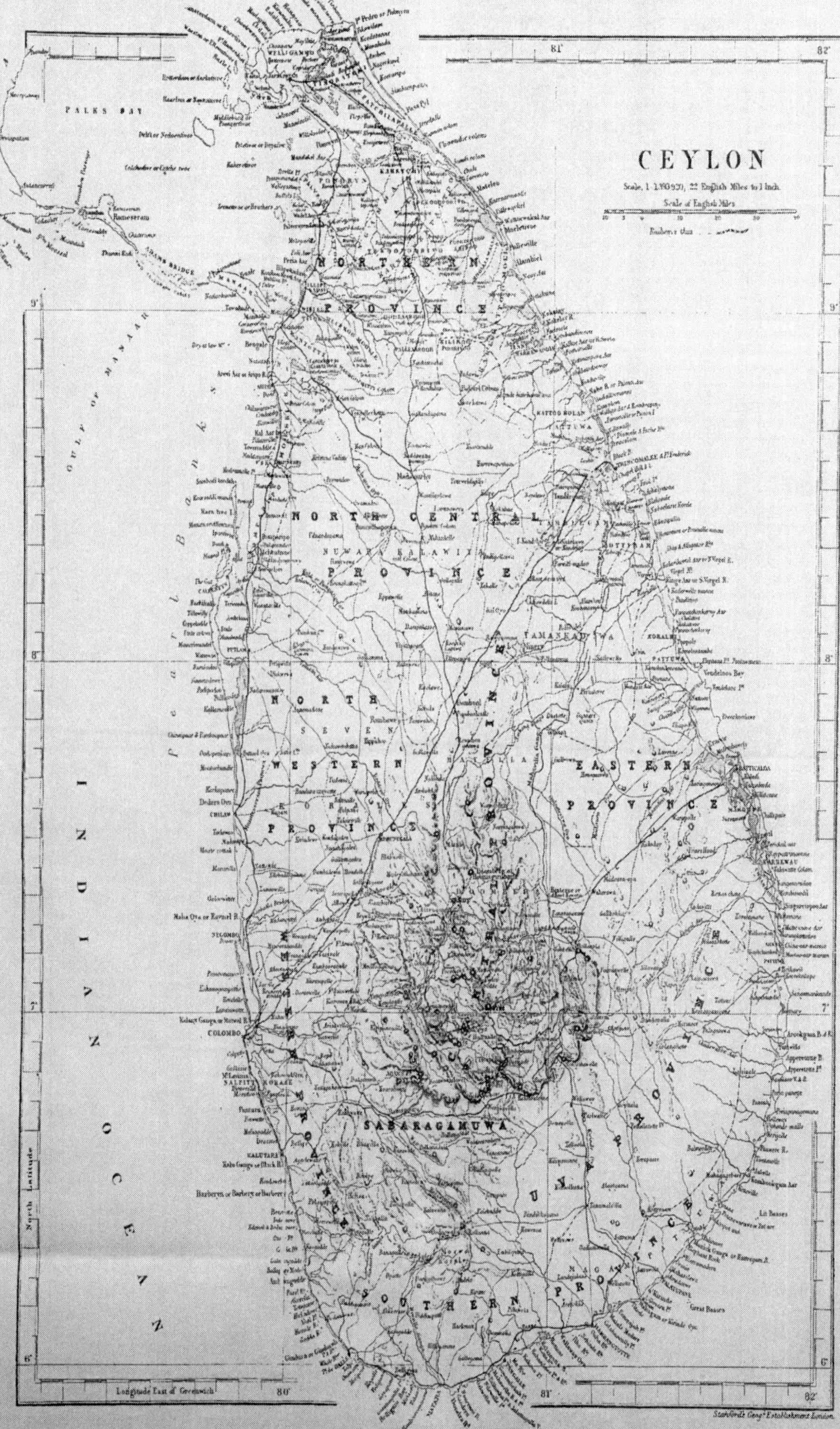
CEYLON
Scale of English Miles
PALKS BAY
GULF OF MANAAR
INDIAN OCEAN
NORTHERN PROVINCE
NORTH CENTRAL PROVINCE
NORTH WESTERN PROVINCE
EASTERN PROVINCE
SABARAGAMUWA
SOUTHERN PROVINCE
UVA PROVINCE
TRINCOMALEE
BATTICALOA
COLOMBO
KALUTARA
Rameseram
ADAMS BRIDGE
Longitude East of Greenwich
North Latitude
Stanford's Geog. Establishment, London

APPENDIX.

NOTE I.

I HAVE always held to the tradition, verbally communicated to me, regarding the antiquity of our family, and without placing undue importance upon it as a distinction, I have felt the necessity of maintaining my position and reputation as the descendant of a long line of ancestors. This feeling has been of great use to me in my up-hill struggle through life; for, while conscious that no distinguished antecedents of my forefathers could in any way compensate for individual deficiency in myself, it proved an invaluable stimulus to personal exertion and determination of purpose, without which I must have totally failed. The knowledge that my family can be traced back as useful and distinguished members of the communities in which they have lived for many generations, has given me the ardent desire, I have ever felt to emulate their example, and to prove myself not altogether unworthy of them.

The following is a copy of the original grant of Arms given to our family :—

GRANT OF ARMS, BY WILLIAM HERVY, ESQ., CLARENCEUX, KING OF ARMS, TO JOHN SKYNNER, ESQ., 10*th July*, 1557.

To all and singuler as well kinges herauldes and Officers of armes as nobles gentilmen and others which these presentes shall see or here, William heruye esquire otherwise called Clarencieulx princi-pall heraulde and kinge of armes of the sowthe Easte and weaste parties of Englande from the ryuer of Trente sowthwarde sendith due commendac'ons and greatinge. ffor asmuche as auncientlie from the beginnynge the valiaunte and vertuouse actes of excellente parsons haue ben commendid to the worlde with sondrie monumentes and remembrances of theire good deseartes. Emonges the which one of the chefiste and moste vsuall hath byn the bearinge of signes and tokens in shildes called armes the which are noné other thinges then euidences and demonstrac'ons of prowes and valoure diuerslie distributed accordinge to the qualleties and Deseartes of the persons that suche signes and tokens of the diligent faithfull and cowragious might appeare before the negligente cowarde and ignorante and be an efficiente cawse to move stirre and kindle the harttes of men to the ymytac'on of vertue and noblenes, Euen so hath the same ben and yet is contynuallie obseruid to the intente that suche as haue don com'endable seruice to theire prince or contreye either in warre or peace maye both receiue due honor in their liues, and also deriue the same successiulie to theire posteretie after them. And beinge required of John Skyn'er in the countie of Lincolne esquire receiuer of the honor of Bollingbroke, sonne and heire to Robert Skynner of Excetor in the countie of Deuon gentilman, to make searche in the register and recordes of myne Office for the auncient armes and creast belonginge to that name and famelie whereof he is descendid, and I fownde the same, And consideringe his auncestors vertue so well begon and so longe continewed I coulde not withoute theire greate iniurie asssigne vnto hym anye other armes then those which belongid to the howse and famelie whereof he is descendid: wherefore in perpetuall memorie of the vertuouse actes and Demerittes reuiued in that person, as by the same deriued from his auncestors, I haue confirmed and graunted to hym and his posteretie the owlde and auncient armes of his auncestors, That is to saye, ermyns thre lozenges sables on everie one a flowredelices golde, And to the Creaste, vpon the heaulme, a Dragons hedd razid azure platey, on the necke two gemelles golde, on a wreathe golde and verte, mantelled gules doublid argent as more plainlie apearith depicted in this margente, which armes heaulme and Creaste I the saide Clarencieulx kinge of armes, by power and auctoretie to myne Office annexed and graunted by letters patentes vnder the greate seale of Englande, haue ratefied confirmed gyuen and graunted vnto the said John Skynner gentilman and to his posteretie with theire due differences to vse beare and shewe for euermor in shildé coate armoure or otherwise and therin to be reuested at his and theire libertie and pleasure without ympediment lett or interrupcon of any person or persons. In wittnes whereof I the saide Clarencieulx kinge of armes haue signed these presentes with my hande and putt therevnto the seale of myne Office and the seale of myne armes. Geuen at London the tenthe of July in the yeare of owre lorde godd 1557, and in the fourthe and fifte yeares of the reigne of owre souereigns Lorde and Ladye phellippe and Marye by the grace of godd kinge and Queene of England Spayne fraunce bothe Cicelles Jerusalem and Ireland deffendors of the faith Archedukes of Austrishe Dukes of Burgondie Millane and Brabant counties of Haspurge flaunders and Tyroll.

Will. Hervy al's clarencieulx
King of Armes.

The name of Skinner is of Danish origin from the word *Sken.* At Herald's College is to be found at the 28th page of the 23rd volume of MS. pedigrees in the handwriting of Robert Dale, from 1703 to 1713—Blanch Lion, Poursuivante extraordinary, afterwards Richmond Herald, the following;—

"The name of Skenner is a name in the Kyngdom of Ingland that came with the elegetematt William Duke of Normandy, who mayd conquest of the Kyngdom; the first of the name of Skenner being a Knight named Sir Robartt Skenner, born in Normandy, who for his good services done unto the Conqueror was made a free Denneson in the aforesaid Kyngdom. He married in the county of Lincone unto the daughter and heayre of Sir Robartt Bolingbroke, Knight, of the rase of Saxony; from him is descended 28 Desenttes whereof six wher Knights, they all of them lyvinge as gentlemen of name and sortte." The arms are then described and the pedigree set forth. It is signed thus,—"Yours to command, HAMLETT SONCKYE."

Transcribed from an ill-written, rude draft or pedigree, in eight sheets of paper pasted together, at the top whereof is joined another sheet with an atchievement of two coats and crest in colours.

Ita Testor, ROBERT DALE, Blanch Lion.

In the eighth year of Edward I., it appears by an *Inqusito post mortem* that the name was spelled Le Skynnere.

The earliest wills registered at Lincoln are in 1515; and the will of Robert Skynner (grandfather of Sir Vincent Skynner,

Receiver of the Honour of Bolingbroke,) bears date 1535; the registers of Bolingbroke, commencing 1561, have the marriage of Vincent Skynner, 1569; and frequent entries of the name, sometimes registered as a Christian-name, in other families.

Among the many branches of the family—(for there are sixteen different coats of arms assigned to them of which I have copies)—it may be said in support of the old pedigree, that the tradition exists that they were established by the munificence of the Conqueror whom they claim as kinsman.

The following very ancient account of the Conqueror's mother may well be considered with reference to such claim :—

"Edmund Ironside, says a Saxon Genealogist, had two sons, Edwin and Edward, and an only daughter whose name does not appear in history, because of her wilful conduct, seeing that she formed a most imprudent alliance with the King's skinner, that is 'Master of the Robes.' The King in his anger banished the skinner from England with his daughter. They went to Normandy where they lived on public charity, and had successively three daughters. Having one day come to Falaise to beg at the Duke Richard's door, the Duke, struck with the beauty of the woman and her children, asked who she was. 'I am an Englishwoman,' she said, 'of the Royal blood.' The Duke, on this answer, treated her with honour, took the skinner into his service, and had one of his daughters brought up in the Palace. She was Arlotte, or Charlotte, the mother of the Conqueror."

It is accepted as true, in all histories, that the Conqueror, being opposed by his father's family, set them aside, and put forward the connections of his mother. In support of this account, it may be stated that on a monument in the Gloucester Cathedral, to the memory of Robert, Duke of Normandy, brother of William, the Conqueror, there exists on its pedestal the exact arms which have been worn by the Skinner family—it is presumed, ever since this asserted connexion.

John Skynner, the grantee of the aforesaid arms, was appointed by letters patent from the king, Edward VI., on October 10th, in the first year of his reign, 1548, "Receiver of the honour of Bolingbroke and all the King's castles, lordships, manors, lands, &c., parcel of the Duchy of Lancaster, in the county of Lincoln, for life." He appears to have occupied this office till the twenty-fifth year of Queen Elizabeth's reign, 1583, when it is supposed he died, as from the twenty-sixth year of Queen Elizabeth's reign the office devolved upon Sir Vincent Skynner, of Thornton College, Lincolnshire.

The family of Skynner,* after the Conquest, originally settled in Lincolnshire, where this John Skynner, Receiver of Bolingbroke, resided, though it would appear that at an earlier period some of the members settled in Devonshire, where the name is frequently met with, and where we find at Barnstaple that Richard Skynner was mayor in 1538, and again in 1551, being "Member of Parliament for that prosperous town in 1557 and 1558."

Sir Vincent Skynner, who succeeded John Skynner as Receiver of the Honour of Bolingbroke, Lincolnshire, was M.P. there from 1572 to 1585. We also find that among the worthies of Exeter, in the earliest records, even before the Conquest, they were the stewards or provosts, whose governing powers were eventually merged in the mayor, but who were always "Free men" of the city, and till the reform of municipalities in the year 1835 the stewards of the city were judges of the ancient court of record, called the Provost's Court, and were men of station and respect, among whom were—

"Aldred Skinner, 1203, 5th of John."
"Michael Skinner, 1314, 8th of Edward II."
"William Skinner, 1620, 18th of James I."

With reference to our ancestor, Lieutenant-General William Skinner, Chief Engineer of Great Britain, it may not be superfluous to add to the account of his connection with the old Danish family before referred to, some notice of his more immediate ancestors. He was probably descended from John Skynner, Receiver of the Honour of Bolingbroke, for he and his descendants use the same amorial bearings, as did also the General's grandfather, William Skynner, Mayor of Hull, 1665, as appears by the arms on the seal affixed to this William's will and engraved on his monument.

It may be interesting to mention here, with reference to our

* Skenner, or Skynner, or Skinner.

coat of arms, that on one occasion a friend was staying with us, well versed in Heraldry, who, on looking at the grant of arms to our family, remarked that the three Fleur de Lys on the shield should all be the same size, not one larger than the other two, as shown on our grant of arms. Some time afterwards I was visiting Gloucester Cathedral, and on examining the monument in the nave, to Robert, Duke of Normandy, I saw, on one of the shields on the monument, the three Fleur de Lys, exactly similar to those presented to our family, the lower one considerably larger than the two above; proving that our grant of arms is correct.

But to return to William Skynner, Mayor of Hull. On January 31st, 1660, he paid a fine of £30 to free himself from the office of Chamberlain, but on the 16th October, 1662, he was elected Alderman, and was sworn in on the 18th October. On the 25th September 1664, he was appointed Mayor.

Of the Mayor, we know that his mother was Mary, sister of that distinguished prelate, John Cosins, Bishop of Durham, born at Norwich, November 30, 1595. "During William Skynner's Mayoralty, on the 16th August 1665, at a cost of £169, he entertained, at his magnificent mansion in Lewer Lane, the Duke of York, afterwards James II., and the Duke of Buckingham and his retainers. The fabric of the house still remains, but the basement is divided into several shops, and its glory has departed." Mr. A. M. Skinner, Q.C., writes: "In 1868, I saw an old man of 80 years of age, who remembered its beautiful gardens when he was a boy, but the growth of the town has obliterated all traces of the existence of these pleasure grounds."

Before William Skynner's death, however, he left Lewer Lane, and built a fine house in High Street, *alias* Hull Street, on the east side, next the haven, called Hull Haven. The sum thus expended, shows some whimsical humour as to the details of calculation on the part of the rich Alderman, for a memorandum, now existing, states that the building cost £3,333 3s. 3¾d.—a large sum at that time.

While Mayor, William Skynner gave to Hull "two large candlesticks, snuffers, and a pan in silver." He left, by Will, a competent Legacy that 8 dozen of Bread—"to hold which there is a conveniet place made in the Church—should for ever be distributed to the poor, the first Sunday of every month."

William Skynner, the Alderman's eldest son, was a strong partisan of James II., and he, with his kinsman, William Hayes, in 1689, refused, as Alderman, to take the Oaths of Allegiance to King William III., and "each was displaced from office, and had to pay down £40, as the Act directed, for the use of the poor."

The only son of his great uncle, Bishop Cosin, to the great grief of the Bishop, had become a Roman Catholic, and "William Skynner did, some time after this, like his kinsman, become a Roman Catholic also."

John Skynner, the Alderman's second son, was twice Mayor of Hull—in 1661 and 1679. During his first Mayoralty he erected, at his own expense, a hospital, placing on it this inscription :—

"Da, dum tempus habes, tibi, propria Manas hæres, duferet hoc nemo, quad dabis ipse Deo.

"G. C., 1661. E. C."

"Give, while you 've time, yourself your own heir make,
For what you give to God, shall no man take."

His wife, Eleanor, who died in 1662, not only took part in this good work, but was a great benefactress to an institution then known as "The Curious Modern Library."

He presented to the Corporation, on his second Mayoralty in 1679, "a guilt cup and cover."

John Skynner's daughter, Elizabeth, was born in April 1665, the same year in which her father was honoured by the visit of James II. At the age of sixteen, she married the eldest son of Anthony Lambert, who died after three years, leaving her a widow at the age of nineteen. A few years afterwards she married Talbot Edwards, who had served at Tanjiers, in 1677, under Churchill, as a Royal Engineer.

Talbot Edwards was a brother-in-law of Sir Martin Beckman, Chief Engineer of Great Britain, who, in 1689, was appointed to construct the citadel of Hull. He brought his brother-in-law with him on his staff, and it was on this occasion that Talbot Edwards, met his wife.

"It appears that young Talbot Edwards, on the 10th of September 1690, purchased a license to marry, at St. Mary's Church, the beautiful young widow of 25, and on the 21st day of the same month, they were married. She died in the Tower of London, and was buried there on the 24th May 1717. Her husband, Captain Talbot Edwards, Second Engineer of Great Britain, died the 22nd April 1719, and was also buried in the Tower of London, beside his wife. Mrs. Talbot Edwards adopted her nephew, William Skynner, who afterwards became General, and Chief Engineer of Great Britain. Talbot Edwards left to him his books, papers, and plans, including Sir Martin Beckman's sword, &c., having already shaped his course in life by preparing him for the Engineers, into which service he entered within three weeks of his uncle's death, viz. on the 11th May 1719.

In 1662, among other offices that had been suspended, or abolished, was restored that of the Keeper of the Crown Jewels in the Tower of London, which had always been held by a person of eminence, and which was now conferred on Sir Gilbert Talbot; but the emoluments having been lost, Talbot assigned the duty, with the diminished profits, to Talbot Edwards, possibly a kinsman of his own.

CORPS ARCHÆOLOGIA.

Under the above heading an account was given in the *Royal Engineers Journal* for October 1878 of the attempt of Col. Blood to steal the Crown Jewels from the Tower of London in 1673, when Mr. Talbot Edwards, the father of the Engineer Officer of that name, and the father-in-law of another Engineer Officer, Sir Martin Beckman, was Deputy Keeper. This account was taken from a manuscript in a catalogue of maps and plans, formerly the property of General Skinner, Chief Engineer of Great Britain, and presented to the Royal Engineers' Institute by his relative, Capt. M. W. Skinner, R.E. Talbot Edwards, the son of the Deputy Keeper of the Crown Jewels, married a Miss Skinner, aunt of General Skinner, and thus the three Engineers — Beckman, Edwards, and Skinner—were connected by family ties.

Capt. M. W. Skinner has sent us an extract from Stowe's *Survey of London*, giving an account of the theft of the Crown Jewels and the part that young Talbot Edwards bore therein; as it is a much more detailed narrative, it may be interesting to many who have not access to Stowe's work, while it is well that it should be recorded in our "Corps Archæologia."

"THE TOWER OF LONDON.

"THE CROWN STOLLEN.

"*The Imperial Crown and Globe stollen away, but recovered.*—But among all the memorable Accidents that have happened in the Tower, hardly any History of our Country can equal that cunning, audacious and villanous Attempt of one Blood in K. Charles the Second's Time, in stealing the Crown, and his Camerade the Globe, out of the safe Place where they with the rest of the Regalia were kept; and carrying them out of the Tower; though they were discovered at last and seized. A faithful Relation deserves to stand upon record. And such a Relation is this that follows, which I had from the Favour of Mr. Edwards himself, the late Keeper of the Regalia.

"*The manner how Mr. Edwards.*—About three Weeks before this Blood made his Attempt upon the Crown, he came to the Tower in the Habit of a Parson, with a long Cloak, Cassock and Canonical Girdle, and brought a Woman with him whom he called Wife. Altho' in truth his Wife was then sick in Lancashire. This pretended Wife desired to see the Crown; and having seen it feigned to have a Qualm come upon her Stomach, and desired Mr. Edwards (who was Keeper of the Regalia) to send for some Spirits, who immediately caused his Wife to fetch some; whereof when she had drunk, she courteously invited her upstairs to repose herself upon a Bed: Which Invitation she accepted, and soon recovered. At their Departure they seemed very thankful for this Civility.

"About three or four Days after, Blood came again to Mrs. Edwards, with a present of Four Pairs of White Gloves from his Wife. And having thus begun the Acquaintance; they made frequent Visits to improve it: She professing that she should never sufficiently acknowledge her Kindness.

"Having made some small Respit of his Compliments, he returned again, and said to Mrs. Edwards that his Wife could discourse of nothing but of the Kindness of those good People in the Tower. That she had long studied, and at length bethought herself of a handsome way of Requital. You have, said he, a pretty Gentlewoman to your Daughter, and I have a young Nephew who hath two or three Hundred a year Land, and is at my Disposal. If your Daughter be free, and you approve of it, I will bring him hither to see her, and we will endeavour to make it a Match.

"This was easily assented to by old Mr. Edwards, who invited the Parson to dine with him that day, and he as readily accepted of the Invitation; who taking upon him to say Grace, performed it with great Devotion, and casting up of Eyes, and concluded his long-winded Grace, with a hearty Prayer for the King, Queen, and Royal Family. After Dinner he went up to see the Rooms, and seeing a handsome Case of Pistols hang there, he exprest a great desire to buy them, to Present a Young Lord who was his neighbour. That was his Pretence, but his Purpose probably was to disarm the House against the Time that he intended to put the Design in Execution.

"At his Departure (which was with a Canonical Benediction of the good Company) he appointed a Day and Hour to bring his young Nephew to his Mistress; and it was that very day that he made his Attempt; viz. the 9th of May, about Seven in the Morning, An. Dom. 1673.

"The Old Man was got up ready to receive his Guest, and the Daughter had put herself into her best Dress to entertain her Gallant when behold Parson Blood, with three more came to the Jewel House, all Armed with Rapier Blades in their Canes, and every one a Dagger, and a pair of Pocket Pistols. Two of his Companions entered in with him, and the Third stayed at the Door, it seems for a Watch. The Daughter thought it not modest for her to come down till she was called, but she sent the Maid to take a view of the Company, and to bring her a Description of the Person of her Gallant. The Maid conceived that he was the intended Bridegroom who stayed at the Door, because he was the youngest of the company; and returned to her young Mistress with the character that she had formed of his Person.

"Blood told Mr. Edwards, that they would not go up Stairs till his Wife came, and desired him to shew his Friends the Crown to pass the time till then. As soon as they were entered the Room where the Crown was kept, and the Door (as usually) was shut behind them, they threw a Cloak over the Old Man's Head, and clapt a Gag into his Mouth, which was a great Plug of Wood, with a small Hole in the Middle to take Breath at. This was tyed on with a waxed Leather, which went round his Neck. At the same time they fastened an Iron Hook to his Nose, that no Sound might pass from him that Way neither.

"When they had thus Secured him from crying out they told him that their Resolution was to have the Crown, Globe and Sceptre. And that if he would quietly submit to it they would spare his Life, otherwise he was to expect no Mercy. He thereupon forced himself to make all the Noise that possibly he could to be heard above: Then they knocked him down with a Wooden Mallet, and told him that if yet he would lie quietly, they would spare his Life, but if not, upon the next Attempt to discover them, they would Kill him, and pointed three Daggers at his Breast. But he strained himself to make the greater Noise: Whereupon they gave him Nine or Ten Stroaks more upon the Head with the Mallet (for so many Bruises were found upon the Skull) and stabbed him into the Belly.

"Whereat the poor Man, almost Eighty Years of Age fell, and

lay some time entranced. One of them kneeled on the Ground to try if he breathed; and not perceiving any Breath come from him said, He is dead I'll warrant him. Mr. Edwards came a little to himself, heard his Words; and conceived it best for him to be so thought, and lay quietly.

"Then one of them named Parrot put the Globe into his Breeches. Blood held the Crown under his Cloak. The Third was designed to file the Sceptre in two, (because too long to carry) and when filed it was to be put into a Bag, brought for that Purpose.

"But before this could be done, young Mr. Edwards (Son of the Old Gentleman) who had attended upon Sir John Talbot into Flanders, and upon his first landing in England, was with Sir John's Leave come away Post to see his Old Father, chanced to arrive at the very Instant that this was acting; and coming to the Door the Person that stood Centinel for the rest asked him with whom he would speak? He made Answer, He belonged to the House. But young Edwards, perceiving by his Question, that he himself was a Stranger, told him, that if he had any Business with his Father he would go and acquaint him with it; and so went up, where he was welcomed by his Mother, Wife and Sister.

In the meantime, the Centinel gave notice of the Son's Arrival, and they forthwith hasted away with the Crown and Globe, but left the Sceptre, not having time to file it. The Old Man returning to himself got upon his Legs, pulled off the Gag (for they concluded him dead, and surprized with the Son's unexpected Arrival, had omitted to tye his Hands behind him) and cryed out, Treason! Murther!

"The Daughter hearing him, hastened down, and seeing her Father thus wounded ran out upon the Tower Hill, and cried Treason, The Crown is stolen. This gave the first Alarm: And Blood and Parrot making more than ordinary Haste, were observed to jog each other with their Elbows as they went, which causes them to be suspected and pursued. By this time, young Mr. Edwards, and Captain Beckman, upon the Cry of their Sister, were come down, and left their Father likewise to run after the Villains; but they were advanced beyond the main Guard; and the Alarm being given louder to the Warder at the Drawbridge, he put himself in posture to stop them. Blood came up first, and discharged a Pistol at him. The Bullet (if any there were) missed him, but the Powder or Fear made him fall to the Ground; whereby they got safe to the little Wardhouse Gate; where one Sill, who had been a Soldier under Cromwell, stood Centinel; who altho' he saw the other Warder shot made no Resistance. By whose Cowardice, or Treachery, the Villains got over that Drawbridge, and through the outward Gate upon the Wharf, and made all possible haste toward their Horses, which attended at St. Katherine's Gate, called the Iron Gate; crying themselves, as they ran, Stop the Rogues. And they were by all thought innocent, he being in that grave Canonical Habit, till Captain Beckman got up to them. Blood discharged his Second Pistol at Captain Beckman's Head, but he stooping down avoided the Shot, and seized upon the Rogue who had the Crown under his Cloak; yet had Blood the Impudence, altho' he saw himself a Prisoner, to struggle a long while for the Crown; and when it was wrested from him said; It was a gallant Attempt (how unsuccessful soever) for it was for a Crown.

"A servant belonging to Captain Sherburn seized upon Parrot, before Blood was taken. There was such a Consternation in all men, and so much Confusion in the Pursuit, that it was no wonder some innocent Persons had not suffered for the Guilty. For young Edwards overtaking one that was bloody in the Skuffle, and supposing him to be one of those who had murthered his Father, was going to run him through, had not Captain Beckman cryed, Hold, he is none of them.

"And as Captain Beckman made more than ordinary haste in the Pursuit, the Guards were going to fire at him, supposing him to be one of the Rogues; but one of them who by good Fortune knew him, cryed out, Forbear: He is a Friend. Blood and Parrot being both seized (as hath been said) Hunt, Blood's Son-in-Law, leaped to Horse, with two more of the Conspirators, and rid far away. But a Cart standing empty in the Street, chanced to turn short, and Hunt run his Head against a Pole that stuck far out; but he recovering his Legs, and putting his Foot in the Stirrop, a Cobler running to enquire after the Disaster, said: This is Tom Hunt, who was in that bloody Attempt upon the Person of the Duke of Ormond; Let us secure him. A Constable being accidentally there, seized him upon that Affirmation, and carried him before Justice Smith. Who upon his confident Denial of himself to be Hunt, was about to let him go; but the Hue and Cry coming, that the Crown was taken out of the Tower, he was committed to safe Custody.

"Young Edwards proposed to Lieutenant Rainsford, to mount some of his Soldiers upon the Horses that were left, and send them to follow the rest that escaped; but he bad him follow himself if he would: It was his Business: And led the Fellows Horses into the Tower, as forfeited to the Lieutenant.

"*Hunt.*—Hunt (as hath been said) was Son-in-Law to Blood, and trained up in his Practices.

"*Parrot.*—Parrot was a Silk-Dyer in Southwark; and in the Rebellion had been Major-General Harrison's Lieutenant.

"*Blood.*—Blood was the Son of a Blacksmith in Ireland; a Fellow that thought small Villainies below him. One of his virtuous Camerades, having received Sentence of Death in Yorkshire for some Crime, he rescued out of the Hands of the Sheriffs Men, as they were leading him to the Gallows. He, with others, laid a

Design in Ireland, to surprize the Castle of Dublin, and the Magazine therein, and to usurp the Government.

"*Duke of Ormond.*—But being discovered by the Duke of Ormond the Night before the intended Execution, some of them were apprehended and suffered as Traitors. Whose Death Blood and the rest of the surviving Rogues bound themselves by Solemn Oath, to revenge upon the Duke's Person. This occasioned his Third Enterprize. For he, with five or six more of his Associates (whereof Hunt was one) well mounted, came one Night up to his Coach side, before he came to his own Gate, dwelling then at Albemarl House, took him out of his Coach, forced him up behind one of the Horsemen, and were riding away with him as far as Berkely House. Where the Duke threw himself off the Horse with the Villain, who had tied the Duke fast to him. The rest turned back, discharging two Pistols at the Duke; but taking their Aim in the Dark, missed him. By this Time the Neighbourhood was alarmed, and the Rogues having Work enough to save themselves, rid for it, and got away.

"It was no small Disrepute to that hellish Contriver amongst his Camerades, to fail in a Project which he had laid so sure, and represented to them so easy to be effected. Therefore, to redeem his Credit with them, he entered immediately upon the Contrivance of another, that should fully recompence all former Miscarriages, with an infallible Prospect of Gain, and the Reputation of a daring Villany; Which was that of sharing the Regalia.

"In the robustious Struggle for the Crown, as was shewed before, the great Pearl and a fair Diamond fell off, and were lost for a while, with some other smaller Stones. But the Pearl was found by Katharine Maddox (a poor Sweeping Woman to one of the Warders) and the Diamond by a Barber's Apprentice; and both faithfully restored. Other smaller Stones were by several Persons picked up and brought in. The fair Ballas Ruby, belonging to the Sceptre, was found in Parrot's Pocket. So that not any considerable Thing was wanting. The Crown only was bruised and sent to repair.

"Young Mr. Edwards went presently to Sir Gilbert Talbot; and gave him an Account of all that had passed. Who instantly went to the King, and acquainted his Majesty with it. His Majesty commanded him to make haste to the Tower, to enquire how matters stood; to take the Examination of Blood and the rest; and to return and report all to him. Sir Gilbert accordingly went and found the Prisoners (whose Wounds had been already dress'd) with their Keepers in the White Tower.

"Blood lay in a Corner dogged and lowring, and would not give a Word of Answer to any one Question.

"His Majesty was in the mean time persuaded by some about him to hear the Examination himself. And the Prisoners were forthwith sent for to Whitehall. Nothing else could possibly have saved Blood from the Gallows. But that which ought to have been his surer Condemnation, proved to be his Safety. For all men concluding, that none but those who had the Courage to adventure upon such a daring Villany as that of the Crown, could be guilty of the Practice upon a Peer of that Magnitude as was the Duke of Ormond; especially the Parliament then sitting. Amongst other Questions therefore it was thought fit to interrogate him, Whether he had not a Hand in that Assault? For the Authors of it were as yet Altogether in the Dark.

"*Blood examined before the King.*—Blood (as if he had valued himself upon the Action, and possibly suspecting that the King might have made some Discovery of it already) without any manner of Scruple or Hesitation, confessed he had. It was then asked him, Who his Associates were; He answered, that he would never betray a Friend's Life; nor never deny a Guilt, in Defence of his own. It was next asked him, What Provocation he had to make so bold an Assault upon the Duke of Ormond? He said, the Duke had taken away his Estate, and executed some of his Friends; and that he and many other, had engaged themselves by solemn Oath to revenge it.

"And lest any of his audacious Villanies should lessen the Romance of his Life, by lying concealed in his Examination about the Crown, he voluntarily confessed to the King (but whether truly or falsely, may very well endure a Question, as I shall endeavour to shew anon) that he had been engaged in a Design to kill his Majesty with a Carbine from out of the Reeds by the Thames side, above Battersea; where he often went to swim. That the Cause of this Resolution in himself, and others, was his Majesty's Severity over the Consciences of the Godly, in suppressing the Freedom of their Religious Assemblies. That when he had taken his Stand in the Reeds for that Purpose, his Heart was checked with an Awe of Majesty; and he did not only himself relent, but diverted the rest of his Associates from the Design.

"He told his Majesty, that he had by these his Confessions, laid himself sufficiently open to the Law; and he might reasonably expect the utter Rigor of it; for which he was (without much Concern of his own) prepared. But he said withal, that the Matter would not be of that Indifference to his Majesty; inasmuch as there were Hundreds of his Friends, yet undiscovered, who were all bound to each other by the indispensible Oaths of Conspirators, to revenge the Death of any of the Fraternity upon those who should bring them to Justice. Which would expose his Majesty and all his Ministers to the daily Fear and Expectation of a Massacre. But on the other side, if his Majesty would spare the Lives of a few, he might oblige the Hearts of many; who (as they had been seen to do daring Mischiefs) would be as bold, if received into

Pardon and Favour, to perform eminent Services for the Crown.

"*Fanaticks.*—And he pretended such an Interest and Sway amongst the Fanaticks, to dispose them to their Fidelity, as though he been their chosen General, and had them all entered in his Muster Roll.

"*Pardoned.*—In short, Blood and his Associates were not only pardoned, and set free; but the Arch Villain himself had 500£. per Ann. conferred upon him in Ireland, and admitted into all the Privacy and Intumacy of Court. Mr. Edwards had the Grant of 200£. and his Son 100£.

"*A continuation of this Narrative, F. S. Sir Gilbert Talbot.*—I have, since the Writing of what is above said, met with a Continuation of Blood's stealing the Crown, in Mr. Edward's M.S.S. writ, as it seems, by Sir Gilbert Talbot. Which is as follows. What his Operation had been among the Quakers, (who are his most beloved Sect above all others, and in whose Synagogue he hath his eminent Seat) the World is yet to learn; except it be, that he had multiplied their Congregations, and increased their Swarms in all Counties. But where lies his Majesty's Service in all this? Oh! they are kept quiet, and do not molest the Government. Indeed the Quakers have ever been reputed an innocent, harmless kind of Madmen: But he must be as mad as they, that can think them so, while Blood is of their Congregation.

"*Some Censures thereupon.*—Since this Villain's Crimes then are visible to all Mankind, and his Merits altogether incomprehensible, every Man will take the Liberty to conjecture, what Consideration could possibly beget his Pardon. His Crimes were without Controversy the highest Breaches of Human Laws: Murther acted upon a poor old Gentleman for defending his Trust; and Murther intended to be acted upon a Great Peer, with all the Circumstances of Contempt: A Design laid to surprize the King's Castle; a violent Seizure of his Crown and Sceptre; and a confessed lying in wait to destroy his Person. It requires a great Measure of Mercy in a Prince (for it is not decent to attribute it to anything else) to forgive such Injuries, done to himself. But it is above his Mercy to pardon the Offence committed against another, because Heaven, which is all merciful, forgiveth not the Trespasses which we commit against our Neighbours, without Restitution. Yet the Lord Arlington came in his Majesty's Name to the Duke of Ormond to tell him, that he would not have Blood prosecuted, for Reasons which he was commanded to give him. The Duke replied, That his Majesty's Command was the only Reason that could be given, and that therefore he might spare the rest. It was a gallant Answer of his Grace, and such as well became the Loyalty of his Family. But it is a great Pity in the mean time, that the World should want the Knowledge of his Lordships's Reasons, which had Weight enough in them to smother a Matter of that high Concernment, to the Dishonour of Justice, and the Dignity of Peerage.

"How great a Misery soever it is to the World Blood and his Associates were not only pardoned and set free, but the Arch Villain himself had the fore mentioned Land conferred upon him in Ireland; and that meritorious Person admitted into all the Privacy and Intimacy of the Court. No Man more assiduous than himself in both Secretaries Offices. If any one had a Business in Court that stuck, he made his Applications to Blood, as the most industrious and successful Sollicitor. Nay, many Gentlemen courted his Acquaintance, as the Indians pray to the Devils, that they may not hurt them.

"Blood had no body but his own black Deeds to advocate for him. Yet thus was he rewarded. And although many sollicited for old Mr. Edwards; and had raised their Arguments from his Fidelity, Courage, and Wounds received; yet all that could be obtained for him was a Grant of 200£. out of the Exchequer, and 100£. to his Son, as aforesaid. The Payment whereof was so long delayed, and his Chirurgeons calling upon him daily for Satisfaction for their Drugs and Pains, he was forced to sell his Order for 100£. Ready Money and his Son his for 50£. and lived not long to enjoy the Remainder. For he died within a Year and a Month after the Wounds received.

"*Reflexions.*—But now to reflect a little, as I promised, not only upon the mysterious Redemption of this Rogue from the Gallows; but upon the (never to be enough wondred) Recompence for his Villanies, of 500£ per Ann. A Reward which the most meritorous Vertue have seldom met with. Let us therefore consider him first, as taken in so flagrant a Crime, that no Plea could possibly lie in favour of his Life, nor no Hopes could be so impudent as to expect it. Observe then what he doth. He maketh a voluntary Confession of three other rapping Crimes. One his Attempt upon the Duke of Ormond. And his alledged Provocation to that, was by Consequence a Confession of his Conspiracy upon the Castle of Dublin. This much he thought necessary to acknowledge to shew his Power and Audacity; that in case he were brought to Execution, he should stand recorded in Story to have died like a daring Sinner, and not as a petty Malefactor. Then he declareth freely and of his own Accord, his Intention to assassinate his Majesty in the River. I ask any man of Reason, What other Consideration could move him to that Confession? But to bring in this other Part of his Story, he was to tell his Majesty that his Heart relented, being surpriz'd with Awe and Reverence of his Person, (he had none of his Crown) and that he (not) only forebore the Execution himself, but dissuaded his Associates likewise from it. There is so great a Probability, that this professed tender Forbearance of his, tended only to dispose his Majesty (who of all Mankind is captivated with Good Nature) to return the like Mercy towards him, that with the good Favour of Mr. Blood's Check of Conscience, which diverted him from the Execution, it is easy to be conjectured, that there was never any such Design really laid; but that the Story was feigned to work upon his Majesty's Tenderness towards him.

"But lest that should not prevail, Blood seemed not to be at all troubled with the Apprehension of his own Death, for which he stood prepared; but it grieved him, forsooth, to consider the sad Consequence of it; Which would be an Attempt of Revenge upon the Person of the King and his Ministers, by the surviving Conspirators, bound by Oath, &c. So that (if Mercy were defective) he could try what Fear could operate; and lest both these should fail, he hath another Fetch in store; which is to persuade them to pardon him upon the Score of good Politicks; by shewing how useful an Instrument he can be to quiet the Minds of all the disaffected Party, and secure the Government from popular Insurrections, if his Life may be spared.

"I cannot easily be persuaded to believe that this Proffer of Service in Blood could much prevail upon his Majesty's judgment; because it was natural to conclude, that he who is able to quiet a Party, is likewise able to irritate it; and that he who is bribed by 500£. per Ann. to do the one, may be gained with 1000£. per Ann. to do the contrary. And what Security can there be, that he will not, but the bare Word of a Villain.

"*History here repeats itself.*—In the meantime, nothing can more betray the Weakness of a Government, than that it should have Recourse to such Instruments to support it. Nor can Anything make the Authority more despisable, than that it should be terrified from the Execution of Justice upon the greatest Malefactor that History, from the Creation hither, recordeth, for fear that Blood's Ghost should rise, or his surviving Confederates meditate Revenge. Besides, it is as far from Reason, that a man of Blood's Principles should be trusted with the Power and Interest that must go to the Managing of a Party, as that those who trust him should expect any good Services from the confessed Author of so many black Deeds, or Heaven give a Blessing to the Endeavours of such an impious Creature."

[*Exact copy of spelling.*]

Lieutenant-General William Skinner, son of Thomas Skinner, who was the youngest son of John Skinner, Alderman of Hull, was born in the West Indies on the Island of St. Christopher in 1699 or 1700. He was an engineer of excellence and merit in the reigns of George I., II., and III. He was a studious youth, and seems to have acquired early so much knowledge of Mathematics and the Theory of War as to have attracted the notice of Colonel Armstrong, the Chief Engineer, who procured a warrant for him from Earl Cadogan, Master of the Ordnance, as Practitioner Engineer, his commission dating from the 11th May, 1719, with a salary of 3s. a day. From 1720 to 1722 he assisted at the works at the Gun Wharf at Plymouth, after which he was despatched to Minorca to superintend under his chief's orders the erection of extensive fortifications there, and being highly commended for diligence and ability was selected to form one of the party of engineers entrusted with the first general survey of Gibraltar, and in 1729 he bore his part bravely during the siege of that place, and afterwards passed there many years of his life.

The General made many plans of Gibraltar, some of which are preserved in the British Museum, and testify to his assiduity in the public service, and his proficiency as an engineer. Skinner was recalled from Gibraltar, where he had succeeded Jonas Moore as chief engineer (Moore having been killed at the siege of Carthagena), and sent to Scotland in order "to erect such fortresses as would effectually control the disaffected Highlanders, after the rebellion in the north of England was fairly crushed." He entered on this new duty in December 1746. He describes travelling at that period as very fatiguing and difficult, and tells a melancholy tale of bad roads, storms, torrents, and frosts, which severely tried one used so long to the genial climate of the south of Spain.

Public work in Scotland of a various and very important character occupied Skinner for several years. He describes a thrilling scene when the 42nd Highlanders were to be augmented by an addition of 500 men to the regiment, how one morning at Inverness, where he was staying with the Laird, MacIntosh, a batch of fifty Highlanders offered themselves for enlistment as soon as the Laird appeared at the window. all the men bearing the name of Macpherson from Badenock.

Late in 1755, Skinner was sent to Ireland to make surveys and reports, being specially ordered there by the Duke of Cumberland. He visited every battery and inspected all the defences most carefully, working chiefly at Dublin, Cork, and other frontier garrisons. He reported on each, suggested improvements and repairs, but the authorities proved supine, and his papers and plans were shelved, only to be disinterred thirty years later.

On the completion of his Irish service Skinner resumed his duty in the Highlands, and on the 1st May, 1757, received from the King the rank of Colonel. Before this time he held no important military status, though he was previously appointed Chief Engineer of Gibraltar.

On the 19th May he was honoured with the royal patent constituting him Chief Engineer of Great Britain, and was often consulted on any difficult question concerning military engineering both at home and abroad. The great defences of Fort George, Fort Augustus, Edinburgh Castle, and the fortifications at Milford, Plymouth, Portsmouth, and a host of other places, bear testimony to his powers and to his industry.

Small cessation from labour was given to Skinner. Scarely had he accomplished the Milford work when Government, becoming alarmed for the safety of Gibraltar, sent him back to the Rock to make all sure in case of attack, and, having done this most satisfactorily, he returned to England and to his old work in the North, where Fort George was approaching completion, and was finally considered a perfect model of a fort.

In 1760 Skinner was sent to Belle Isle on, probably, some secret mission, as a preliminary to the anticipated descent upon the place. In 1761 he was commissioned as Major-General, and the following year his patent as "Chief Engineer of all the garrisons, castles, forts, blockhouses, and other fortifications in Great Britain" was renewed by George III.

But Fort George seems to have been the ruling passion of Skinner's life. He drew up still more elaborate plans and details, and finally presented the Board of Ordnance with a finely executed model of the completed works, as he would wish to see them. This model was kept for fifty years in the Tower of London and then removed to the Royal Engineers' Institute at Chatham, where it is often admired, though little is remembered of its indefatigable originator.

Once more, in 1769, he was consulted concerning the safety of Gibraltar, when he gave his opinions very decidedly, and differed considerably from those of other officers, whose plans had been submitted to the authorities.

In 1770 Skinner was commissioned as Lieutenant-General, still retaining his post as Chief Engineer of Great Britain. Here his record of public work ends, but his quick discernment and clear head were constantly made use of whenever occasion required, and his judgment was seldom at fault. He never relaxed his efforts even when advanced in years, dying in harness at the last, at his old residence at Croome Hill, Greenwich, on the 25th December 1780, in the 81st year of his age, having served uninterruptedly for nearly sixty-two years.

He was buried at St. Alphage Church, Greenwich. The following inscription is over the vault :—"To the memory of Lieutenant-General William Skinner, who died the 25th day of December 1780, having served sixty-one years an Engineer, twenty-three of which Chief of Great Britain."

Skinner was presented with the freedom of many of the most important cities of the United Kingdom; but the only diplomas which have been preserved are the following :—

Inverness, dated 10th April 1747
Stirling, dated 9th September 1747
Edinburgh, dated 17th October 1748
Perth, dated 25th October 1748
Aberdeen, dated 3rd June 1750
Athlone, dated 7th January 1761.

* * * * * * *

The collection of old maps, plans, drawings, and manuscripts of Sir Martin Beckman, Talbot Edwards, and General Skinner, some as old as 1660, which have been in my possession since my father's death in 1829, and which I had handed over to my son Monier Williams Skinner, Royal Engineers, have, I am happy to say, been accepted by the Committee of the R.E. Institute at Chatham, while the Committee of the Royal Engineer Mess have been good enough to accept and to place in their mess-room a portrait of General Skinner, R.E.

The following are copies of documents on the subject :—

"Chatham, 17th August 1875.

"MY DEAR MAJOR SKINNER,

"The picture and box of plans, &c., arrived in due time and in good order.

"The former I handed over to the Mess Committee, the latter to the Library Committee. I now have the pleasure of enclosing for the information of yourself and your son the Committees' resolutions in acknowledgment of these valuable contributions to the corps.

"I beg that you and your son may also accept my individual thanks for these gifts, and I am pleased to think that the interest in these gifts is enhanced from the fact that a descendant of General Skinner is now serving in the corps.

"Believe me, with kind remembrances to your son,

"Yours sincerely,

"(Signed) T. L. Gallwey, Col. R.E.,

"Commandant S.M.E."

The Committee R.E. Mess pass the following resolutions, viz. :—

"That the gift from Major Skinner, C.M.G., and Lieutenant Monier Skinner, R.E., consisting of a portrait of the late General Skinner, R.E., who was Chief Engineer and senior officer of the corps from 1757 to 1780, be accepted on behalf of the officers of the corps, and be placed in the R.E. Mess with the portraits of other distinguished members of the corps.

"2nd. That the thanks of the officers of Royal Engineers be conveyed to Major Skinner, C.M.G., and to Lieutenant Monier Skinner, R.E., for their valuable gift.

"3rd. That the president R.E. Mess notify to the Commandant S.M.E. the above resolutions, with a request that they be communicated to Major Skinner, C.M.G., and Lieutenant Monier Skinner, R.E.

"(Signed) Arthur Leahy, Colonel R.E.,

"President Mess Committee.

"August 11th, 1875."

"R.E. Institute,

"Brompton Barracks, Chatham,

"August 12th, 1875.

"Sir,

At a meeting of the Library Committee held on the 11th instant the following resolution was passed.

"The Committee accepts with pleasure the kind present from Major Skinner, C.M.G., and Lieutenant Monier Skinner, R.E., of a large collection of papers and plans, and begs leave, in the name of the officers of the corps, to tender their heartiest thanks.

"The President of the Library Committee is requested to inform the Commandant specially of this resolution, and to ask him to be kind enough to communicate it to Major Skinner and Lieutenant Skinner.

"I therefore send you this letter, and I have the honour to be,

"Sir,
Your most obedient servant,
(Signed) C. N. Martin, Major R.E.
President Library Committee, S.M.E.

"To the Commandant, S.M.E., Chatham."

* * * * * *

When the General was at Portsmouth in 1761, erecting fortifications there, he was assisted by Lieutenant—afterwards General Gotha Mann, R.E., and by a curious coincidence my son Monier W. Skinner, then a Lieutenant, R.E., when stationed at Portsmouth in 1874 to 1876, was associated with Gotha Mann, then also a Lieutenant, R.E., in pulling down those same fortifications which had become out of date; so the two grandsons were employed in destroying the fortifications erected in 1761 by their ancestors, which fortifications were then important ones. In pulling down these works, a skeleton was found with a big nail driven right through the skull; the skeleton measured 6 feet.

But to resume my account of the General, he married Margaret Caldwell and had only one son, William, Captain in the 94th Regiment, which formed part of the force under Lord Rollo, who on the 23rd April 1761 left New York with 2,000 men, on an expedition against the Island of Dominica. On the third day after their departure the fleet was dispersed by storm, and Lord Rollo reaching Guadaloupe with only 400 men received an augmentation of 300 men from that garrison, and on the 4th of June, sailed thence with 700 men and occupied Roseau the capital of Dominica. His scattered, storm-tost forces did not reach the island till July 15th, the 94th Regiment being amongst them; on their arrival the conquest of Dominica was made complete, and the possession of it secured to Great Britain.

On the 27th August 1761, Captain William Skinner, the General's only son, was drowned at Coulehault on the coast of Dominica.

The following extract is taken from the report of his death made to Lord Rollo, Governor of the Island.

"The loss you suffer by it, my Lord, is so much the greater, as he was an exceedingly good officer, much of a gentleman, endowed with great merits and rare qualities, and a thorough good Christian; in a word, all that constitutes the well-bred person of distinction; and leaves behind him infinite concern for his loss."

At the time of this sad occurrence the General was *en route* to the recently captured Island of "Belle Isle," and is said to have seen a vision of it.

It is a curious coincidence that my own father, on his death-bed at Woolwich in 1829, had a vision of my brother Willie's death, who was drowned on his voyage to Ceylon. General Thorndike, R.A., who was then a subaltern in my father's Battery has often told me that my father distinctly saw my brother standing by his bedside dripping wet, and when my step-mother came into the room he begged her to see that "Willie had dry clothes to put on, or he would take cold, as he had been in the water." My mother thinking he was wandering, left the room to satisfy him that she was attending to Willie; but she made a note of the day and hour, and at that very time my brother fell overboard and was drowned. So his mother was not altogether unprepared for the sad news when it reached her months afterwards.

In 1830, when, as Deputy Assistant Quartermaster-General, I was building a suspension bridge at Ambepoose in Ceylon, Sir Edward Barnes drove down the road on one of his tours of inspection, and arrived at the bridge earlier than he had named. Not expecting him so soon, I had gone up to my bungalow, which overlooked my work, and had left a friend of mine, George Cripps, at the bridge, in case Sir Edward should arrive in my absence, which he did. On getting out of his carriage, I saw him speaking earnestly to Cripps. Instantly the conviction possessed me that he was communicating to my friend the death of my father, of whose illness I had never heard. At that time communication with England was both slow and of infrequent occurrence. My friend spent the day with me, and on his leaving the following morning for his station, Kornegalle, of which district he was the Government Agent, he sent me back a note to say that in the room he occupied I should find a coat of his, in the pocket of which I should find an Army List of the latest date. I went direct to the Obituary, where I at once found my father's death recorded.

I have stated these as curious facts connected with the name of William Skinner, which may interest my readers, and now resume the history of my family.

Captain William Skinner, of the 94th Regiment, married, *very* young, Hester, the daughter of Colin Lawder, of Berwick-upon-Tweed, of the family of Sir John Dick Lawder. Tradition relates that the united ages of bride and bridegroom did not exceed 30. Three children were the result of this marriage: William Campbell Skinner, Captain, Royal Engineers; Thomas Skinner, Colonel, Royal Engineers; and Margaret, who married the Right Honourable Sir Evan Nepean, Bart.

Colonel Thomas Skinner, R.E., married a daughter of Barry Power, Esq., and had eight children, the eldest, William Thomas Skinner, Colonel, Royal Artillery, being my father. He was born at Gibraltar in 1780, during the siege, my grandmother being the first to be wounded, by a shell bursting over the castle, while she was nursing her son.

The third son, Robert, was also born at Gibraltar, in 1786, and was a captain in the Newfoundland Fencibles. He distinguished himself by his daring bravery and great activity during the American War, while on the Quartermaster-General's staff in Canada, between the years 1812 and 1815. On the 11th November 1813, he was publicly thanked on the field and in General Orders for his gallant conduct. He died from over fatigue while on service.

The second son, George, was a captain in the navy. The fourth and fifth were both in the army, the former of whom, Charles, died from his wounds, and the latter, Frederick, in the West Indies.

Even the daughters seemed imbued with the soldier's spirit. Harriet married Captain George Prescott of the 7th Fusiliers, who on the 12th July 1812 fell, "when nobly leading his men to the charge at the battle of Salamanca." Mrs. Prescott had followed her husband's marches with his regiment, from the time of its embarbation at Cork. When the tidings of his death reached her, in an agony of grief, and dressed in male attire, she sought his body on the field of battle and recovered it. This incident I have been told formed the subject of a tragedy called "The Heroine of Salamanca," which was subsequently acted in London. The beautiful Mrs. Prescott afterwards married Edward, the fourth son of Sir William Gibbons, Bart., LL.D.

Colonel Thomas Skinner, Royal Engineers, my grandfather, when stationed at Newfoundland in 1795, received orders to raise a force for the protection of that settlement; and with reference to this service, I have found several letters from the Duke of Kent and other public officers of the day. I will, however, only insert the following from Sir William Waldegrave, Governor of Newfoundland. showing how ably Colonel Thomas Skinner performed his duties.

"Fort Townshend, 8 August 1797.

"Sir,

"No words can express the satisfaction I felt, and still feel, on the perusal of your letter of this day's date, enclosing me the very loyal declaration of the non-commissioned officers, drummers, and privates of His Majesty's Royal Newfoundland Regiment which you have the honour to command.

"Although I never have for a moment doubted the loyalty of these gallant men, yet 'tis impossible to read the noble sentiments of their honest hearts, but with that delight which honest worth ever inspires.

"I must request that you will be pleased to make these my sentiments known to your regiment as soon as possible, together with my most sincere assurance, that so long as I find in these brave soldiers that true spirit of loyalty of which they may now so justly boast, I shall ever feel a pride in considering myself as their friend, and in promoting their interests to the utmost of my power. As the first step towards this, I shall embrace the earliest opportunity of transmitting their very soldier-like and constitutional declaration to His Grace the Duke of Portland, in order that His Majesty may know that he has not in his whole army a more gallant, loyal, and well-disposed regiment than the Royal Newfoundland.

"I cannot, Sir, conclude this letter without expressing to yourself, and the officers of your regiment, the very high sense I entertain of your own and their military merit, as, without the greatest exertion and the most unremitting attention, no regiment could have been brought in so short a period into such high order and good discipline as that which now characterises His Majesty's Royal Newfoundland Regiment.

"I beg you will direct this letter to be inserted in the General Orders as a memorial of my admiration, and the approbation of a regiment which so justly merits my applause and esteem.

"I am, Sir,

"Your most obedient and very humble servant,

"(Signed) WM. WALDEGRAVE,

"Governor.

"Colonel Thomas Skinner,

"Commanding the Royal Newfoundland Regiment."

His eldest son, Lieutenant-Colonel William T. Skinner, R.A., married, first, Anne, daughter of Lord Chief Justice Williams, of St. John's, Newfoundland, and, secondly, Marie Monier, daughter of Doctor Monier, Royal Artillery, descendant of a Huguenot refugee family. They had three children. Harriet, who married Arthur Carter, son of Judge Carter, Newfoundland; Monier, who died in infancy; and myself.

My father afterwards married a daughter of John Remmington, Esq., of Barton-end House, Gloucestershire, and had nine children.

On the 19th December 1838, I married Georgina, daughter of Lieutenant-General George Burrell, C.B. The following is an extract from the *Gentleman's Magazine* of March 1853. After mentioning General Burrell's death, at Alnwick, on the 4th January 1853, they add: "This distinguished officer was the second son of John Burrell, Esq., of Littlehoughton, Northumberland, and Barbara Peareth, his wife. He was born at Longhoughton in that county on the 26th February 1777, and entered the army as ensign in the 15th Regiment in 1797; was promoted to lieutenant in the same year, and to captain in 1805. On his passage to the West Indies that year the transport, in which he had embarked, was attacked by a large French schooner privateer, which was beaten off with great loss. He became major in the 90th Light Infantry in 1807; was at the capture of Guadaloupe in 1810, and served during the war in Canada in 1814 and 1815. He proceeded to the continent in 1815, but arrived too late for the battle of Waterloo. Having marched with his regiment to Paris, he remained there until the Army of Occupation was formed in December, and returned to England in July 1816.

"In 1820 he went to the Mediterranean, where he held the civil and military command of Paxo, one of the Ionian Islands, for upwards of five years, and received high commendation from the Regent, and civil authorities of that island. He attained the rank of colonel in 1830, and returned to England in 1832 with the 18th Royal Irish, and in 1836 was ordered with that regiment to Ceylon, where he remained till 1840. In 1837 he received the local rank of major-general, and acted as Commandant at Colombo and also at Trincomalee. In May 1840 he proceeded to China, and commanded the troops at the first capture of Chusan. He was appointed Governor of that island, which, with the command of the troops, he held until February 1841, when the island was restored by the Commissioner of the Government, in consequence of a treaty with the Chinese authorities. This not being ratified, hostilities were renewed, and the Major-General commanded a brigade at the attack on the heights above Canton, which brigade carried and destroyed the Tartar camp under the walls of the city. General Burrell continued to command a brigade in China until peace was made in July 1842.

"He received the thanks of both Houses of Parliament for his services in China, and in 1844 Her Majesty was graciously pleased to include him in the list of officers receiving rewards for distinguished services. In 1851 he was promoted to the rank of lieut.-general, and in February 1852 was appointed Colonel of the 39th Regiment.

"General Burrell married, first, Miss Scott, daughter of Sir John Scott, Knight of Ireland, and secondly, Marianne Theresa, daughter of the Rev. Dr. Thomas, of Claydagh, Co. Carlow, and was therefore connected with the Irish house of Lisle, while he was the lineal descendant of one of the oldest families in the North of England."

It will be seen by the foregoing that all the members of my family have been, with scarcely an exception, either in the army or navy for many generations. My mother's brother, Colonel George Williams, at the age of twelve years is said to have "joined General Burgoyne's army in America, and was present at the

Battle of Stillwater; after which he accompanied Lady Harriett Acland on her memorable expedition down the Hudson to join her husband in captivity, but was not made prisoner by General Gates, on account, it is supposed, of his extreme youth; for afterwards we find him carrying the flag of truce into the enemy's lines on the capitulation of Saratoga. At the conclusion of the American War he joined H.M. 20th Regiment, and served with it during twenty-three years in Jamaica, St. Dominico, and in Holland, and on the staff of General Crampagné in Ireland, during the French invasion of 1798. In 1800 he quitted the army, and from that time, until the passing of the Reform Bill, figured in the political history of Lancashire as the stern and consistent supporter of civil and religious liberty. He represented Ashton in the first Reform Parliament, and died at the age of eighty-seven. He is supposed to have been the last survivor of the army which surrendered at Saratoga.

Though all my *immediate* ancestors have been naval or military men, we have had many distinguished relatives in Holy Orders and at the Bar. Space will not admit of my doing more than mentioning the names of some of those whom I am proud to claim as members of our family.

Robert Skinner, Bishop of Worcester, born 10th February, baptized 12th February 1590, "was the last bishop consecrated before the commencement of the Civil War, and the only one, who remained, at great peril, during the time of the Commonwealth, steadfastly at his post, in his own diocese at Oxford, comforting the clergy that were left. He secured, by the indulgence of the ruling powers, a license to preach, and never, at any time, desisted from reading prayers, preaching, and discharging those duties which he had undertaken at his ordination." . . . "It is said that, with the exception of Bishop King, who ordained Archbishop Dolben, in 1656, and of Bishop Duppa, who ordained Archbishop Tenison about 1659, he was the sole bishop who conferred Holy Orders during the interregnum, and that, at his death, he had, himself, ordained more priests than all the bishops then surviving him."

A copy of a sermon preached by him, before the King at Whitehall, on the 3rd December 1634, is to be found in the Bodleian Library at Oxford, He was successively Bishop of Bristol,

Oxford, and Worcester, and died at the age of 80. He is "buried at the east end of the choir of the Cathedral Church at Worcester."

The Bishop's eldest son, Matthew Skinner, was born in 1624; he became a scholar of Trinity College, Oxford, in 1640, and was elected Fellow in 1644.

In 1662 he was returned by the Commissioners as one of the gentlemen qualified for the honour of being made a "Knight of the Royal Oak," an order then contemplated. He died in 1698. His eldest son, Matthew, was born in 1689, and at the age of fourteen was admitted a scholar of St. Peter's College, Westminster. In 1709 he was elected student of Christ Church, Oxford. On coming of age, he acquired the family property at Welton, Northamptonshire, and in 1716 was called to the Bar, and joined the Oxford circuit. In 1721 he was elected Recorder of Oxford; three years afterwards Serjeant-at-Law; and in 1734 was made "The King's Serjeant," the highest rank at the Bar. The same year he was elected M.P. for the city of Oxford.

He resigned his seat for Oxford in 1738, and was made Chief Justice of Chester and Flint, and also of Denbigh and Montgomery. He conducted for the Crown, as Prime Serjeant, on the 28th July 1746, the prosecution of Lord Kilmarnock for high treason, taking precedence, by virtue of his patents, of the Attorney General. On October 21st, 1749, he died at Oxford, Premier King's Serjeant, Chief Judge of Chester, and Recorder of Oxford. He was buried in Christ Church Cathedral.

Another member of this family was the Right Honourable Sir John Skynner, Knight, Lord Chief Baron. Sir John, like his kinsman, Matthew, above mentioned, was a scholar of St. Peter's College, Westminster, and in 1742 was elected student of Christ Church, Oxford, taking his degree, B.C.L., in 1750. He was called to the Bar in 1748, and joined the Oxford circuit. He was one of the counsel present in court at the Worcester Assizes on the 15th March 1757, when, between 2 and 3 o'clock, P.M., as Sir Eardley Wilmot began to sum up in the last cause, a stack of chimneys fell through the roof, killing many. The counsel then in court, being five in number, saved themselves under the stout table; and of these, four—Aston, Nares, Ashurst, and Skynner—afterwards became judges.

Sir John Skynner, in 1768, was elected M.P. for Woodstock, and in 1771 became a bencher of Lincoln's Inn, on being made a King's Counsel.

In 1776 he was elected Recorder of Oxford, with the freedom of that city; while holding that office he presented "a soup tureen, cover, and ladle, the gift of the Right Honourable Sir John Skynner, Recorder of the City, for the use of the Mayor, 1789."

On December 1st, 1777, he was made Lord Chief Baron of the Exchequer, and received the honour of knighthood.

In 1787 he was sworn in as a member of the Privy Council. He died in 1805 at the advanced age of 82. The excellent picture of the Chief Baron, by Gainsborough, is in the hall at Christ Church, Oxford. . . . .

I cannot close this account of our ancestors without mentioning the name of Allan Maclean Skinner, who by his kind and able assistance, has done much to help me in tracing back our pedigree. He was the son of Richard, and grandson of Stephen Skinner; was educated at Eton, took his degree of B.A. at Balliol College, Oxford, was called to the Bar, at Lincoln's Inn, in 1834, and joined the Oxford circuit. He was appointed Revising Barrister in 1837, Recorder of Windsor in June 1852, and Deputy Recorder of Gloucester in the same month. He resigned the office of Revising Barrister in 1857, on being appointed one of Her Majesty's Council. "He was invited, by the Society of Lincoln's Inn, to be a Master of the Bench, in 1857; and was appointed Judge of County Courts in South Staffordshire in 1859."

NOTE II.

General Fraser, in his Report, dated 28th February 1841, to the Assistant Military Secretary, gives the following Statement of Charges incurred for Caffrees and Coolies employed under the officers of the Quartermaster-General's Department in Surveying operations, from 1833 to 1840:—

	£	s.	d.
1833	28	17	7½
1834	41	17	6
1835	79	1	2¾
1836	52	15	7½*
1837	32	17	6
1838	55	6	10½
1839	76	13	7
1840	69	14	10½†
	£437	4	9¾

* A considerable portion of this was expended in tracing the road from Colombo to Ratnapora.

† This includes Captain Gallwey's pay and allowances, amounting to £21 18s.